A Montana Historical Society Guide

A Traveler's Companion to Montana History

by Carroll Van West

Montana Historical Society Press • Helena

1986

Cover photographs by John Smart

Cover design by Glenda Clay Bradshaw

92 93 94 95   6 5 4 3

Library of Congress Cataloging-in-Publication Data

Van West, Carroll, 1955-
       A traveler's companion to Montana history.

       (A Montana Historical Society guide)
       Bibliography: p.
       Includes indexes.
          1. Montana—Description and travel—1981-   —Guide-
books. 2. Historic sites—Montana—Guide-books.
I. Title. II. Series.
F729.3.V36 1986   978'.0433   85-31072
ISBN 0-917298-12-8

The activity that is the subject of this book has been financed in part with Federal funds from the National
Park Service, Department of the Interior. However, the contents and opinions do not necessarily reflect
the views or policies of the Department of the Interior.

Contents

East Gallatin Valley, Gallatin County, ca. 1905. *Over the centuries, human beings have left their mark on the face of Montana, creating historical landscapes of trails, roads, structures, farms, and towns. You can see patterns in these landscapes, such as those found in the relationships between this well-ordered farm, the flat Gallatin Valley, and the Bridger Mountains near Bozeman.*

Historical Landscapes of Montana

"High, wide, and handsome"—that's how Joseph Kinsey Howard described Montana; as a description of Montana's geography, it is hard to better Howard's phrase. Traveling in the eastern third of the state, you will see a wide open prairie, a landscape of beauty and surprising variety. This high plain is crossed and cut by some of the most famous rivers in western history: the Missouri, the Yellowstone, the Powder, and the Tongue. This is also a landscape of fertile bottomlands, impressive uplands, and dramatic coulees.

Western Montana's geography contrasts starkly with the eastern plains. The northern Rocky Mountains provide a stunning backdrop to the Bitterroot, the Flathead, and the Madison valleys, three of the most bountiful valleys in the state. In this part of Montana, you will see dense forests, cascading rivers, and snowcapped peaks.

In central Montana, you can see where the eastern plains meet the western mountains. Standing in the middle of a Hill County wheat field, for example, you can see the Sweetgrass Hills to the west and the Bears Paw Mountains to the south. This is the landscape that inspired western artist Charles M. Russell.

Human activity in Montana dates back to at least 10,000 B.C., but only the last 200 years are well documented. Thousands of years of history are only partially understood, even by experts; and the conclusions presented in this book about Montana's prehistory are necessarily tentative.

Ten thousand years ago, prehistoric groups hunted animals not commonly associated with Montana, such as huge mammoths and bison and a type of camel. These Indians had developed hunting techniques and tools that allowed them to exploit the country's resources, but they could only produce enough food to support a small population.

In about 5500 B.C., Montana's climate became warmer and drier, and the Native Americans' lives changed. The change in climate had driven animals from

C. V. West, photographer, MHS SHPO

Pryor Mountains, Crow Indian Reservation, Big Horn County. *Ancient rock cairns, vision quest sites, and ceremonial structures are part of the historical landscapes found in the Pryor Mountains. The Crow Indians look to these mountains as a source of spiritual strength.*

the valleys and flatlands to the uplands, and the Indians moved to higher elevations to hunt. Most Native Americans remained in the high country until the climate changed again about 2,500 years later and the animals returned to the plains and lowlands.

Indians adapted well to the changes in climate. They lived in bands of less than 20, gathering together in larger numbers only during the fall for bison hunts and religious ceremonies. They traveled on foot, with dogs as their only pack animals.

Native Americans with tribal names that we recognize did not come to Montana until recent times. About 800 to 900 years ago, Shoshonean groups began to push into Montana, and by the 1500s they controlled most of present-day Montana east of the Continental Divide. During the 1600s, however, many of these Indians began to leave Montana for lands to the southwest outside of present-day Montana. When Lewis and Clark explored Montana in 1805-1806, however, some Shoshoni Indians were living in southwestern Montana.

During the 1500s, the Kootenai and Kalispell occupied parts of western Montana. The Crow Indians arrived during the 1600s and occupied much of the Yellowstone Valley; and by the late 1700s, the Blackfoot Confederacy, the Atsina, and the Assiniboine had moved into northern Montana.

The Native Americans' way of life changed rapidly during these years. The plains Indians had obtained European trade goods—metal tools, knives, cloth, and beads—long before they saw whites. Once the Indians of the northern plains

C. V. West, photographer, MHS SHPO

Ulm Pishkun, Cascade County. *Native Americans killed bison by driving them off steep cliffs and outcroppings. There is still evidence of the slaughter areas built at the base of these cliffs, part of the Native American historical landscape in Montana.*

established trade with Canadian posts, they exchanged bison meat and animal furs for guns and ammunition. Obtaining horses from southern tribes, however, brought the most profound changes to the lives of the plains Indians. Horses gave them greater mobility and prosperity, allowing them to hunt and kill larger numbers of bison and to use the environment's resources to greater advantage.

By the mid 18th century, most of the tribes that are now considered Montana Indians resided near or within the future state boundaries. In eastern and central Montana, the Crow and the Blackfoot Confederacy were dominant, and the Flathead increasingly became the most powerful tribe in western Montana. Whites moving westward pushed the Atsina (Gros Ventre), the Cree, and the Assiniboine off their land and into north central and northeastern Montana, while the Sioux and Northern Cheyenne moved into the extreme eastern area of Montana.

By the early 1800s, Canadian fur traders, American explorers Meriwether Lewis and William Clark, and English explorer David Thompson advertised Montana's fur riches, especially the valued beaver pelts. The Americans soon dominated the Montana fur trade, save for northwestern Montana where British and Canadian companies operated. The trade expanded to include most of the region's larger animals, and by 1850 the bison were as important a resource to the fur traders as to Native Americans.

A decade later, whites discovered a resource that the Indians had usually ignored—gold. Thousands flocked to the region, creating instant towns in southwestern Montana: Bannack, Virginia City, and Nevada City. In 1864, Mon-

Birney Day School, Northern Cheyenne Indian Reservation, Rosebud County. By 1900, *most of Montana's Indians lived on reservations, where Indian children were often separated from their parents and boarded in schools established by whites—another important part of the Native American landscape.*

tana became a U.S. territory, and other gold strikes sparked additional rushes: Last Chance Gulch (Helena), Pioneer, Emigrant Gulch, and Confederate Gulch (Diamond City). Later discoveries of silver and gold created more boom towns: Marysville, Garnet, Castle, Elkhorn, and Philipsburg. During the 1880s, railroads arrived to haul away the territory's mineral riches and to freight in manufactured goods. Montana achieved statehood in 1889, and five years later Helena became the state capital.

Montana Indian tribes, who had already suffered great losses of life from epidemic diseases, found it difficult to protect their hunting land from the miners, merchants, farmers, and ranchers who flooded into Montana. The Black Hills gold rush pushed the Sioux and Cheyenne into Montana's Tongue and Powder river valleys, pitting Indians against whites for control of southeastern Montana. During the 1870s, Native Americans fought to protect their way of life and white Americans waged war for complete control of Montana's resources. The U.S. Army and its Crow and Shoshoni allies defeated the Sioux and Northern Cheyenne, and the government forced the Native Americans in Montana onto reservations.

Mineral wealth and building Montana's railroads—the Union Pacific, Northern Pacific, and Great Northern—fueled the state's development. Helena, Butte, and Great Falls became major cities. Farmers prospered and stock-growers took advantage of the free grass ranges of eastern Montana. The winter of 1886-1887,

F. J. Haynes, photographer. Haynes Found. Coll. MHS Photo Archives

Northern Pacific train, Upper Missouri Valley, Broadwater County, 1883.
In 1883, the Northern Pacific completed its line through Montana, bringing the territory new immigrants. The railroad created a transportation corridor—a new historical landscape of towns, depots, bridges, and other community and commercial structures.

the harshest on record, discouraged many stock-growers, but the cattle and sheep business rebounded and remained central to Montana's economy. Once the Dawes Act of 1887 opened the Indian reservations to white settlers, more and more farmers began to convert the buffalo-grass prairie of eastern and central Montana into checkerboard fields of hay, wheat, and other grains.

From 1900 to 1920, the homesteading boom brought thousands of newcomers to Montana with the promise of land and prosperity. Towns like Broadus, Plentywood, Square Butte, and Circle developed overnight. Tilling a dry land, however, was difficult, and many failed at farming. Thousands deserted the state, leaving behind a landscape of abandoned farms, schools, and churches.

During the 20th century, Montanans developed more of the state's resources. Northwestern Montana's forests, first cut during the 1880s, became the basis for an expanding forest products industry. Oil was first discovered in several places at the turn of the century, and wells are still producing in Glacier, Richland, and Fallon counties. Strip mining southeastern Montana's coal began during the 1920s and has expanded dramatically since the 1960s. Throughout this century, hydroelectric powerhouses on the state's waterways have provided power for Montana's homes and industries.

Human activity in Montana is reflected in its landscape. Although white Americans built railroads, towns, and strip mines and had the greatest effect on the landscape, Native Americans also shaped the land. The Indians built struc-

Walter B. Dean, Jr., photographer, MHS Photo Archives

Colstrip, Rosebud County, 1929. *Industrial development brought dramatic changes to many landscapes in Montana. The Northern Pacific created a new historical landscape in southeastern Montana when it stripped away grazing land to mine coal for its locomotives.*

tures, beat pathways across Montana, and used resources to their advantage. That the Native Americans did nothing to compare with the Colstrip coal mines or the Fort Peck Dam illustrates basic cultural and technological differences between whites and Native Americans.

White Americans have always viewed the land and its resources as commodities—objects that can be owned, traded, and, most importantly, accumulated. Montana Indians, at least until the final years of the fur trade, believed that nature's bounty could be used to support life; but it could not be accumulated, separated from the landscape forever. Indians and whites altered the landscape differently, not only because of their respective technological achievements but also because of their differing views about Montana's resources. The evidence of Indian and white activity that we see on the land make up the historical landscapes that inform us about our past.

What we see on the face of Montana are historical landscapes of great diversity, reflecting centuries of human activity. These historical landscapes are easily obscured; but if we look carefully, we can still see and appreciate them. What we discover is a fascinating set of patterns on the landscape.

A Traveler's Companion to Montana History is designed to introduce people to the rich and fascinating history that can be found in these landscapes. The physical settings for many important events in Montana's history have changed little during the last 100 years, and there are still many physical remnants of Montana's prehistoric past, the exploring expeditions, the activities of miners, cowboys, and

C. V. West, photographer, MHS SHPO

Powder River Valley, Custer County. *Native Americans lived in harmony with nature, using and reusing the region's natural resources. From laying out tipi rings to building bison kill sites, the Indians created subtle but enduring patterns in Montana's river valleys, mountains, and plains.*

Native Americans, and the lives of homesteaders. Looking at these historical landscapes, travelers can see Montana history in new ways and discover a past that textbooks cannot present.

The land always reflects people's need to use or to preserve the environment, so almost every place is a historical landscape. Most historical landscapes—plowed fields, buffalo jumps, mine shafts—are man-made, but Montana's mountain passes and other natural resources also played a vital role in shaping the state's history.

In this book, "historical landscape" describes a fairly large area—a mining district, a river valley, a transportation route—that encompasses the land, the vegetation, and a wide range of structures and sites, some of which are historically related and others that might be quite different in origin and use. Although some landscapes might not strike you as being particularly beautiful, you can see how nature has combined with the patterns of human activity to create a landscape that has a beauty all its own.

Each chapter begins with a summary of the region's history, followed by a description of the region's major landscapes and a series of highway routes (labeled A, B, C, D) that are keyed to important historical themes. A *Traveler's Companion* is also indexed by person and by place name. There are seven chapters, each representing a region of the state: Chapter 1 describes the valleys and badlands of the lower Yellowstone country; Chapter 2 takes you along the Hi-Line, a landscape that has been indelibly shaped by the Great Northern Railway;

John N. DeHaas, Jr., photographer, MHS SHPO

Madison County Courthouse, Virginia City, Madison County, 1963. *Those who came to Montana's mining country created a new historical landscape of deep mines, ramshackle camps, and settled towns with wooden and brick homes, commercial buildings, streets, and roads.*

Chapter 3 describes the Judith Basin country and another major railway, the Milwaukee Road; Chapter 4 lets you travel over the prosperous plains and into the mountains of the upper Yellowstone Valley; Chapter 5 lets you explore the forests and the beautiful valleys of northwestern Montana; Chapter 6 takes you to the Butte-Helena-Philipsburg historic mining region; and Chapter 7 tells about the early days of Bannack and Virginia City.

As you travel Montana's highways, remember that the state's historic sites are fragile and the information they contain is invaluable. Whether the site is on public or private land, it is illegal to dig for artifacts or to remove objects from a site, so treat the land and historical remnants with care. Many historic sites are on private land; *please do not enter any private property without the owner's permission.* If we are to leave a heritage for future Americans to enjoy, we must protect our historical resources just as we protect our natural resources.

While writing A *Traveler's Companion to Montana History,* I accumulated many debts. I did the research for this book while under contract to the State Historic Preservation Office (SHPO) at the Montana Historical Society. I especially thank Marcella Sherfy and everyone at the SHPO for their support throughout the project and Bill Lang and Marianne Keddington at the Montana Historical Society Press for their careful and considerate editing of the original manuscript. I also thank Lory Morrow, Becca Kohl, and John Smart of the Montana Historical Society Photograph Archives for their care in locating, checking, and producing the photographic prints used in this book.

C. V. West, photographer, MHS SHPO

Flathead Valley, Montana Road 382, Sanders County. *The patterns in historical landscapes—such as trails, cultivated fields, mining districts, railroads, and communities—are scribed on the land and are evidence of how generations of Montanans have used and abused our natural resources.*

I offer a special thank you to many Montanans who shared their thoughts about the state's historical places. In preparing this book, I traveled a distance roughly equal to the circumference of the earth and met with over 20 of Montana's local historical societies. Without their encouragement, suggestions, and friendliness, driving all of those miles would have been a burden, not a special delight and wonderful experience.

I thank the Fort Benton Kiwanis Club, the Blaine County Historical Society, the Phillips County Historical Society, the Valley County Historical Society, the Sidney Kiwanis Club, the Fallon County Historical Society, the Powder River County Historical Society, the McCone County Historical Society, the Custer County Art Museum, Dave Rivenes for his wonderful television interview in Miles City, the Rosebud County Historical Society, the Musselshell County Historical Society, the Park County Historical Society, the Three Forks Historical Society, the Eureka Historical Society and Museum, Eleanor Clack for her tour of the buffalo jump in Havre, Manson Bailey for his tour of the Valley County Museum, the Butte Historical Society, Ralph Karmen for his tour of Saco, the Westerners of Helena, the Great Falls Genealogical Society, the Dillon Kiwanis Club, the Sanders County Historical Society and Museum, the Sun River Historical Society, the Carbon County Historical Society, and the Big Horn County Museum.

Carroll Van West, September 1985

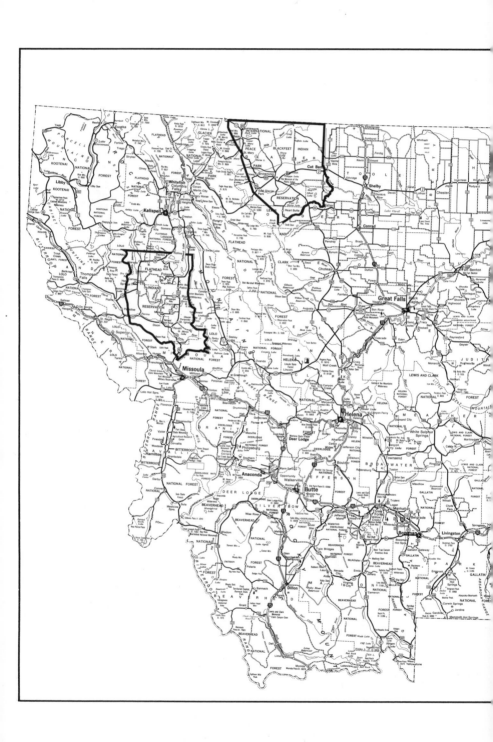

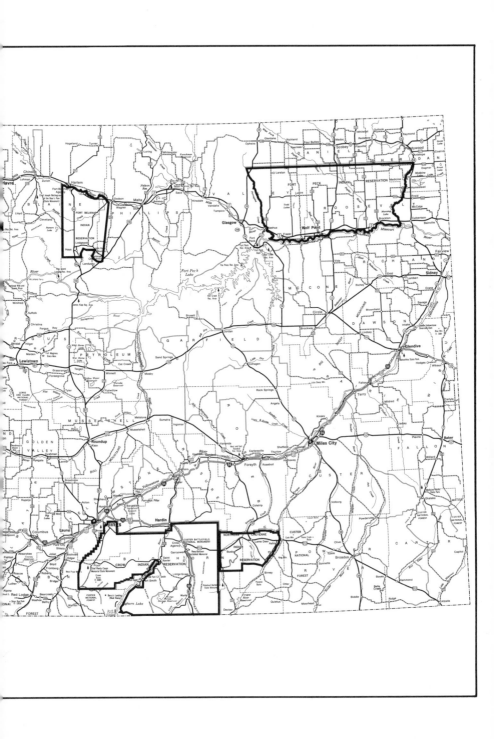

Remnants of Captain John Mullan's 1862 military road, Powell County

A Traveler's Companion
to Montana History

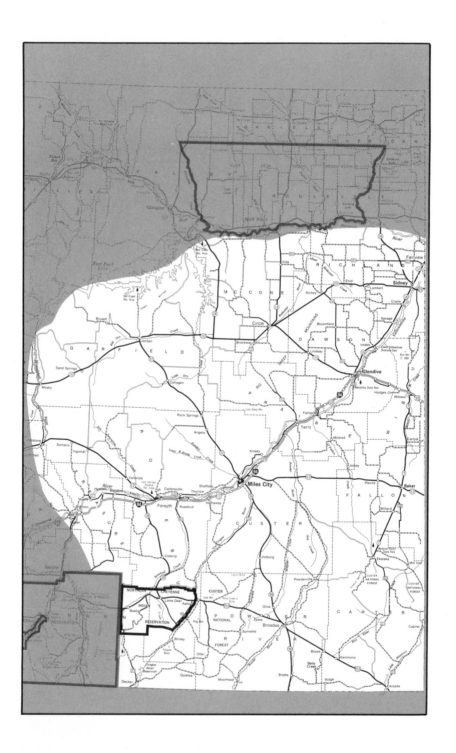

Chapter 1

The Lower Yellowstone Country

Fantastic shapes, rolling plains barren of trees and sparsely covered with grass, strikingly beautiful river valleys, and land laced with rich seams of coal all make up the southeastern Montana landscape. You can stand near the border of Carter and Fallon counties on Montana Highway 7 and see a landscape unlike any other in Montana. In this forbidding country, the elements have shaped sandstone outcroppings into eerie formations. When the Sioux and Northern Cheyenne entered these "badlands" 150 years ago, they called the formations "medicine rocks" and used the area as a center for religious ceremonies where they replenished their spiritual faith and celebrated the Great Spirits who lived there.

Few people have ever lived in Montana's badlands; most have preferred the valleys of the Yellowstone River and its major tributaries—the Bighorn, the Powder, the Tongue, and the Rosebud—where natural resources are rich and varied. Looking closely at this landscape, you can see that in southeastern Montana this combination of resources is usually found in the river valleys. For hundreds of years Native Americans had hunted herds of bison, elk, and deer in the fertile Yellowstone Valley. The Indians burned cottonwood and aspen logs during long winter nights; in times of extreme hunger, they ate the trees' bark; and the valley's foliage sheltered them from the elements.

Explorers and fur traders in the mid 19th century looked for a different resource in the rivers and streams of southeastern Montana—beaver pelts, which were in great demand in both eastern and European markets. Except for the valley's cottonwoods and aspens used to build trading posts and to fuel fires, the traders generally ignored the resources that the Indians valued.

By the 1880s, settlers had replaced the rich buffalo grass on the benchlands with neatly plowed rows of oats, barley, and wheat, and stock-growers had moved in large herds of cattle. The land began to assume the patterns you see today as you look from the towns of Moorhead on the Powder River, Kinsey on the Yellowstone River, and Birney on the Tongue River. At these places, you can see the natural resources of the river valleys that the Indians relied on. You can also see how farmers and ranchers created a new landscape by using the river valley resources.

During the 20th century, the rolling but sparsely vegetated plains of southeastern Montana lured those who believed that modern technology could transform the thin layer of topsoil into prosperous farmland. Soon homesteaders were settling on the land. Irrigation ditches crisscrossed the uplands, watering the land below, and farmers plowed more and more acres. Within a few years, it became clear that the land could not sustain that much intensive agriculture. Crops failed, lives were ruined, and the plains of southeastern Montana took on a new look. In section after section, abandoned farms remind us of the homesteaders' dreams and struggles; and when a heavy wind kicks up a dust storm on the rolling plains, it is easy to see why so many of them failed.

Look again at that country and consider the resources that lie below the ground. Today, oil wells literally surround the towns of Sidney and Baker, and surface deposits of coal have heated many southeastern Montana homes for decades. With such vast coal reserves and with the price of energy from foreign sources so high, developers have been drawn to the region's underground resources. In Rosebud County, thousands of acres of land have been stripped away to uncover coal that is then burned at a massive power-generating plant at Colstrip. More and more, the mining landscape of southeastern Montana has come to resemble a man-made badlands.

Landscape 1: The Lower Yellowstone River Valley

The Yellowstone River is the last major free-flowing river in the U.S. The river's resources have served people for centuries, but this human activity has done little to change the character of the river or the surrounding landscape. The cottonwoods and aspens provided shelter for Native Americans and gave settlers logs for their homes, fuel for their fires, and wood for the steamboats that once braved the river's swift, treacherous currents. The Yellowstone's most valuable resource, its water, quenched the thirst of tired warriors on bison hunts, floated boats of commerce, and irrigated farmers' crops. The lower Yellowstone Valley is wide at some places and narrow at others; it contains rich topsoil in some counties and valuable rangeland in others. The valley is a mosaic of historic sites, prosperous wheat farms, and cattle ranches.

The Yellowstone country is more than just the land watered by the *Roche Jaune*, the name applied to the river by early French fur trappers. This landscape also includes the Yellowstone's major tributaries—the Bighorn, the Tongue, and the Powder rivers and Rosebud Creek. These streams and their resources—cottonwoods, beaver, bison, and rangeland—attracted Native Americans, fur trappers, and settlers.

Route 1: The Confluence of the Missouri and Yellowstone Rivers

Montana Highway 200 and North Dakota Highway 58

After reaching the mouth of the Yellowstone in 1806, William Clark wrote in his journal that whoever controlled the confluence of the Missouri and Yellowstone rivers could control the northwestern fur trade. To reach the area where the two rivers meet, take Montana Highway 200 from Fairview to the

Granville Stuart sketch of Fort Union, 1866. In 1805, Meriwether Lewis reported that the confluence of the Missouri and Yellowstone rivers was a "most eligible site" for a permanent trading post.

North Dakota line, leave North Dakota Highway 58, and follow the signs to the Fort Union National Historic Site.

It is not surprising that Clark suggested that the Americans be the ones to build a trading post here. But the Canadians, led by Kenneth McKenzie, acted first and constructed Fort McKenzie in the late 1820s. McKenzie hoped that the Blackfoot Confederacy, the Atsina, and the Assiniboine would follow the Missouri River and that the Crow would follow the Yellowstone River to his fort. At this strategic crossroads, he would control the trade of all Indian tribes in the Northwest.

The location also appealed to the prosperous American Fur Company, owned by John Jacob Astor. By building a fort at the confluence of the two rivers, Astor hoped to dominate the Indian trade and to develop the navigation of the Yellowstone and the Missouri. In 1829, using some of the cottonwoods along the Missouri's banks, the American Fur Company built Fort Union. Kenneth McKenzie joined the Americans and became the post's administrator.

Throughout the 1830s and 1840s, Fort Union was the center of the Upper Missouri fur trade. Traders bundled the beaver pelts and bison robes gathered by Native Americans and free trappers and loaded them onto steamboats headed for St. Louis. The post expanded considerably during these years; in the spring and summer, men took to the surrounding woods, cutting logs for new living quarters and splitting cottonwoods for their fireplaces and the insatiable steamboat boilers. What had begun as a simple trading post became an imposing log stockade, requiring the labor of dozens of men and timber from acres of land.

During the 1860s, federal soldiers dismantled Fort Union and used its logs to build Fort Buford about a mile downriver on the Missouri. The foundations that remain at Fort Union have been designated a National Historic Site, administered by the National Park Service, and interpretative films and a self-guided tour are available.

Route 2: The Lower Yellowstone Irrigation Project
Montana Highway 16, from Sidney to Intake

On Montana Highway 16 between Sidney and Glendive, you can see many signs of farming success—grain elevators, plowed fields, large farming complexes, and herds of cattle—but the irrigation ditches and canals are the most important signs. Without the establishment of the Lower Yellowstone Irrigation Project in 1905, there would be few successful farms along this stretch of highway.

Signs marking the canals and irrigation ditches of the Lower Yellowstone Irrigation Project stand at several places along Montana Highway 16, but the best place to stop and consider the effect that irrigation has had on the Yellowstone Valley is at the Intake fishing access. Here the irrigation diversion dam and the project's main canal transport water to the farmers of Richland and Dawson counties. The gravel road to the fishing access crosses the main canal.

The Bureau of Reclamation initiated the Lower Yellowstone Irrigation Project in 1905, but the project developed slowly because farmers had little experience with irrigated land and ranchers were wary of diversified agriculture. Between 1910 and 1920, however, Dawson County's population soared from 2,500 to 25,000. Instead of a few scattered ranches between Sidney and Glendive, there now stood the towns of Crane and Savage. The population boom justified the creation of Richland County from the northern portion of Dawson County. Sidney became the county seat of the new county, and county officials constructed an impressive neoclassic courthouse. The irrigation project became a major element in the development of agriculture in the Yellowstone Valley when a large sugar beet factory opened in Sidney in 1925. Irrigation had transformed part of this last Montana frontier into a prosperous agricultural region.

Route 3: Early Settlers and Stock-growers in the Lower Yellowstone Valley
Route A: Interstate Highway I-94, from Glendive to Wibaux
Route B: Montana Highway 7, from Wibaux to Ekalaka

Between Glendive and Wibaux on I-94, you can see a landscape where prehistoric Indians and, centuries later, railroad officials and stock-growers established some of eastern Montana's earliest settlements.

Route A: Interstate Highway I-94, from Glendive to Wibaux

About 400 years ago, migrating Indians moved into the Yellowstone Valley just west of Glendive, where they built a village overlooking the river. The place where the village once stood is the Hagan archaeological site, which is a National

MHS Photo Archives

Douglas and Mead Block, Glendive, Dawson County, 1897. *Henry Douglas, a commissary agent for the Northern Pacific, built Glendive's first tent store in 1881, helped plan the townsite, and was a partner in the Douglas & Mead Mercantile Company, which closed in 1954.*

Historic Landmark. Here along the banks of the Yellowstone River stood earth-covered lodges and tipis (portable homes made from pine poles and bison hides) that housed hundreds of people. The Native Americans made the earth lodges using cottonwoods for the frames, riverbank clay for the covering, and a layer of buffalo grass for the roofs. Nearby, small plots of land were under cultivation, producing squash, tobacco, and other plants. The Hagan site is on private property and is closed to the public. Do not trespass.

Few white settlers lived in the present-day Glendive area until 1880-1881, when a small village developed on the mesa south of Glendive Creek in anticipation of the arrival of the Northern Pacific Railroad. But railroad insiders who knew where the tracks would be laid formed the Yellowstone Land and Colonization Company and established Glendive on the flatland beside the Yellowstone River, 34 miles west of the North Dakota state line.

The first Northern Pacific train arrived in Glendive on July 4, 1881, and from the beginning the town had all the characteristics of a typical railroad boom town. Local residents constructed 150 buildings between July 20 and November 30, 1881, and one 1881 visitor remembered Glendive as "a wild frontier town, mostly board shacks and log cabins," populated by hundreds of railroad employees who often "got gloriously soused" at the town's 20-odd saloons.

But Glendive's days as a "wild west" town lasted only a few months. By 1884, the town had become an important commercial center on the lower Yellowstone River, the railhead for shipping buffalo robes, buffalo bones, and cattle. As the local editor reported, "Glendive is essentially a railroad town, as the surrounding region is a stock country."

Wibaux, 26 miles east of Glendive on I-94, was perhaps the most important stock-growing center in eastern Montana; and for the past century, this country has contained some of the best stock-growing land in the state. Bison once dominated this land; but in the late 1870s and early 1880s, ranchers brought in large cattle herds, which multiplied on the open range and made stock-growing profitable. During this time, westerners, easterners, and foreigners rushed to be part of the "Beef Bonanza" in southeastern Montana.

At first there were resources and room for everyone; the region's creeks promised enough water, and the grasslands seemed endless. The number of cattle on the range increased dramatically; and by the mid 1880s, over 400,000 head of cattle grazed the land in southeastern Montana. But prosperity did not last long.

The winter of 1886-1887 devastated the cattle industry in Montana. Heavy snows fell, followed by a warming trend that melted some of the snow. Then the brunt of the storms hit, with temperatures dropping to 40 degrees below zero, leaving a thick coat of ice over the open range. Then more snow fell. Cattle died by the thousands. Some companies lost 90 per cent of their stock as fortunes suddenly became bankruptcies.

Despite the devastation, there were survivors. On Orgain Avenue in Wibaux stands the headquarters of one such "spread," Pierre Wibaux's W-Bar Ranch. A white house built in 1884, the W-Bar headquarters and ranch house is listed in the National Register of Historic Places. Wibaux, an immigrant from France, conducted his business from this building and owned rangeland stretching from eastern Montana into western North Dakota. After the disastrous winter of 1886-1887, Wibaux realized that the open-range days were over, so he leased and purchased grazing land throughout eastern Dawson County and in Wibaux County. By the 1890s, his ranch had over 65,000 head of cattle and Wibaux was known as the "Cattle King of Eastern Montana."

Route B: Montana Highway 7, from Wibaux to Ekalaka

The land along Montana Highway 7, from Wibaux 80 miles south to the town of Ekalaka, is prime stock-growing country. As you look for physical remnants of the open-range era, keep in mind that ranchers and stock-growers only built substantial ranch headquarters, such as Wibaux's white house, after they had achieved some success. The first building on most eastern Montana ranches was a "dug-out" to house the headquarters. Basically a hole in the side of a hill, a dug-out had a dirt roof supported by heavy log beams and covered by sod to make it waterproof. The front of the structure was closed off by cottonwood logs into which a small door and a smaller window were cut; on the inside, hides covered a dirt floor. Early ranchers claimed that dug-outs were "warm and pleasant during the coldest weather." As you travel along Montana Highway 7, look for abandoned dug-outs on the south side of hills and bluffs, where they were built to protect the cowboys from harsh northern winds.

No dug-outs remain at the Mill Iron Ranch, which is located about 15 miles northeast of Ekalaka near the post office and general store at Mill Iron, but its original buildings, dating to 1885, still stand. The ranch buildings were strategically placed against a large cliff to the north, sparing the ranch hands some of the coldest winds. Mill Iron Ranch is a good example of the social organization that developed on most Montana ranches. The mess hall and kitchen shared one building, a foreman's house was separate from the cowboys' bunkhouse, and the ranch headquarters was in another building. The Mill Iron Ranch is now part of another ranch and is on private property. Do not trespass.

Route 4: Navigating the Yellowstone River
Interstate Highway I-94, from Terry to Miles City
U.S. Highway 10, from Terry to Miles City

There are three good locations where you can imagine steamboats and other early river crafts navigating the Yellowstone River: where the interstate crosses the Yellowstone River near Fallon, where Montana Highway 22 crosses the river in Miles City, and at the Powder River State Monument on U.S. Highway 10 about six miles west of Terry. During late spring and summer, the section of the Yellowstone between Terry and Miles City is deep enough to accommodate large boats. Despite the swift and treacherous current, over 100 years ago steamboats puffed along this part of the river.

Before steamboats arrived, no one truly "navigated" the Yellowstone. The Indians crossed the river in bullboats—haphazard tub-like vessels made on the spot by stretching bison hides over freshly cut willow tree frames and waterproofing them with buffalo grease. Members of the Lewis and Clark expedition used canoes and bullboats, and early fur traders relied on canoes, keelboats, and mackinaws. Keelboats were about 60 to 75 feet long with a beam of 16 feet, a draft of about 4 feet, and a rectangular-shaped "cargo box" set in the middle. Mackinaws were much better suited to the river's currents. They were smaller boats, 50 feet long with a beam of about 12 feet and with flat bottoms that were sharp at each end. Ideally suited for floating down the river, both crafts were powerless when facing upstream into the Yellowstone's current. As you look eastward up the river, you can imagine teams of men on the river bank struggling to pull a flatboat or mackinaw up the mighty Yellowstone.

When steamboats arrived, transportation on the Yellowstone changed dramatically. The first boats came during the 1870s, courtesy of the U.S. Army, which established several supply depots on the river. The Powder River State Monument, located at the confluence of the Powder and Yellowstone rivers on U.S. Highway 10, marks the site of one of these military bases. To reach this monument, take exit 169 from I-94, travel northeast on U.S. Highway 10, and stop at the highway historical marker. Near Terry on U.S. Highway 10, Prairie County citizens have marked the location of Terry's Landing, a key supply depot during the war against the Sioux and Northern Cheyenne in 1876-1877. After the Sioux war, the army established Fort Keogh, a permanent base near the confluence of the Tongue and Yellowstone rivers and the primary military establishment in eastern Montana. The fort, located just west of Miles City, can be seen from I-94 at exit 135.

L. A. Huffman, photographer, MHS Photo Archives

Fort Keogh, Custer County, ca. 1878. *"The officers' quarters were all double buildings, and the allowance of quarters for a captain was two rooms and a kitchen. [But] a little ingenuity got a additional room on the ground floor. Of course the upper story was only an attic, but with the high mansard roof and dormer windows, four completely furnished rooms were easily obtained and a Captain got seven rooms and a kitchen."—* officer's son at Fort Keogh.

Fort Keogh was named for Capt. Myles Keogh, who died at the Battle of the Little Bighorn. Soldiers began building the fort in 1877 and finished it a year later, using the resources at hand and materials brought in by steamboat. Rough lumber came from the trees on nearby Pine Hill, and bricks were burned on the spot. Until the Northern Pacific Railroad arrived in Miles City in 1881, steamboats delivered most of the fort's supplies.

Today, the only buildings remaining from the 1880s are two officers' quarters and a warehouse. But it is possible to imagine the patterns of the fort and its appearance when steamboats docked along the banks of the Yellowstone. The fort was diamond-shaped and had no stockade. The commanding officers' quarters was at the west point of the diamond, and the officers' quarters were situated along the sides. There were six large barracks for enlisted men and a bakery, granary, storehouse, guardhouse, hospital, stables, library, and pool hall—in all, 60 major buildings. It was the largest fort in Montana Territory.

Fort Keogh operated as an army post until 1900, when it became an army horse remount station. Eight years later, the U.S. Department of Agriculture converted it into a livestock experiment station.

The steamboat era came to an end in the early 1880s with the construction of the Northern Pacific Railroad through the Yellowstone Valley. Army officers welcomed the change; the Yellowstone's swift currents, shallow depth, and tricky course had cost them many valuable shipments.

Route 5: The Fur Trade in the Lower Yellowstone Valley

Interstate Highway I-94, from mile marker 113 rest stop (near Rosebud) to mile marker 42 rest stop (near Custer)

You can get a breathtaking view of the Yellowstone Valley at the Rosebud rest stop on I-94, located at mile marker 113. Looking to the west, you can see a portion of the river where fur traders once concentrated their activity, a 52-mile stretch from present-day Rosebud to the town of Bighorn near the mouth of the Bighorn River. Although there are no visible remains of the fur-trade era on the landscape today, the natural resources that you see are what the fur traders found so inviting over 150 years ago.

If you look to the north as you cross the bridge at mile marker 104 on I-94, you can see the mouth of Rosebud Creek. This stream was populated with beaver, and it served as a passageway to the rich hunting lands of the Bighorn Mountains. Many fur-bearing animals also lived in Sarpy Creek (I-94 exit 72), which empties into the Yellowstone near Sanders. Fur traders also used the Bighorn River, which joins the Yellowstone near Bighorn (I-94 exit 49), to reach the rich hunting territory of southern Montana and northern Wyoming.

The foliage in this part of the Yellowstone Valley is thick, and traders found plenty of cottonwoods, aspens, and other trees for fuel and for building. A substantial number of tipis, belonging to the Crow Indians, stood along the river bluffs and elsewhere throughout the valley. For the traders, success was almost guaranteed in this section of the valley because of the neighboring Indians, plentiful game and fur-bearing animals, and wood for shelter and fuel.

The trappers first hunted beaver, the source of the felt used in high-fashion hats during the late 18th and early 19th centuries. They placed their traps in swampy depressions and along the many small streams that flow into the Yellowstone. During the 1830s, when beaver pelts were no longer in fashion, Indian and white trappers hunted bison in the valley, which was literally black with bison herds. Buffalo robes were popular as floor coverings, carriage and sleigh robes, and overcoats. Trappers also hunted deer, antelope, and elk.

The first white traders in the Yellowstone Valley were Canadians, who soon discovered that the Crow did not care much for the beaver trade. As Antoine Larocque complained during his visit in 1805, the Crow "seemed to desire that I go away. I had in my possession twenty-three beaver skins; in their opinion, that is a very large number and a great many more than we needed." A year later, William Clark surveyed the Yellowstone Valley and claimed its furs for the U.S. John Colter, a member of the Lewis and Clark expedition, returned to the Yellowstone country with eager fur trappers rather than going back to St. Louis with everyone else. Colter later became an important mountain man, leading trapping parties in the valley for the next several decades.

In 1807, trappers led by Manuel Lisa of St. Louis built Fort Remon, the Yellowstone's first trading post and the first permanent structure built by white men in Montana. Located near present-day Bighorn at the mouth of the Bighorn River, the fort was constructed on flat bottomland accessible to both river traffic and the Indians who traveled overland. You can reach the site by taking I-94 exit 49 and going about two miles northeast on U.S. Highway 10 to the old Bighorn River bridge. There are no remains of this small trading post made of cottonwood logs.

Lisa and his trappers abandoned Fort Remon in 1811. The opposition of the powerful Blackfoot Confederacy kept the Americans from extending their influence along the Yellowstone, and for more than a decade, no trading posts were built in the Yellowstone Valley. During the 1820s, Americans returned to the mouth of the Bighorn River and constructed Fort Benton. The fort was temporary, hastily constructed with cottonwood logs, and quickly abandoned after large numbers of Crow refused to trap and prepare beavers and other small fur-bearing animals for the traders.

Not until the fur trade included bison did the Crow become willing partners with the Americans. The American Fur Company built Fort Union near the mouth of the Yellowstone River in 1829 and encouraged the Crow to exchange buffalo robes there. But the Crow didn't like traveling to Fort Union, fearing the wrath of the Blackfoot Confederacy, and asked for a more centrally located trading post. In 1833, the Americans built Fort Cass at the mouth of the Bighorn River. Unlike its predecessors, Fort Cass was a substantial trading post. Within its tall cottonwood stockade, traders lived year-round, exchanging manufactured products for beaver pelts and other furs and, not incidentally, learning to understand Crow customs. By learning about Crow culture, traders improved their trading skills and helped to strengthen the ties between the whites and the Crow. As expected, exchanging buffalo robes dominated the trade at Fort Cass; Crow and free trappers traded 120 pounds of beaver pelts and about 4,500 buffalo robes during the 1834-1835 season.

You can leave I-94 at exit 49 and travel about two miles northeast to the fishing access site at the Bighorn River bridge. If you look north to the mouth of the Bighorn River, you can imagine the scene at Fort Cass during a typical trading season. The tipis of many Crow families were clustered around the fort, with the Crow women outside busily preparing recently skinned bison hides. The women stretched "the hide tight on the ground and there let it dry" before cutting and scraping "the fleshy side until it becomes thin and smooth." After soaking the hide for two days in "a mixture composed of the brains and liver of the animal mixed together," they stretched the hide on the ground again and "beat and rubbed [it] with a paddle until it [became] perfectly soft and dry." Outside the stockade walls, there were also small garden plots, which produced fresh food for the traders.

Both inside and outside the fort, traders treated the Crow men royally to ensure their continued cooperation. Before the actual trading took place, company employees staged ceremonies where they presented the Indians with blankets, beads, tobacco, and other desirable objects. The Native Americans were the dominant partners in the trade, and they expected to be treated as allies, not as employees. The Crow supplied finished buffalo robes and protected the Americans from Blackfoot Confederacy warriors. Without the Indians' cooperation, Fort Cass would have been a besieged post. Instead, the Crow, mountain men, and fur traders learned to live with each other and entered into a working relationship rarely equaled in Montana history.

Between 1835 and 1857, the American Fur Company built four more trading posts in the Yellowstone Valley to accommodate the shifting campsites of the Crow Indians: Fort Van Buren (1835) and Fort Sarpy I (1850) at the mouth of Rosebud Creek, off I-94 exit 104 near the present-day town of Rosebud; Fort Alexander (1842) at the mouth of Armeils Creek; and Fort Sarpy II (1857) at the mouth of Sarpy Creek. This period of the fur trade had no lasting effect on the landscape; each fort was either burned or dismantled, and beaver and bison still flourished in the Yellowstone country.

Although the fur trade declined steadily during these years, the American Fur Company maintained friendly ties with the Crow. By the terms of the Fort Laramie Treaty of 1851, the U.S. government paid a yearly annuity to the Crow and to other plains tribes, and the trading posts became the conduit for those funds and supplies.

The abandonment of Fort Sarpy II in 1859 was a turning point in the history of the Yellowstone Valley. For two decades, company employees and the Crow had hunted in the valley together. Crow warriors had shared their knowledge as hunters and guides, Crow women had taught the traders how to prepare buffalo robes, and the Crow had protected the American traders and trappers from those who opposed their control of the fur trade. Although the company reciprocated with food and tobacco, metal utensils, clothing, guns, hospitality, and friendship, the trading partnership was unequal. The Americans did not have to exploit their own environment, but the Crow had become economically dependent on the trade and were soon plundering their own land in order to continue their participation.

From 1877 to 1884, hunters and Indians systematically decimated the large bison herds in this part of the Yellowstone Valley, leaving in their wake rotting carcasses and bleached bones. Nearly every bison in the valley was slaughtered by professional hunters and by Native Americans, who continued to rely on the bison as their staff of life. Hunting bison became lucrative once again because of the development of an industrial tanning process that made it profitable to transform the hides into leather. Government officials also encouraged the killing of bison in the belief that if the herds disappeared Native Americans would be forced to change their way of life and would "settle down" and become "civilized."

Hunters sometimes killed 65 bison a day, using .50 caliber Sharps rifles. Placing their heavy rifles on tripods some distance from the herd, the hunters shot the bison, who sensed no danger and continued to graze. The hunters or professional skinners skinned the bison where they fell, and

stretched the hide out on the ground with the flesh side up and left them to dry. After the hunting season was over they would then roll the hides up as best they could and haul them to some location and stack them up to press them in as small bulk as possible. Then they had to haul them to the Yellowstone River, where they were bought by the hide buyers and transported to the Tanner[ies] by boat.

It is difficult to imagine the carnage the hunters left. Granville Stuart, who journeyed through the lower Yellowstone Valley in 1880, reported that

. . . the bottoms are literally sprinkled with carcasses of dead buffalo. In many places they lie thick on the ground, fat and the meat not yet spoiled, all murdered for their hides which are piled like cordwood all along the way.

Stuart found such deliberate waste disgusting: " 'Tis an awful sight," he exclaimed, "probably 10,000 buffalo have been killed in the vicinity this winter." He did not realize just how great the waste had been: over 100,000 hides were sold in Miles City from 1879 to 1883, and from 1881 to 1883 the Northern Pacific Railroad shipped almost 300,000 hides from that town to eastern markets.

One of the busiest towns involved in the buffalo robe trade was the river port of Junction City, located at the head of navigation on the Yellowstone at the confluence of the Bighorn and Yellowstone rivers, across from present-day Custer. Here, entrepreneurs profited from the trade in buffalo robes and bones. There is only one reminder of the town: the grave of William Gridley, an early stage driver, still lies above the site. If you cross the Yellowstone at the bridge on Montana 310 at Custer, you can see Gridley's grave on the river bluffs just west of the junction of Montana 310 and Myers Road.

By 1884, the hunt was over. Even the thousands of bison skeletons that remained on the landscape soon disappeared, as fertilizer companies used them to make phosphates and sugar companies wanted them for carbon deposits. In 1885, one company shipped 400,000 pounds of buffalo bones to the East, and the trade in bones brought additional prosperity to the recent settlers of southeastern Montana.

Next to vanish was the grass that had fed the bison. Cattlemen preferred hay to buffalo grass, and later settlers replaced what natural grass remained with wheat, barley, oats, and other grains. You can stop anywhere along the 52-mile stretch of the Yellowstone Valley from Rosebud to Bighorn and look at the valley's natural resources. The foliage, the animals, and the water are the only physical reminders of the fur trade era; the tipis, the trading posts, and the great bison herds are gone forever.

Route 6: The Tongue River Valley
Route A: U.S. Highway 212, at Ashland
Route B: Montana Road 332 and Montana Road 314, from
Birney Day School Village to Decker

The Tongue River is the primary tributary of the Yellowstone River in southeastern Montana; but compared to the Yellowstone Valley, the Tongue River Valley is undeveloped. The valley has the same valuable rich bottomland and foliage found in the Yellowstone Valley and large deposits of coal near the Tongue River Reservoir at Decker. Ranches are scattered along Montana Road 332, but there are no towns. Only where the upper Tongue River splits the Northern Cheyenne Indian Reservation and the Custer National Forest are there settlements of any size.

L. A. Huffman, photographer, MHS Photo Archives

Birney Day School Village, Northern Cheyenne Indian Reservation, Rosebud County, ca. 1900. *"To make the education of the young Indians effective they should be separated from their parents and savage surroundings and placed in the midst of civilization. . . ."*—Major J. S. Brisbin

Route A: U.S. Highway 212, at Ashland

Much of the history of the Tongue River Valley centers on the Northern Cheyenne Indian Reservation, whose eastern border runs along the Tongue River in Rosebud County. Traveling west on U.S. Highway 212, you will first encounter Ashland, home of the St. Labre's Indian School. Established as St. Labre's Mission by Jesuit priests in the early 1880s, the school's founders hoped that here, along the valley's rich bottomland, they could transform the Northern Cheyenne into successful farmers. By 1884, the mission included a home for the priests, a church, and a school, each built from cottonwood logs taken from trees along the banks of the Tongue River. Although the missionaries had only limited success converting the Northern Cheyenne, the Indian school is still a thriving concern and is a center for religious and cultural activity.

About 20 miles south of Ashland on the west side of the Tongue River is Birney Day School Village, a small town built in the early 1900s. The Bureau of Indian Affairs financed the village's construction, reasoning that if Northern Cheyenne children were educated by white teachers in a "civilized" town setting they would grow into "Americanized" adults. The white teachers at the Birney school introduced their 47 students to the "three R's," but their primary concern was teaching the boys to be farmers and the girls to be housewives.

The day school was abandoned in the late 1960s, but many Cheyenne families remain in the village. The original schoolhouse burned in 1936, and the one you see now dates to 1940. The teachers' homes stand a few hundred yards east of the school, and several log buildings, some possibly dating to the 1890s, lie along dirt streets between the school and the houses. Such "Indian towns" were laid out using dwellings that had been moved from other parts of the reservation. The early log houses were built low to the ground, and it was a shattering experience for the Cheyenne to live in them after generations of living in tipis. Standardized

BIA housing, constructed during the last two decades, surround the log dwellings. The village also has a Mennonite church (dating to 1910) and a Catholic church (dating to 1929); both still hold services for the community.

Route B: Montana Road 332 and Montana Road 314, from Birney Day School Village to Decker

From Birney Day School Village, travel southeast, cross the nearby Tongue River bridge, and take Montana Road 332 (a gravel road) southwest toward the town of Birney. You are now in the middle of the Tongue River Valley and will see several cattle ranches. To see other important historic landscapes, continue on Montana Road 332 to its junction with Montana Road 314 and turn south toward Decker.

The land along Montana 314 has been treated harshly. The river has been dammed, creating the Tongue River Reservoir, and men and machines are stripping away the surrounding land, mining the coal underneath. Piles of slag and the rumble of coal trains greet visitors to Decker, a town with only a school and a combination post office and store. Hundreds of people have worked in the Decker coal mines since the 1970s, but coal mines and huge earthmovers are the only physical evidence they have left behind. There are no homes or businesses in Decker. The miners live and shop in Sheridan, Wyoming, about 25 miles south on Montana Road 314, and they drive across the state line every day to go to work. Modern transportation has nearly eliminated the need for the boom towns that once sprung up in Montana whenever a new mining venture began.

Also on Montana 314, about five miles north of its junction with Montana 332, is the Rosebud Battlefield State Monument, which is listed in the National Register of Historic Places. Here, on June 16, 1876, Crow and Shoshoni warriors, who were fighting with the U.S. Army, saved the Americans from an embarrassing defeat at the hands of Sioux and Northern Cheyenne warriors. The battle set the stage for George A. Custer's defeat at the Battle of the Little Bighorn on June 25, 1876. Interpretive signs at the monument also describe a prehistoric bison kill, which is located adjacent to the monument.

Route 7: The Rosebud Creek Valley
Route A: U.S. Highway 212, from Lame Deer to Busby
Route B: Montana Highway 39, from Lame Deer to Colstrip

The land watered by Rosebud Creek in southern Rosebud and Big Horn counties was the location of some of the most important events and developments in the history of Montana. In 1884, the federal government created the Northern Cheyenne Indian Reservation. For years, the tribe had struggled to regain their homeland along the Tongue River. About 40 years later in the Rosebud Creek Valley, the Northern Pacific Railroad developed Montana's first coal strip mines.

Route A: U.S. Highway 212, from Lame Deer to Busby

Rosebud Creek runs through the Northern Cheyenne Indian Reservation, home of the Northern Cheyenne for over a century. Tribal and agency headquarters are located at Lame Deer at the junction of U.S. Highway 212 and Montana Highway 39. Busby, which is located 16 miles west of Lame Deer on U.S. 212, is another major Cheyenne settlement. Busby once had an agency school and hospital.

The Cheyenne lived in present-day Minnesota and Wisconsin until the pressure of westward-moving Americans forced them to leave their homeland. They migrated to the Dakotas and the Black Hills, but the pressure continued; and in 1830 the Cheyenne people divided, one group going south, the other remaining with their allies, the Sioux, in the Black Hills and in southeastern Montana. U. S. government officials promised the Northern Cheyenne a permanent home there, in the land of the *Noaha-vose*, the Sacred Mountain.

During the early 1870s, however, the Northern Cheyenne had their homes invaded once again when gold rush fever hit the Black Hills, and in 1874 they moved to the valleys of the Tongue and Powder rivers. The Sioux joined them the following year. Although the two tribes had suffered years of epidemic diseases and inter-tribal warfare, they valiantly fought to protect their rights and their land during 1876-1877. The Cheyenne agreed to live on a reservation on the condition that they could remain in the Yellowstone country. But that was another promise that the government wouldn't keep.

The government sent the Northern Cheyenne south to live with the Southern Cheyenne in Indian Territory (present-day Oklahoma). In 1878, Northern Cheyenne chiefs decided to risk everything in a heroic trek home to the country of *Noaha-vose*. Soldiers tracked the Indians and captured them on the northwestern plains, incarcerating them at Fort Robinson, Nebraska. After several years of residence at Pine Ridge on the Sioux Indian Reservation in present-day South Dakota, the Northern Cheyenne finally went home in 1884 to the newly created Northern Cheyenne Indian Reservation.

Government officials believed that the Cheyenne should be farmers. But as Wooden Leg tried to explain to the whites, the Cheyenne believed that

it is wrong to tear loose from its place on the earth anything that may be growing there. It may be cut off, but it should not be uprooted. The trees and the grasses have spirits. Whatever one of such growths may be destroyed by some good Indian, his act is done in sadness and with a prayer for forgiveness because of his necessities, the same as we were taught to do in killing animals for food or skins.

Wooden Leg explained why much of the reservation remained untouched. "We revere especially," he continued,

the places where our old camp circles used to be set up and where we had our old places of worship. There are many of such spots on our reservations. White people look at them and say: "These Indians are foolish. There is good land not plowed." But we like to see these places as they were in the old times. They help to keep in our hearts a remembrance of the virtues of the good Cheyennes dead and gone from us.

The Northern Cheyenne's attachment to the land—as embodied in the concept of *Noaha-vose*—remains strong today.

C. V. West, photographer, MHS SHPO

Colstrip Electrical Generating Plant, Rosebud County. *This coal-fired plant remains the center of controversy because of high construction costs and potential deterioration of environmental quality.*

Route B: Montana Highway 39, from Lame Deer to Colstrip

The land north of Lame Deer on Montana Highway 39 has few trees and little vegetation, but lying just underneath the thin layer of topsoil are tons of coal. About nine miles north of Rosebud Creek in the Rosebud uplands is a scene that would have shocked early residents of this region—the coal mines at Colstrip. Strip-mining, which began at Colstrip in 1924, is similar to a large-scale excavation project. Explosives first loosen the soil and then huge mechanical shovels remove the topsoil and mine the coal.

The Northern Pacific Railroad, which owned the land, used this vast coal reserve to supply fuel for its steam engines. When it switched to diesel fuel in 1958, the Northern Pacific sold its mines to the Montana Power Company, which began strip-mining again in the late 1960s. Since then, the Western Energy Company, a subsidiary of Montana Power, has greatly expanded mining operations, stripping away additional thousands of acres to supply its planned power plant.

Colstrip's most imposing feature is the Colstrip Electrical Generating Plant. Owned by several northwestern utilities and costing over $500 million, the Colstrip Plant began operations in the 1970s. Two 500-kilovolt power lines transmit electricity throughout Montana to other northwestern states.

Montana Highway 39 follows the old Northern Pacific track from the mainline in the Yellowstone Valley to the town of Colstrip. The similarity of materials and construction techniques in the town's buildings that were constructed in the late 1920s and early 1930s is a reminder that Colstrip began as a company town. And the similarity of the drab prefabricated buildings and dwellings constructed by the Montana Power Company during the last 10 years is a reminder that Colstrip remains a one-industry town. New prefabricated buildings are intermingled with original brick and frame structures, creating an interesting urban landscape. Wooden cottages, mobile homes, the old main street, and the new shopping center coexist in a town that lives on the work and wealth of the mines.

Landscape 2: The Badlands of Southeastern Montana

"Badlands" conjures up images of a lifeless landscape with windblown shapes and unusual scenery. Some areas of Montana's southeastern corner, such as Makoshika State Park off I-94 at Glendive, fit this description. Makoshika contains the most spectacular badlands in the state, where the wind has carved eerie and colorful shapes from the sandstone.

Although most of Wibaux, Fallon, and Carter counties do not contain formations such as those found at Makoshika, people called this area "badlands" for decades after southeastern Montana was settled. On Montana Highway 7, you can stand on a large hill overlooking the landscape north of Ekalaka and compare the barrenness of the countryside to the hills, rock outcroppings, and forests that make up the Custer National Forest south of Ekalaka.

An even more desolate region of Montana lies in the area bordered by the Musselshell River to the east, the Missouri River to the north, and the Yellowstone River to the south. Between Jordan and Miles City on Montana Highway 22 or between Circle and Jordan on Montana Highway 200, there are few people and little vegetation. The locals accept the barrenness of their land with humor. In the "Rock Springs National Forest," for example, located just south of Garfield County near Rock Springs on Montana Highway 22, there is only one tree.

During the winter, snow frames the picturesque colors of the sandstone outcroppings and hillsides in Garfield, McCone, Prairie, and northern Rosebud counties, but the harshness of the land becomes apparent once the spring thaw is over. The topsoil is not only thin in this area, it is often nonexistent. Until just after the turn of the century, conventional wisdom had it that the land was only good for stock-growing; there was too little topsoil and the rain came too infrequently for farmers to succeed.

During the homesteading boom, however, the railroads and land speculators convinced many Americans that southeastern Montana had good land. Thousands came, creating towns like Baker, Circle, and Broadus. When the boom busted in the 1920s, most left, abandoning their homesteads. Along Montana Highway 7, Montana Highway 200, and U.S. Highway 212 are the remains of their homes, reminders of the homesteaders' dreams in this dry land.

The topsoil is still poor and the rain scanty in this region of Montana, but new wealth has been found in the petroleum and natural gas that lie underneath this dry and desolate region. Oil and gas wells are now prominent features on the southeastern Montana landscape.

Route 8: The Medicine Rocks
Montana Highway 7, near Ekalaka

Standing ominously on the plains near the border of Fallon and Carter counties are the Medicine Rocks. When Theodore Roosevelt visited here in 1883, he observed: "Altogether it was as fantastically beautiful a place as I have ever seen; it seemed impossible that the hand of man should not have something to do with

Medicine Rocks State Park, Carter County. *For centuries, Native Americans came to these rocks, where they prayed to the Great Spirit for guidance, strength, and protection.*

its formation." Native Americans drew a different conclusion about the oddly shaped sandstone formations and eerie feeling of the Medicine Rocks: the land must have been touched by the Great Spirits.

The Sioux called the country *Inyan-oka-la-ka*, or "rock with hole in it." The Medicine Rocks, which stretch for several miles, have ceremonial and religious significance for Montana Indians. It is a place where they often gathered to pray to the Great Spirits and to ask for spiritual guidance. Within the park, several stone circles mark the location of Native American camps, and there is a large medicine wheel, a stone circle used in religious rites. In the hills visible on the horizon, Indians found sources of red and blue pigments for the ceremonial paints they wore at the Medicine Rocks.

Route 9: Homesteading in Montana's Badlands

Route A: Montana Highway 200, at Circle
Route B: U.S. Highway 12, at Baker
Route C: Montana Highway 22, from Miles City to Jordan
Route D: Montana Highway 59, from Miles City to Biddle

Whites first settled Montana's southeastern badlands region during the 1880s and transformed the landscape by stocking the range with cattle. Some 20 years later, when the homesteading fever took hold, settlers crowded into the area and transformed the landscape once again, carving out dry-land farms from the arid region. Homesteaders soon discovered that there wasn't enough good land for everyone, and many failed. They left the land, but during their tenure they had created several towns. Transportation systems defined the nature of these homesteading communities. There were railroad towns, such as Circle, the county seat of McCone County, which was served by the Northern Pacific Railroad, and Baker, the county seat of Fallon County, which was served by the Chicago, Milwaukee, St Paul & Pacific, later known as the Milwaukee Road. And there were towns that relied only on dirt roads and later paved highways, such as Jordan, the county seat of Garfield County, and Broadus, the county seat of Powder River County.

Route A: Montana Highway 200, at Circle

Located at the junction of Montana Highway 200 and Montana Highway 13, Circle is one of the region's trading centers. Settlers began building Circle in 1904, but the town didn't boom until the first homesteaders arrived in the early 1910s. In 1914, the Great Northern platted a new townsite one-half mile away from the original village. Assuming that the railroad would build a spur line to the new town, residents of "old" Circle moved to "new" Circle. The Great Northern never built southward into Circle; but in 1929, the Northern Pacific Railroad extended a spur line from Sidney to Circle and continued on to Brockway. Highway 200 generally follows this railroad route.

By 1915, Circle had two banks, a newspaper, and the Gladstone Hotel. The two-story Gladstone—which still stands, with additions, on Montana Highway 200—had 20 sleeping rooms and served as a temporary home for the hundreds of homesteaders who flooded into McCone County. The hotel added 10 new sleeping rooms when it enjoyed a second burst of prosperity during the post-World War II oil boom in McCone County. The Gladstone is listed in the National Register of Historic Places.

Route B: U.S. Highway 12, at Baker

Baker, located at the junction of Montana Highway 7 and U.S. Highway 12 in Fallon County, was created when the Milwaukee Road extended its line from Evarts, South Dakota, to the West Coast. Many of Baker's buildings date from 1915 to 1918, when hundreds of homesteaders came to this corner of southeastern Montana. Baker's railroad corridor is still largely intact, and the spatial arrangement created by its Milwaukee depot and the neighboring Baker Hotel, an imposing brick building dating to 1916, symbolizes the railroad's importance to the town. Despite the Milwaukee Road's bankruptcy in the late 1970s, Baker has remained prosperous because of recent oil discoveries in Fallon County.

Route C: Montana Highway 22, from Miles City to Jordan

Jordan is the most isolated county seat in the contiguous 48 states. From 1910 to 1920, thousands of homesteaders came to this area hoping to find a better life. Today, just over 1,600 people live in this large county, in a land shaped by the physical remains left by those who found nothing but hardship in the "Big Dry."

Life was always difficult in Garfield County. The first homes were tiny, with one or two rooms. Some homesteaders built log houses; others constructed dug-

C. V. West, photographer, MHS SHPO

Abandoned homestead, Montana Highway 200. *Early Richland County residents had a favorite saying: "There is some of this homesteading land that you can't raise hell on with a gallon of whiskey."*

outs, tar-paper shacks, sod houses, and even houses made of gumbo clay. Only half had screens to keep out the grasshoppers and mosquitoes. The land never delivered the bounty that the homesteaders expected. In 1930, after two decades of settlement, only 25 of the county's 1,077 farms had piped water, and only 8 of those had running water in the bathrooms. Ranchers have moved many of these early homes to their spreads, converting them into chicken coops and storage sheds. On Montana Highway 200 east of Sand Springs and on Montana Highway 22 near Cohagen, you can spot the old homestead dwellings by looking for storage sheds with window openings or chimneys.

The primary reason that Garfield County did not grow was its isolation. Fifty years ago, Jordan, the county seat, was farther away from a rail connection than any other county seat in the U.S. Only a quarter of the farmers had trucks, and it took a week to carry produce to Miles City by horse and wagon. Most county roads were unimproved dirt roads or tracks across the prairie. There was no electricity until 1951 and no telephone service until five years later. The railroad never arrived.

The county's isolation is apparent in the Garfield County High School Dormitory in Jordan, which houses students who live too far away to go home every day. At one time, there were several such dormitories in Montana; but Garfield County's is the only one that still operates as a home for high school students.

C. V. West, photographer, MHS SHPO

Cross Ranch, Powder River County. *Established in the 1890s, the Cross Ranch is still a working ranch and its distinctive ranch house is still being used.*

Route D: Montana Highway 59, from Miles City to Biddle

Broadus, located in the Powder River Valley on Montana Highway 59, is 79 miles south of the railroad hub of Miles City. Like Jordan in Garfield County, highways are Broadus's only link to the rest of Montana. But because of the valley's plentiful resources, Powder River County residents have enjoyed more prosperity than those in Garfield County. In Powder River County, farmers and ranchers have discovered the value of the river valley's bottomland; and at Belle Creek, in the county's southeastern corner, there have been major oil discoveries. Broadus also has the advantage of being on U.S. Highway 212, which receives substantial commercial and tourist traffic.

In the middle of Broadus, surrounded by a town square and most of the town's major businesses, is a newly constructed county courthouse. This large one-story brick building is a reminder that homesteading towns such as Broadus can survive and prosper in an era of modern agriculture.

Ranching has also played an important role in Powder River County's history, and you can see an unusual type of ranch house about 26 miles south of Broadus near Biddle. The old ranch headquarters of the Cross Ranch, organized by Major S. F. B. Biddle, dates to the 1890s. Biddle's ranch headquarters has a unique design, with a hip roof and a porch that encircles the building. The ranch buildings were constructed with logs from the head of nearby Ranch Creek. Biddle's eastern background is evident in the care he took in building his ranch headquarters and in landscaping the surrounding land. The Cross Ranch is on private property. Do not trespass.

Seventy-four miles north of Broadus on Montana Highway 59 is Miles City, the county seat of Custer County and the commercial center of southeastern Montana. Located at the confluence of the Tongue and Yellowstone rivers, Miles City is the oldest settlement in the region, created in 1876-1877 by entrepreneurs who located their businesses next to the recently established Fort Keogh. The settlement, located four miles from Fort Keogh, was called Miles Town until 1878, when the government opened for settlement a 10-square-mile portion of the military reservation east of the Tongue River. The residents of Miles Town moved to the area and named the new town Miles City.

From 1878 until the mid 1880s, Miles City was the region's leading settlement. It had "the appearance of a lively up-to-date town. A garrison full of soldiers and the usual complement of followers and citizen employees made a good payroll. This was enlarged by the earnings of a small army of government contractors' new, high salaried clerks in the stores and the continued influx of the tenderfoot." Miles City's main street (now U.S. Highway 10) became an important transportation artery through the northern plains, connecting Bozeman and Fort Keogh in Montana to Fort Buford, Deadwood, and Bismarck in the Dakotas.

The arrival of the Northern Pacific Railroad in 1881 further strengthened Miles City's position as southeastern Montana's leading trade center. Entrepreneurs established several new businesses and, as Walter Cameron recalled, "in these places could be seen doctors, merchants, lawyers and other varieties of professional men as well as the common laboring men jostling and crowding each other in their efforts to see what was going on in the place."

The presence of the U.S. Army in the Yellowstone country created the need for Miles City over 100 years ago, but the town changed when the Northern Pacific arrived. By 1881-1882, Miles City had become one of the classic cattle towns of the American West. Cattlemen trailed their herds for hundreds of miles from Montana's central and eastern ranges to the railhead at Miles City, and the town responded by building sizable and busy cattle corrals and loading docks and by providing entertainments for cowboys that were typical of other cattle towns.

Many of the storefronts along Main Street date to the late 19th century. Today in Miles City, the Northern Pacific depot on Pacific Avenue and the Montana Bar at 612 Main are reminders of a time 100 years ago when cowboys, railroad workers, soldiers, and store clerks kicked up the dust along these streets.

When the Milwaukee Road built to Miles City in the early years of this century, the town underwent another change. In 1906, the Milwaukee Road had accepted Miles City's offer of a free right-of-way through town. The railroad built through the city's northern section, creating a new boom in settlement and construction. You can still see the Milwaukee's depot on N. 9th Avenue and many of the warehouses, grain elevators, hotels, and rooming houses still stand in nearby residential and commercial districts.

Miles City, Custer County, 1884. *During the early 1880s, Miles City was the major trade center in eastern Montana. Each year, Montana stock-growers shipped thousands of carloads of cattle to markets in the East, making Miles City the territory's leading "cowtown."*

Ranch on the Tongue River, Custer County, 1894. *Many ranchers in eastern Montana altered the prairie with irrigated gardens and orchards. Their fences, homes, outbuildings, and grazing lands created new patterns on the landscape.*

Burlington Northern tracks and U.S. Highway 2 in Glacier County

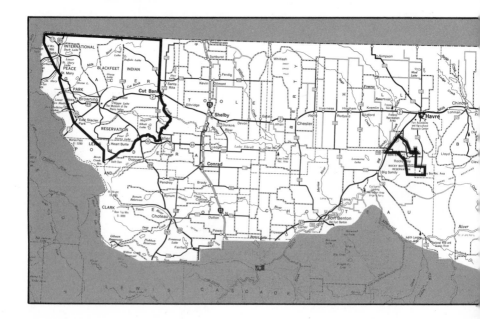

Chapter 2

The Hi-Line Country

The country east of the Continental Divide and north of the Missouri River has been called the Hi-Line for the last 100 years, but you won't find the state's highest mountains here nor is the altitude unusually high. "Hi-Line" is a term Montanans use to describe the Great Northern Railway, its route, and the surrounding area.

When you travel along U.S. Highway 2, you can see why northern Montana residents use a railroad route to define their country. Whether the tracks follow the Milk and Missouri rivers or stretch across the wheat fields of north central Montana, there is no escaping the railroad's presence. The grain elevators, passenger depots, and warehouses that line the iron rails dominate the region's built environment.

Two hundred years ago, however, the tribes of the Blackfoot Confederacy—the Piegan, Kainah, and Siksika—rode across these prairies and claimed them as their domain. The Indians marked the landscape with trails of conquest, such as the Old North Trail, which runs roughly parallel to U.S. Highway 89. Remnants of the old trail, which Confederacy Indians used to travel as far north as

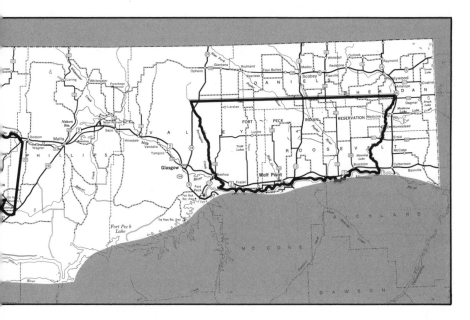

Calgary, Alberta, and as far south as New Mexico, can be seen in Glacier and Pondera counties.

The fur-bearing animals that lived along the rivers and streams of northern Montana lured the first white Americans. During the 1830s, the American Fur Company took control of the Upper Missouri fur trade, establishing a trading partnership with the Blackfoot Confederacy and its allies, the Atsina. By the 1840s, the company had constructed Fort Benton at the head of navigation of the Missouri. Steamboats regularly supplied the trading post during the 1860s, making Fort Benton Montana's major river town and home to the trading companies of T. C. Power and I. G. Baker. On U.S. Highway 87 at the highway marker for Fort Benton, you can look from the river bluffs and see a natural basin and river landing and imagine how a prosperous trade center emerged here during the 1860s.

Despite the wealth of natural resources on the northern plains and in the river valleys, permanent white settlers did not come to northern Montana until the St. Paul, Minneapolis & Manitoba Railroad (later known as the Great Northern Railway) physically linked the northern plains to major eastern population centers and eastern markets. Laying the first rails in Minot, North Dakota, on April 2, 1887, the Manitoba reached the present-day Havre area by early September. Speculators, entrepreneurs, and railroad officials hurried to lay out towns along the new railroad line.

At the outset, Glasgow, Malta, Chinook, and Havre were primarily shipping points for the large stock-growing concerns that ran cattle throughout the Milk River country. Later, during the early 1900s, the homesteading boom turned these small towns into commercial centers, and villages such as Rudyard, Kremlin, and Inverness developed along the railroad's sidings. These homesteading towns retain a commanding position on the landscape, but they are no longer important commercial centers. Automobiles and the creation of U.S. Highway 2 made a handful of towns—Cut Bank, Shelby, Havre, Glasgow, and Wolf Point—into the region's major trade centers.

Landscape 3: The Hi-Line

On U.S. Highway 2 east of Browning, you can stop at Cut Bank, Dunkirk, Chester, or Hingham and see rolling prairie stretching as far as the eye can see. But this land, with its alternating strips of wheat and fallow land, is only a part of the region's diversified topography.

At Havre, the county seat of Hill County, you can look to the northwest and see the Sweetgrass Hills and to the southeast and see the Bears Paw Mountains. Havre is in the Milk River Valley, which is a source of timber, rich bottomland, and water for irrigation. U.S. Highway 2 follows the Milk River for many miles until the river empties into the Missouri near Nashua.

The Hi-Line also passes through Marias River country. Formed by Birch and Cut Bank creeks and Two Medicine River, the Marias's headwaters are on the southeastern corner of the Blackfeet Indian Reservation. From there the river flows to the southeast, eventually joining the Missouri River at Loma on U.S.

Highway 87. The valley created by the Marias possessed important resources for Native Americans: trees, water, and fur-bearing animals. But the relative narrowness of the valley convinced white homesteaders to settle elsewhere.

Huge herds of bison once grazed on the Hi-Line's plains, on the rolling hills of the uplands, and in the "Missouri Breaks," where Native Americans lived and hunted. This same country later became an open range, where stock-growers grazed their large herds; it is now largely the domain of wheat farmers. Indians worshipped in the Sweetgrass Hills and the Bears Paw Mountains, and whites searched these same hills for mineral treasures. The Hi-Line is a land of varied resources.

Route 10: The Great Northern Railway
U.S. Highway 2, from Shelby to Bainville

The Great Northern Railway parallels U.S. Highway 2, which stretches across Montana for almost 440 miles from Browning on the eastern boundary of Glacier National Park to Bainville near the North Dakota state line. The Great Northern was the brainchild of James J. Hill, a midwestern businessman who was persuaded by several Montanans to extend his railroad west of Minot, North Dakota. Marcus Daly, president of the Anaconda Copper Company, wanted a northern line to compete with the Union Pacific in order to decrease the cost of freighting his copper from Butte. Paris Gibson told Hill that a railroad across northern Montana could attract settlers and allow Gibson's town at the Great Falls of the Missouri to become the "new Minneapolis" of the Northwest.

Hill had grander plans. He envisioned the creation of commercial markets that would keep his trains running around the clock, and he planned to control all of the railroad traffic in the region. Beginning in Dakota in the spring of 1887, his crews worked feverishly and reached Great Falls by mid October. Hill quickly added a spur line out to the surface coal mines at Sand Coulee, east of Great Falls. His subsidiary line, the Montana Central Railroad, linked Great Falls and Helena by November and Butte by the following year.

By the turn of the century, Hill and his partners had also gained control of the Northern Pacific and the Chicago, Burlington, and Quincy railroads. With this empire, Hill controlled Montana's railway traffic, and he prospered as his railcars headed east to Chicago hauling copper from Butte, gold from Marysville, silver from Granite, and cattle from Havre. But the cars returning to Montana arrived virtually empty. There were too few settlers along the Hi-Line during the 1880s and 1890s to provide a market for eastern manufactured products.

Hill also faced competition from a new transcontinental railroad, the Chicago, Milwaukee, St. Paul & Pacific, better known as the Milwaukee Road. The Milwaukee Road officials planned to build the railroad through southern and central Montana and vigorously promoted the new route and encouraged thousands to settle along the line. The railroad's advertisements flooded not only urban centers in the East but many European cities as well.

Hill responded by launching his own promotional campaign to entice settlers to Montana and North Dakota. He preached that dry farming techniques and ir-

C. V. West, photographer. MHS SHPO

Depot, Rudyard, Hill County. *The Rudyard community made its reputation as a grain producer early in its history. In 1914, it shipped more wheat down the Hi-Line than any town between Shelby and Havre.*

rigation in northern Montana would make it possible for Americans to exchange their factory jobs for farming. Tens of thousands responded to the advertisements, and during the first two decades of the 20th century Hill's railcars were filled with homesteaders headed to northern Montana. But by the 1920s, drought seared the land and the homesteading boom had become a bust. Jim Hill's cars ran empty once again.

Regardless of the effects of drought and depression, the Great Northern Railway continued to dominate the lives of those who lived along the Hi-Line and directly influenced how their towns looked and developed. Montana's first towns—the mining camps—had developed haphazardly, each with a distinctive look as settlers fitted their houses and businesses to the particular topography of the mining district. But the towns along the Great Northern were carefully planned by engineers and landscape architects. These towns were similar in appearance, usually having either a "T-style" or "strip" design.

To see how the Great Northern influenced town development, begin at Shelby and travel east on U.S. Highway 2 for 42 miles until you reach Chester. Chester originally stood north of a curve in the Great Northern line along Cottonwood Creek; but in 1907-1908 railroad officials decided to straighten the bend, forcing the entire town to move to its present location south of the tracks.

Rudyard (about 20 miles east of Chester) and Kremlin (21 miles east of Rudyard) in Hill County are excellent examples of T-style railroad towns. In Rudyard and Kremlin, running east and west of the depots are the railroad tracks and imposing grain elevators, which form the top part of the "T." In Rudyard, run-

C. V. West, photographer, MHS SHPO

Abandoned building, Cottonwood, Hill County. *Located miles from the Great Northern Railway, Cottonwood was established in 1910 as a small farming community in the eastern Milk River Valley.*

ning north of the depot and in Kremlin running south is each town's business strip, which forms the stem of the "T." T-style town plans diverted pedestrian and vehicle traffic away from the railroad and usually placed the Great Northern depot at the "head" of the town, with every business except the grain elevator flowing from this symbolic position of power. There was little doubt about what was the most important institution in these towns.

In a strip or symmetrical town, such as Saco and Dodson in Phillips County, you can see a different arrangement of businesses, space, rails, and elevators. In Dodson, over 90 miles east of Kremlin, the railroad splits the town in two, with the grain elevators and depot on one side and the business district on the other. At Saco, 45 miles east of Dodson, looking north from the tracks that run in front of the town's abandoned bank—an impressive two-story brick building—you can see several decaying wooden buildings that once comprised the town's main business district, which included the post office, the telephone exchange, and the hotel. Sixty years ago, Saco was a "T" town, but it changed when U.S. Highway 2 replaced the Great Northern Railway as the primary transportation route in northern Montana. The businesses that survived the change moved to new locations along the highway, and Saco became a strip town.

The railroad's influence is more difficult to see in other towns along the Hi-Line. Wolf Point, 91 miles east of Saco, is the county seat of Roosevelt County. The town was established as a railroad division point in 1917. At the old stockyards, on the north side of the tracks across from the depot, there was once a 20-stall roundhouse, a 50-room dormitory for "layover" railroad employees, and several homes

Grain elevators, Lothair, Liberty County. *The rigors of homesteading toughened many northern Montanans. It "got so we could live on nothing," recalled Selmer Helland.*

for permanent railroad workers. But in 1925, the railroad abolished the division point, and hundreds of residents left the community. Decades of hard times followed until the late 1940s and 1950s, when oil was discovered in Roosevelt County, returning prosperity to Wolf Point.

Fifty-four miles east of Wolf Point on U.S. Highway 2, the Great Northern's depot in Culbertson is a reminder of the railroad's social and economic importance to the small towns along the Hi-Line. The depot replaced the post office or general store as the place where villagers could swap local gossip and hear the latest news about distant cities from arriving passengers and from the telegraph office. For many Montanans, the depot was a center of community in a land of isolation with indirect connections to the rest of the country.

The Great Northern's steel rails, wooden ties, and raised roadbed created a corridor through northern Montana. Two prominent features of the corridor, telephone lines and electric power lines, kept rural Montanans in touch with the world and supplied them with a constant source of energy.

At Bainville in Roosevelt County, about 15 miles east of Culbertson, you can see how the arrangement of rails, ties, and roadbed created a corridor between Chicago and Seattle, connecting Montana to major eastern and western markets and introducing urban values to a largely rural population.

The railroad imposed a pattern on the lives of those who lived in towns along the Hi-Line. The railroad employees' work day, for instance, did not begin at dawn and end at sunset. Because of bureaucratic organization and precise round-the-clock schedules, working for the railroad in Bainville was similar to working a factory shift in Cleveland, Ohio. Even townspeople who didn't work for the railroad found that the rhythms of the train traffic influenced everyday activities.

The corridor established by the Great Northern Railway connected the citizens of Bainville, Malta, and Glasgow with the rest of America and its conspicuous consumption, industrial grandeur, and hurried pace of life. You can stand at Bainville and imagine what local residents must have thought when luxurious passenger trains, with individually owned cars, rolled through on their way to Seattle,

Chicago, or summer resorts in Glacier National Park. For rural Montanans, these special trains symbolized the wealth and power held by those men who owned the railroad and manufactured the goods the trains carried. Sixty years ago, those who lived along the corridor believed that they had only to reach out to the tracks to feel the pulse of a mighty nation.

Route 11: Homesteading on the Hi-Line
Route A: Montana Roads 232, 241, and 242
Route B: U.S. Highway 2, from Havre to Shelby
Route C: U.S. Highway 87, at Montana Road 432 exit in Big Sandy
Route D: Montana Highway 16, at Montana Road 258 at Reserve

One of America's last homesteading booms took place in northern Montana during the first two decades of this century. Novelist Wallace Stegner has best described the look of the land after homesteaders had transformed the prairie into farms:

On that monotonous surface with its occasional ship-like form, its atoll of shelter-belt trees, its level ring of horizon, there is little to interrupt the eye. Roads run straight between parallel lines of fence until they intersect the circle of the horizon. It is a landscape of circles, radii, perspective exercises—a country of geometry.

Most of the homesteaders came to the Hi-Line to take advantage of the homestead acts of 1909 and 1912, which offered up to 320 acres of land free to those who could build a house and improve the land in three years—"prove up" on the claim. Others came to claim the unallotted land on the Indian reservations. Another group purchased their land from private owners. All who came endured the hardships and celebrated the triumphs of homestead life.

The northern Montana homesteading boom took place for three reasons: First, the Great Northern Railway provided inexpensive transportation to the settlers' new homes and created a transportation system that could carry their crops to market. Second, speculators and promoters, along with Great Northern officials, persuaded many Americans that technological advances in dry farming techniques and irrigation could transform the dry, upland plains into a farming wonderland. Third, the government offered free land and opened the Indian reservations to white settlement.

For those who already lived along the Hi-Line, the boom must have been something to behold. In 1910, the federal land office at Great Falls processed over 1,000 land claims a month; and on one evening that spring, 250 homesteaders disembarked from Great Northern cars in Havre. On one day in 1913, a Great Northern conductor took up 503 tickets from people bound for Montana's plains; three years later, 1,200 homesteaders arrived in Havre during March. The migration affected the entire state. In 1900, Montana's population reached over 240,000; 20 years later, the state had almost 550,000 residents, many of them homesteaders.

You can see the remnants of those frenetic days along several routes in northern Montana. Barns, silos, frame homes, school buildings, and other structures convey a sense of what the homesteaders' life was like on the Hi-Line during the 1910s and 1920s.

Route A: Montana Roads 232, 241, 242

The historical landscape along Montana Road 232 in Hill County, Montana 241 in Blaine County, and Montana 242 in Phillips County provides clues about the nature of homesteading on the sparsely vegetated rolling hills of Montana's uplands in communities that were often located miles from the mainline of the Great Northern Railway.

You can leave U.S. Highway 2 in downtown Havre at the exit for Montana Road 232 and travel along the eastern border of the Milk River Valley. About 30 miles northwest of Havre is the homesteading community of Cottonwood, first settled in 1910, where local citizens have put up a monument honoring the settlement's history. A few hundred feet from the monument is Cottonwood Community Hall, a well-preserved wooden building constructed in 1914, with some of the town's remaining buildings standing a few hundred yards to the south. North of the community hall is St. John's Catholic Church, built in 1928.

At Simpson, about six miles south of the Canadian border and eight miles north of Cottonwood, the Spring Coulee and Border one-room schoolhouses have served the people of northern Hill County for most of this century. These buildings have been placed together, and their good condition attests to the community's pride in its past.

Forty-two miles east of Havre is Montana Road 241, which branches from U.S. Highway 2 at Harlem and winds through another upland historical landscape that was shaped by homesteaders. Turner, 31 miles north of Harlem, dates to 1913, when Henry Turner built a store to serve both American and Canadian homesteaders. After the homesteading bust 15 years later, the Great Northern constructed a spur line from Saco to Turner. When railroad officials decided to survey the new townsite two and one-half miles south of town, "old" Turner residents quickly relocated to "new" Turner. The passenger depot and the large grain elevators still remain in Turner, but the weeds now stand tall along the railroad corridor. Nevertheless, Turner retains a strong community spirit, which can best be seen in the historic American Lutheran Church, a social center for the many Scandinavian-American families who live there today.

The Saco spur line ended at Hogeland, a small town about 10 miles west of Turner. When railroad officials located a town here in 1928, the largest settlement in this part of Blaine County was at Woody Island Creek, some miles away. But once again the railroad was a more powerful magnet than community allegiance, and by the fall of 1928 almost everyone at Woody Island had moved to Hogeland. As in Turner, the railroad corridor still exists at Hogeland, although it is rapidly deteriorating. Unlike Turner, Hogeland no longer has a school. Its large two-story brick schoolhouse, built in 1936, housed the primary grades on the first floor and the intermediate and junior high grades on the second floor. The school is a strong statement of Hogeland's hopes as it emerged from the Great Depression. Many of those dreams were dashed by the 1950s, however, as the difficulty of farming in the "Big Flat" of Blaine County drove most of the town's citizens to more promising regions.

Forty-six miles east of Harlem at Malta is the exit for Montana Road 242. Wallace Stegner, who lived along the Whitewater Creek drainage just north of Montana Road 242 in Canada, remembered a desolate and beautiful land, a place where the vastness of the sky and the enormity of the prairie makes you "acutely aware of yourself." As you drive on Montana 242 north toward Loring, you will see abandoned farms and irrigation ditches, given up by those who failed to scratch out a foothold on this rugged terrain.

Loring and Whitewater are still community centers for settlers on the Whitewater Creek drainage. A Great Northern spur line once served both towns, but the large grain elevators in Loring are now the only link the town has with its railroad past. The passenger depot in Whitewater still stands, but it is no longer located on the tracks. It has been moved to another part of town and is now a private home.

Route B: U.S. Highway 2, from Havre to Shelby

West of Havre along U.S. Highway 2, you can see many abandoned homesteads. Those small buildings that have a window opening or chimneys or the remains of chimneys may well be homesteaders' houses. Many of those buildings are now used for storage or for chicken coops.

Most of the abandoned buildings along this route are second generation (or later) homes, constructed once the farm was successful. A woman homesteader in Blaine County, for instance, recalled that she and her husband first built a 9- by 12-foot "shack" to which they had added a 10- by 12-foot room by the end of their first summer there. Not until five years later did they attach to "this contraption" a "modest 3-room house, with an attic." These abandoned homesteads appear to be isolated, connected to nothing but the land; but considered together, they comprise a historical landscape that provides evidence of the migration to the Hi-Line three generations ago.

Homesteaders may have felt isolated on the Hi-Line, but that feeling vanished when they stepped into their homes. In the early dwellings, there was an acute lack of privacy. The typical homesteader's house measured about 12 by 18 feet, with two rooms, one doorway, and two or three windows; some had only one room and one door. Most homesteaders covered their windows and doors with wooden flaps that could be left open in warm weather and closed during cold spells. There were few trees on the Hi-Line, so most houses were built of planks instead of logs. These homes were unbearably hot during the summer, but at least the family could seek relief outside. Winter was another matter. Insulation was often make-do, with newspapers covering interior walls and tar paper tacked on the outside, and some homesteaders piled dirt around their shacks to help keep out the cold.

The average homestead also had stables for the livestock, a shed for the plow and other farm tools, and a hen house with several chickens and a rooster. But there were few fences on early Hi-Line homesteads. They were just too expensive to build. In 1915, for example, it cost $220 to fence a typical 320-acre homestead—too much money for most farmers to spend.

Traveling west on U.S. Highway 2 through Rudyard, Gildford, Chester, and Shelby, grain elevators dominate the skyline. These elevators were the key

C. V. West, photographer, MHS SHPO

Barns, Montana Road 432, Chouteau County. *A changing agricultural landscape can be seen in this farm, which combines modern metal granaries with classic examples of a gable roof granary and a broken-angle roof barn.*

C. V. West, photographer, MHS SHPO

Kenilworth Hall, Montana Road 432, Chouteau County. *According to Morris Stewart of northern Chouteau County, isolated homesteaders were compelled to attend as many community events as possible, sometimes traveling through blizzards to attend dances and "midnight lunches."*

businesses in the Great Northern's corridor and are the most imposing physical remnants of the homesteading experience. Looming over all other structures in both small and large towns along the Hi-Line, grain elevators are a symbol of agriculture's importance to the region and represent the farmers' entry into world markets.

As you drive along U.S. Highway 2, you can see an elevator or the remnants of one at nearly every railroad siding. Towns like Ethridge, Devon, and Joplin existed largely because of the grain elevators; and when the elevator companies ceased operations in these places, the towns began to die. Some homesteading ghost towns still have operating elevators, used by local farmers for their own grain storage.

Small towns along the Hi-Line usually had wooden grain elevators. Most elevators were three and a half stories tall, topped with a gabled roof, and built with 2 by 8 planks on the lower half and 2 by 6 planks on the upper half. They had a clapboard exterior, although many elevator operators later added pressed metal siding. Wooden-cribbed elevators work well on the Hi-Line: they do not sweat and they stay free of vermin if they are kept clean and are built properly with seasoned timbers.

In larger towns along the Hi-Line, operators built concrete and steel elevators, which are fireproof and durable but they have a tendency to sweat. While concrete elevators could be constructed quickly in almost any shape, they required materials not locally available and were expensive to build.

By looking at the type of grain elevators found along U.S. Highway 2 or U.S. Highway 87, you can date the economic stability of most towns on this route. Most wooden elevators were built before 1942; and if a town has only wooden elevators, it has enjoyed little economic progress for over 40 years. Those towns with large concrete elevators, however, survived the hard times of the 1920s and 1930s and have enjoyed some prosperity.

Route C: U.S. Highway 87, at Montana Road 432 exit in Big Sandy

If you take a brief detour from U.S. Highway 87 at Big Sandy, 70 miles southwest of Havre, you will see an example of the diversity of rural Montana farm buildings. Along Montana Road 432, most of the barns are examples of the intermontane style, a rectangular structure with an open and uncovered loft that is very popular throughout the West. The region's dry climate allows farmers to leave their hay exposed to the elements, and many leave huge piles of hay in the field. Because most farmers leave their stock on the range, the intermontane style of barn needs no large area for animals.

While the barns on Montana Road 432 are basically in the same style, they have many different types of roofs, including the straight lines of the simple gable roof, the three-bay wide roof, the broken-angle roof, the gracefully curved gambrel roof, and some with cupolas. The modern corrugated metal cylinders on the landscape compare strikingly with the early wooden granaries, which often appear to be miniature barns. There are also several abandoned two-story farmhouses in this area.

Kenilworth Hall, about 15 miles west of Big Sandy on Montana Road 432, is a significant building in this part of Chouteau County. This simple, one-story wooden building, which looks like the top half of a round-roofed barn, played an important role in the local community. Before there were paved roads and automobiles in the area, homesteaders escaped the isolation of their farms and gathered at Kenilworth Hall to enjoy the fellowship of their neighbors as they listened to a politician's plea, a preacher's exhortation, or a fiddler's tune. At such times, homesteaders came together to create a town atmosphere.

Route D: Montana Highway 16, at Montana Road 258 at Reserve

Many homesteaders along the Hi-Line were first or second generation European immigrants, and they influenced every town's history. One particularly good example is Dagmar in Sheridan County. Dagmar is located in the northeastern corner of Montana. From Plentywood, the county seat of Sheridan County, take Montana Highway 16 south to Reserve, then turn on Montana Road 258 and travel east until you reach Dagmar. The Dagmar Lutheran Church remains the community center for the children of Danish immigrants who arrived during the homesteading boom. E. F. Madsen, a former Danish schoolteacher who founded the colony in the fall of 1906, made the land arrangements so that "all any new settlers had to do was to come to Montana, follow the trail out across the prairie, and build their shacks."

The colony produced grain and did well during its first 10 years. Madsen remembered that "modern farm houses and buildings everywhere dotted the prairie; good roads were made and everyone prospered." The drought of the late 1910s and a hailstorm in 1921 ended those halcyon years, and the colony slid into a long period of decline. Little remains in Dagmar today, but the Lutheran church and E. F. Madsen's multi-story home still make a striking appearance on the northeastern Montana countryside.

Route 12: Native American Dwellings in Northern Montana
Route A: U.S. Highway 2, from Poplar to Browning
Route B: Montana Road 243, at Saco

U.S. Highway 2 links the three largest Native American reservations in northern Montana: the Blackfeet Indian Reservation, the Fort Belknap Indian Reservation, and the Fort Peck Indian Reservation. Two centuries ago, the stretch of land between present-day Glacier National Park and the North Dakota state line was the domain of the Blackfoot Confederacy, the Atsina, the Assiniboine, and the Cree. The descendants of these tribes still live in this country.

Whenever you visit northern Montana, stop and think about how the land must have looked before whites arrived. With a bit of imagination and observant eyes, you can recreate the Native American built environment. Two hundred years ago, the typical Native American camp and village contained many types of buildings, each made from the natural resources at hand. The most common remnants of these structures are tipi rings, the stone circles left when Native

MHS Photo Archives

Dane Church, Dagmar, Sheridan County, 1920. *The Dagmar colony's meetinghouse, which was an important social center for Danish Americans in the area, was constructed in 1909 to replace one that had been built of sod.*

Americans moved their camps. These stones—or sod and wood when stones were unavailable—were used to keep the edges of a tipi flat on the ground.

Route A: U.S. Highway 2, from Poplar to Browning

Whenever you travel through a river corridor in northern Montana—whether along the Milk River on U.S. Highway 2 from Havre to Nashua, the drainage of Big Muddy Creek along Montana Highway 16 from Plentywood to Homestead, or where I-15 crosses the Marias River about six miles south of Shelby—you are surrounded by hundreds to thousands of tipi rings in the river breaks and uplands that rise over the river valley. You can see what a tipi looks like in Browning at the Museum of the Plains Indians, located at the intersection of U.S. Highways 2 and 89.

Three of the best marked tipi ring sites in northern Montana lie some distance from a major highway. One well-preserved tipi ring site lies about 20 miles south of Browning on the paved reservation road that runs west from U.S. Highway 89 to the town of Heart Butte.

On U.S. Highway 2, 11 miles west of Havre, is a gravel road heading north toward the Fresno Dam Recreation Area, the site of thousands of tipi rings. The nearby Chain of Lakes, a preglacial channel of the Milk River, constantly waters the surrounding grasslands. Bison were plentiful because of this source of food, so prehistoric groups occupied the area throughout the year. This region was an exceptionally important resource for Montana's prehistoric peoples and is a significant historical landscape.

Along Montana Highway 16 at Lake in Sheridan County, you can visit the Tipi Hills at the Medicine Lake National Wildlife Refuge, a place listed in the National Register of Historic Places. The hills surrounding the lake contain many tipi rings, and there is evidence that many bands of Native Americans used the rich resources of the Medicine Lake area.

C. V. West, photographer, MHS SHPO

Sun Lodge, Heart Butte Road, Blackfeet Indian Reservation, Glacier County. *Canadian fur trader Alexander Henry wrote that "the greatest oath [a warrior] can possibly utter is that the earth and the sun hear him speak."*

Tipi is a Siouxian word meaning "used for dwelling." A tipi is "a cone-shaped tent with a smoke hole at the top for ventilation" built out of bison hides or canvas, rocks and wooden pegs, and lodgepole pine poles. More often than not, the tipi was a "tilted cone," with an oval-shaped floor, a design that allowed the poles of the frame to cross at the top end of the smoke hole, protecting the interior from rain and snow. This design also made the tipi more stable, with the back side facing the prevailing winds, and allowed for more head room at the back of the structure.

Tipis were the Indians' most common dwelling for thousands of years. Once the Indians had acquired horses, they were able to move larger tipis; and sometimes they constructed large tipi lodges, with as many as 30 buffalo skins and 2 or 3 rock-lined hearths. Most Native Americans lived in tipis year-round, even if the camp frequently changed locations. Women maintained their family's tipi and moved it on a travois, a wooden pole frame that Native Americans used to carry their belongings and tipis from camp to camp. Rebuilding the tipi was quick and simple, usually taking no more than 30 minutes.

The poles were the most important parts of the tipi structure. Each tipi required a certain number of poles, depending on its size. A tipi with a diameter of 18 feet, for instance, needed about 18 poles, each at least 21 feet long. The Indians of northern Montana and southern Alberta and Saskatchewan often cut their pine poles in the Little Rocky Mountains, the Bears Paw Mountains, and Canada's Cypress Hills. Stripped of their bark and pointed at their butt end, the poles were smooth and thin, measuring about two inches at the top and four to five inches at the bottom. Only a smooth, straight pole would allow for a tight fit.

Trees are scarce in parts of northern Montana, so the Indians carried their poles from camp to camp. It took a lot of time and work to prepare new poles, and most Indians tried to make a set of tipi poles last for two years. Almost without exception, tipis were covered with buffalo hides that the women had transformed into a tipi cover, usually decorated with religious or personal symbols.

During the 1850s, Edwin Denig, an American Fur Company official at Fort Union, described the tipis he had seen among the northern Montana Indians after the fur trade had brought them greater prosperity:

The tent is stretched on poles from 12 to 20 feet in length . . . each family making one to suit the number of persons to be accommodated or their means of transporting it; therefore their sizes vary from 6 to 23 skins each. . . . the common or medium size being 12 skins, which will lodge a family of eight persons with their baggage, and also have a space to entertain two or three guests. The area of a lodge of 12 skins when well pitched is a circumference of 31 feet.

The tipi was the perfect dwelling for the semi-nomadic hunters of Montana's high plains. In the summer, the Indians rolled the cover up from the bottom to create better ventilation. During the winter, they surrounded their tipis with snow fences.

Native American religious structures were very different from their homes. You can see two examples of the most sacred lodge—the sun lodge—in northern Montana: on the Blackfeet Indian Reservation, along the road between Browning and Heart Butte, and on the Fort Peck Indian Reservation at Frazer, just off U.S. Highway 2. The Fort Peck sun lodge is clearly visible from the highway. Do not enter or remove articles from these lodges; they are sacred religious sites and are on tribal property.

The sun lodge was a large tipi centered on a huge wooden pole, with long poles representing the bands of the tribe leaning against the center pole. During the 19th century, however, the shape of a sun lodge changed dramatically. The tall cottonwood pole remained at the center of the building, but the lodge's shape was a polygon, with other forked posts placed around the center pole. These outside posts, representing the tribal bands, were connected to the center pole "by stringers laid in their forks." Brush and animal skins covered parts of the frame.

Both the Assiniboine and Cree built "long lodges" for certain ceremonies. The Cree *sapohtowa'n* was made from two tripods of cottonwoods placed 25 feet apart with a top ridgepole on the tripods and tipi poles laid against the "ridgepole and in a semicircle around the two tripods." The Cree placed some tipi covers and brush on the lower portion of the lodge, but the top half remained open. Two rock-lined hearths located beneath each tripod kept dancers warm in the *sapohtowa'n*. The Cree *wewahtahoka'n* was a large tipi framework used for special ceremonial dances. The Cree "smoking tipi" religious lodge was built from four cottonwood poles and had a round altar dug into the center of the lodge.

The long lodge of the Assiniboine was much different. Edwin Denig described the Assiniboine's sacred lodge as a "long tent" in which posts are placed "a few yards apart and others transversely, over which are stretched many lodge skins to form one building about 100 yards long and 5 or 6 yards wide." The Assiniboine tied offerings to their god Wakonda on the transverse poles and built a 40-foot-high mast to designate the sacredness of the dwelling.

The sweat lodge was associated with the sun lodge ceremonies and many other Native American rites. According to George B. Grinnell, the Blackfeet sweat lodge was "built in the shape of a rough hemisphere, three or four feet high and six or eight in diameter. The frame is usually of willow branches, and is covered with cowskins and robes." Periodically, heated rocks and a bucket of water were placed inside a rock-lined hearth, producing heat and humidity that made the occupants sweat. You can see a sweat lodge from U.S. Highway 2 at Frazer on the Fort Peck Indian Reservation, located next to the standing sun lodge.

The topography of the river bluffs and creeks of northern Montana was ideal for trapping and killing bison. The Indians drove bison over steep cliffs and then slaughtered them. Using a similar hunting technique, the Piegan women built buffalo pounds, temporary structures made by placing dog travois upright into the ground and then tying them together to create a semicircular fence. Warriors could then either chase bison up a gully or over a cliff into the trap. This type of buffalo pound was a very portable structure, which the Piegan used primarily in the summer.

During the winter, the Piegan used a buffalo pound that was much more permanent. At the bottom of a cliff or slope, warriors set wooden posts in the ground to a height of seven feet and connected the posts with "crosspoles tied in place with rawhide." To support the corral, the Piegan "laid stakes over the lowest crosspole" and planted the butt ends of the stakes into the ground, leaving about three feet of the stakes projecting inside the pound. The stakes were then sharpened. Warriors chased the bison into the traps, and the animals were impaled on the stakes or killed by arrows and spears.

The Assiniboine buffalo pound used in northeastern Montana and southern Saskatchewan differed from that used by the Piegan. It was about 300 feet in circumference, 5 feet high, and usually built on a slope or placed in a wide gully. Its foundation was covered with branches and twigs.

The Assiniboine also built deadfalls to trap small animals. According to one expert on the tribe, this simple trap was "made by planting sticks in the ground with a cross-piece supporting a heavy series of beams loaded with rocks." A post, which supported the trap, served as the trigger. Tied to the trigger was a piece of buffalo meat.

The only bison kill open to the public is the Wahkpa Chu'gn ("Too Close for Comfort") archaeological site in Havre, just off U.S. Highway 2. Listed in the National Register of Historic Places, the site is located behind the Havre shopping mall, and tours can be arranged at the H. Earl Clack Museum on U.S. Highway 2 in Havre. The Indians first used this part of the Milk River Valley about 2,000 years ago; and Wahkpa Chu'gn, which was last used in the mid 1800s, remained a bison kill site long after the Indians acquired horses.

Wahkpa Chu'gn overlooks the Milk River and is a combination buffalo jump and pound used by the Indians who lived in the coulee. They may have chased a large herd over the river bluffs, killing enough animals to meet their needs. The

C. V. West, photographer, MHS SHPO

Wahkpa Chu'gn Bison Kill, Havre, Hill County. *These small sheds protect parts of the bison kill that have already been excavated. Archaeologists have found evidence that Native Americans used this area for hundreds of years as a camping site and as a bison kill.*

pound was a more efficient way to hunt a small herd, since the Indians trapped the bison before killing them. Yet, archaeological excavations indicate that Native Americans often killed more bison than they needed, butchering the animals to take only the choicest cuts of meat.

The other bison kills in northern Montana are not accessible to the public, but when you travel along U.S. Highway 2 in the Milk River Valley from Havre to Nashua or in the Missouri River country from Frazer to Brockton on the Fort Peck Indian Reservation, look for areas of steep river bluffs and deep gullies. Such geographical features made excellent sites for bison kills.

The remains of a much different Native American structure may still stand in the pine-covered Bears Paw Mountains and Sweetgrass Hills to the north of Highway 2. Usually located in thickly timbered high country, the war lodge of the Blackfoot Confederacy was "a most ingenious example of Indian architecture." Traveling Piegan war or hunting parties used three aspens or cottonwoods to build the permanent lodge in the shape of an "L," with willow posts latched to the foundation. They stripped the bark from the trees and placed them, along with twigs and branches, on the foundation's exterior. The warriors completed the war lodge by laying several aspens or cottonwoods around its base to a height of two feet. Large enough to sleep 12 warriors, the lodge had a long, covered entrance made of "heavily forked tree trunks" angled out for at least 10 feet. The war lodge served as a scouting post, a supply base, and, in the worst of times, a fort. Kept in constant repair, a war lodge built in two hours by a dozen warriors might be used for several decades. Both the Atsina and Assiniboine built war lodges of similar design and used them for the same purposes.

One hundred and fifty years ago on the open plains and rolling hills now traversed by U.S. Highway 2, Native American burial structures stood alone on the high plains. The Indians built burial cairns by digging a shallow grave and then placing rocks around the body to protect it from predators. If the deceased had requested it, the Cree would place the body inside a tipi on a hill, recline the body against a willow backrest, and then build a stone wall around it. With the flap closed, the tipi would be left to the elements. The Sioux and Atsina, however, reserved this treatment for very brave warriors, placing the deceased in a tipi, upright, fully dressed, and painted. A thick hedge of branches, dirt, and brush was built to keep animals out.

Both the Assiniboine and Blackfoot Confederacy Indians usually reposed their dead in the fork of a tree, sometimes with a simple foundation to support the body. The Piegan placed important tribal leaders inside a "death lodge," a tent located away from camp and fastened to the prairie with heavy rocks. Tribal members killed the owner's horses in front of the lodge and left them to decay. The most significant part of the memorial was the rocks "piled in lines extending outward from the death lodge in the four cardinal directions," each pile representing a coup of the dead warrior.

Native American women had their own structures. During the summer, for instance, Cree women worked at most of their daily tasks underneath a three-pole shelter covered with boughs or rawhide. The Assiniboine's menstruation lodge, separated from the rest of the camp, was a simplified form of a sweat lodge. Women stayed in the lodge for the first days of their menstrual period, after which they returned to their homes; but they would not sleep with their husbands until menstruation had ended.

Route B: Montana Road 243, at Saco

The country north of the Missouri and east of the Continental Divide has four ecological regions: lowland, transition areas, upland breaks, and upland. The lowlands are the major river valleys, such as the Milk, Marias, and Missouri, and the larger creeks. The transition areas and upland breaks contain broken terrain, such as gullies, bluffs, ridges, and plateaus. Uplands include rolling terrain, hills, and high flatland.

Northern Blaine, Phillips, and Valley counties, particularly the drainages of Frenchman and Whitewater creeks north of Saco, possess some of the best examples of upland landscape in Montana. The number and density of prehistoric archaeological sites indicate that Montana's prehistoric peoples favored this area and indicate how they adapted to the environment.

Before Native Americans acquired horses, moving camp, with tipis and household and food supplies, was difficult and the pace was slow; sometimes it took a week to travel 15 miles across the region's broken terrain. The location and arrangement of tipi rings on the uplands indicate that Indians camped here for long periods of time, often on the leeward side of knolls. It is also likely that group bison kills took place throughout the year, with frequent hunts occurring in the spring. The uplands were also a good place to hunt smaller animals; and the area was rich in the nutritious Indian turnip, a staple of the Indians' diet.

Today on the Hi-Line, grain elevators, railroad tracks, farms, and towns shape our perception of the landscape. It is easy to forget that less than 200 years ago you would have seen tipis, sun lodges, burial lodges, and many other Native American buildings on the open prairie, rolling hills, and river valleys of northern Montana.

Route 13: The Fort Peck, Fort Belknap, and Rocky Boy's Indian Reservations

Route A: U.S. Highway 2, from Frazer to Brockton
Route B: Montana Highway 66, from Harlem to Hays
Route C: U.S. Highway 87, from Havre to Box Elder

Northern Montana is home to four reservations: Fort Peck, Fort Belknap, the Blackfeet, and Rocky Boy's. The patterns on the landscape in the large Fort Peck, Fort Belknap, and Rocky Boy's Indian reservations show how the events of the last 100 years have changed the look of the land. Each reservation, for instance, contains distinct white and Indian population centers. Whites have lived on the reservations for decades, ever since the Dawes Act of 1887 opened them to white settlers. The Dawes Act was intended to "civilize" the Indians by making them property owners. Acting in what they considered to be the Indians' best interests, the federal government gave each Indian a homestead claim and opened the remaining reservation land to white settlement. On these reservations today you can see the traditional and modern patterns of the Native American landscape.

Route A: U.S Highway 2, from Frazer to Brockton

The Fort Peck Indian Reservation for the Santee Sioux and southern Assiniboine is a good place to see how the Dawes Act affected the northern Montana landscape. The major white settlements are within the reservation's boundaries, and since 1877 the agency headquarters has been at Poplar, a town with about 1,000 residents. The homesteading boom actually created two Poplars: one centered on agency headquarters, where most Native Americans lived, and the other a "T" town created by the railroad, where new settlers and agency employees lived. South of U.S. Highway 2 is the town's commercial heart, and to the north stand most of the agency buildings. You can see most of the historic agency structures from the highway. Listed in the National Register of Historic Places, they date to the early years of the reservation and include a hospital (built in 1916), a jail (1920), and a dining hall and kitchen (1920). The academic building and headquarters, built in 1907, is the only remaining building that was constructed before homesteaders arrived at the reservation.

Wolf Point, 21 miles west of Poplar on U.S. Highway 2, is the largest town in northeastern Montana and the region's trade center. When the reservation was thrown open to homesteaders in 1913, many settlers disembarked from the Great Northern at Wolf Point and soon transformed the original reservation landscape into wheat fields. Wolf Point became the homesteaders' commercial center. North of Wolf Point and Poplar along Montana Roads 438, 250, 251, and 344, you can see miles of wheat fields stretching across the reservation landscape. Small towns such as Larslan, Lustre, and Reserve are white farming communities that have developed since 1913. Most Native Americans live near the Missouri River, where they settled in Frazer, Wolf Point, and Brockton on lands allotted to their families over 70 years ago.

Route B: Montana Highway 66, from Harlem to Hays

Before the federal government created the present-day Fort Belknap Indian Reservation in 1888, the northern Assiniboine and Atsina shared a reservation in the Milk River Valley, with an agency headquarters located near Chinook. Assimilation began early in this area, and by 1884-1885 the Assiniboine had built 150 log cabins. In December 1885, the Jesuits opened St. Paul's Mission, and two years later they moved the mission near the mouth of Mission Canyon in the Little Rocky Mountains. The mission, located about one mile from Hays, is still operating.

Federal officials encouraged the development of permanent Indian towns on the new reservation in an attempt to "civilize" the semi-nomadic Native Americans. Officials gave the northern Assiniboine and Atsina window glass, hinges, and locks, and the more prominent tribal leaders received small iron stoves. Two towns were established in the foothills of the Little Rocky Mountains, 50 miles from the scrutiny of the reservation agent who lived at Fort Belknap Agency, along the mainline of the Great Northern just south of the Milk River near Harlem. Hays was located near where the Atsina had lived before the reservation was created, and Lodgepole was established where the northern Assiniboine had resided. The Native Americans in both towns lived in unadorned log cabins with earthen floors and roofs, moving into canvas tipis when summer came.

The government built most of the buildings at Fort Belknap Agency during the 1930s. By 1931, there was an agency hospital with 45 beds, and four years later, the agency buildings included a warehouse, a garage, offices, a clubhouse, and residences for a doctor, educational field agent, and other employees. Despite the agency's growth, most Atsina and northern Assiniboine remained in Hays and Lodgepole.

Opening the reservation to homesteaders did not immediately change these patterns. Fort Belknap's land was ideally suited for stock-growing, but it did not appeal to homesteaders. Consequently, there was never a great demand for the reservation land except by stock-growers. Largely a creature of the Great Northern Railway, Harlem is a typical "T" town. The town, which is located just outside the northwestern corner of the reservation, is the area's primary white settlement and was a shipping point for the stock-growing industry before becoming the supply base for the reservation.

Route C: U.S. Highway 87, from Havre to Box Elder

To the west along U.S. Highway 87, the original Great Northern route from Havre to Great Falls, is the Rocky Boy's Indian Reservation, the last reservation

C. V. West, photographer, MHS SHPO

St. Paul's Mission, Hays, Fort Belknap Indian Reservation, Blaine County.
*This church is part of a century-old Catholic missionary effort that brought Christian
education to Native Americans on the reservation.*

created in Montana. Congress established the reservation in September 1916 for
two groups of landless Indians who had wandered the Montana high plains: a
band of Canadian Chippewa led by Rocky Boy, who had moved into Montana
during the 1880s, and Little Bear's band of Canadian Cree, who had fled Canada
to escape retribution for their role in the Riel Rebellion in 1885. Neither group
found prosperity in the Hi-Line country, and their plight moved several Montanans, including artist Charles M. Russell, who began a subscription list for their
support. "It doesn't look good for the people of Montana," Russell argued,

> if they will sit and see a lot of women and children starve to death in this
> kind of weather. Lots of people seem to think that the Indians are not
> human beings at all and have no feelings. These kind of people would be
> the first to yell for help if their grub pile was running short and they didn't
> have enough clothing to keep out of the cold, and yet because it is Rocky
> Boy and his bunch of Indians they are perfectly willing to let them die of
> hunger and cold without lifting a hand.

Because of lobbying by Russell, William Bole, Frank Linderman, and other Montanans, the federal government created the Rocky Boy's Indian Reservation from
55,000 acres of surplus Fort Assinniboine Military Reserve land. It was not
valuable land, but it gave the Chippewa and Cree an opportunity to escape the
poverty of their elders.

At agency headquarters, also named for Chief Rocky Boy, several original
buildings remain, including some log cabin dwellings. The reservation has expanded over the years to almost 110,000 acres, giving Rocky Boy's a mix of Indian and non-Indian residents similar to that found at Fort Peck and Fort

Belknap. The expansion also added the homesteading town of Box Elder on the Great Northern line between Great Falls and Havre, and the grain elevators there still serve surrounding farmers. The residential pattern at Fort Peck and Fort Belknap is repeated at Rocky Boy's, with most whites settling around Box Elder and most Indians living near the town of Rocky Boy.

Route 14: Chief Joseph Battleground
U.S. Highway 2, at Montana Road 240 exit at Chinook

A short detour off U.S. Highway 2 via Montana Road 240 at Chinook runs south to the Bears Paw Mountains and the site of the Chief Joseph Battleground. The Bear's Paw State Monument, which is listed in the National Register of Historic Places, commemorates the place where in 1877 the Nez Perce Indians surrendered to the U.S. Army.

In 1855, the Nez Perce tribe, then based in Idaho and Oregon, had split over whether or not they should live on an Idaho reservation. The "treaty" Nez Perce agreed to move to a big reservation in present-day Idaho; and in 1863, following the discovery of gold along the Clearwater and Salmon rivers, they even agreed to accept a much smaller reservation. But the "nontreaty" Nez Perce rejected reservation life, and Chief Joseph, the elder, and his people continued to live in Oregon's Wallowa Valley.

In 1871, Chief Joseph's son inherited his position and within a few years was contending with whites who wanted the Wallowa Valley. Chief Joseph, the son, refused to buckle, insisting that his father had never signed any treaty nor had he sold the land. At first, the federal government agreed and allowed the nontreaty Nez Perce to stay in the valley. But the Oregon settlers intensified their protests, and in May 1877 the federal government gave Joseph and his people 30 days to move to the Idaho reservation.

The Nez Perce had no choice but to head east. In June, while the bands were gathered near the Salmon River, three young warriors killed four white settlers. Fearing retribution, Joseph's people hid along the river with White Bird's nontreaty band. Within days, however, local militia and the U.S. cavalry discovered their position and launched an attack at White Bird Canyon. The Indians successfully repelled the attack, and the Nez Perce war of 1877 was underway.

The Nez Perce fled eastward, with the troops of General O. O. Howard close behind. The plan was to escape across the Bitterroot Mountains to eastern Montana, where the Nez Perce hoped that the Crow, their traditional allies, would protect them.

The Nez Perce trek was one of the most courageous acts in American history, as the 800 Indians avoided battle and time and again evaded capture. After withstanding an attack on their camp on the Big Hole River, they packed what remained of their goods and escaped west through Yellowstone National Park to Canyon Creek, north of present-day Laurel, Montana, where they bravely and skillfully fought the army. Failing to gain sanctuary with Crow Indians, the Nez Perce decided to go north to join Sitting Bull in Canada. Their route took them across the Musselshell River near present-day Ryegate. A monument on U.S. Highway 12 near Ryegate marks the river crossing.

From Fort Keogh on the Yellowstone River, Colonel Nelson A. Miles—who the Indians had named "Bear Coat"—set out to prevent Joseph's escape. If they had moved quickly, the Nez Perce probably could have reached Canada, but Chief Looking Glass argued that the people needed rest. On September 30, Miles's troopers caught the Indians along Snake Creek in the Bears Paw Mountains, and a major battle ensued. The Nez Perce found all escape routes blocked, but they held off Miles's forces for several days while the chiefs argued about what to do. White Bird led 300 people to safety across the Canadian border. But Chief Joseph had witnessed enough bloodshed, and on October 5 he surrendered, with Colonel Miles's promise that the Nez Perce could return to the reservation in Idaho. But the federal government had been so embarrassed by the Indians' fighting ability that officials refused to accept the surrender documents, and the Nez Perce were sent to Indian Territory in present-day Oklahoma.

The most famous event associated with the Battle of the Bear's Paw is the speech that Chief Joseph reportedly made during the surrender ceremonies. Even if that great Nez Perce leader made no speech and did not utter these words and they were written by an imaginative journalist, they remain some of the most moving in the long history of Indian-white conflict:

> . . . it is cold and we have no blankets. The little children are freezing to death. . . . Hear me, my chiefs! I am tired. My heart is sick and sad. From where the sun now stands, I will fight no more forever.

Within a decade of Joseph's surrender, cattle herds grazed on the plains; log cabins had replaced the tipis; one- and two-story houses lined the banks of the Missouri and Milk rivers; imposing Fort Assinniboine stood on the high plains; and, most important, the Great Northern Railway stretched from the Dakota state line to the Great Falls of the Missouri.

Route 15: The Fur Trade in the Milk River Valley
U.S. Highway 2, from Nashua to Chinook

Off U.S. Highway 2 east of Hinsdale in Valley County is Vandalia, a tiny village on the south bank of the Milk River. Looking to the east from Vandalia, you can see the quiet waters of the Milk River, the rich bottomland, and the surrounding rolling hills. This is the landscape that greeted the fur traders who came here over 130 years ago, opening the door for the white conquest and development of the Milk River Valley. When the traders reached this point on the river, they knew that they were deep in the territory of the Blackfoot Confederacy; but the lure of a land rich in fur-bearing animals was strong.

Augustin Armel (known also as Hamel) arrived in northern Montana about 15 years after Lewis and Clark. Active in the fur trade with the Blackfoot Confederacy, he married a Piegan woman and worked at almost every major American Fur Company trading post on the Missouri River. The company lost interest in the Missouri River fur trade during the 1850s, and by 1855 Armel had opened his own trading house near present-day Vandalia. Known as Hammell's Houses, Armel's post is believed to be the first trading post on the Milk River.

The post stood alone until 1868, when I. G. Baker of Fort Benton built a small trading post over 70 miles west of Hammell's Houses, just 3 miles east of the mouth of Peoples Creek. Baker's Post, however, closed after a single trading season. The following year, A. J. Smith, James Hubbell, and A. F. Hawley established Fort Browning at the mouth of Peoples Creek (near present-day Dodson). The traders constructed the fort with cottonwood logs taken from the river's banks. This post, located about six miles upriver from Dodson on the south bank of the Milk, was also a sub-agency that supplied the Atsina and Assiniboine tribes with their yearly government annuities.

Durfee & Peck, a northwestern fur trade company, constructed three posts on the Milk River during the early 1870s. Tom Campbell supervised the building of Tom Campbell's Houses near Vandalia in 1870. In 1871, the company hired Abel Farwell to build Fort Belknap on the south bank of the Milk near Chinook. About two miles west of Chinook, on old U.S. Highway 2 (immediately south of U.S. Highway 2), you can still see some of the post's original cottonwood buildings, which later housed an agency headquarters for the Atsina and northern Assiniboine. In 1872, Durfee & Peck constructed a minor post about 12 miles north of the Milk along Frenchman Creek, near present-day Saco, where they traded with the Cree and Metis who had fled to Montana after the first Riel rebellion in 1870.

During the 1870s, most Fort Benton businessmen refused to make major investments in the Milk River fur trade, but I. G. Baker and T. C. Power constructed several posts. Baker hired C. W. Price to build two trading posts along the Milk, one about 3 miles west of Fort Browning and the other about 12 miles east of present-day Havre, near Lohman in Blaine County. In 1879, Power operated Power's Post on the Milk between the mouths of Big Sandy Creek and Beaver Creek. When you stop at Lohman, try to imagine what Baker's and Power's trading posts looked like. They were not the large, stockaded posts found on the Yellowstone River or at Fort Benton, but were temporary affairs built from cottonwoods and canvas.

Because Baker, Power, and Durfee & Peck were only interested in the buffalo robe trade, they had built their posts to exploit the valley's bison herds in the least expensive way. Their posts on the Milk River operated for only one or two trading seasons, serving small, isolated groups of Metis and other Indians who exchanged their furs at prices that heavily favored the traders.

Route 16: "Camp Disappointment" of the Lewis and Clark Expedition

U.S. Highway 2, at the Camp Disappointment Monument, 22 miles west of Cut Bank in the Blackfeet Indian Reservation

In 1805-1806, Meriwether Lewis, William Clark, and their expedition party explored the Northwest for the American government, opening the country to fur traders and, later, to white settlers. In July 1806, on their return from the Pacific

Coast, Lewis and nine men left Clark and the others to explore the country northeast to the headwaters of the Marias River. On their outward journey, members of the expedition had almost mistaken the Marias for the Missouri River. Lewis wanted to travel the Marias, a northern tributary of the Missouri, to find the Missouri's northernmost drainage so that he could determine the northern boundary of the Louisiana Purchase. He also hoped to discover whether there was an easy portage from the headwaters of the Marias to the Saskatchewan River, the favorite route of English fur traders in Canada. If he could find a connection between the two rivers, perhaps Americans could divert the lucrative Canadian fur trade to the Missouri River and so control this valuable resource.

On July 22, Lewis and his party reached a point where he could see Cut Bank Creek winding into the Rockies about 20 miles away. They camped, Lewis wrote in his journal, at a "clump of large cottonwood trees in a beautiful and extensive bottom of the river about ten miles below the foot of the rocky mountains." Off U.S. Highway 2, west of Cut Bank, the Great Northern has constructed a monument to mark the campsite, which is a National Historic Landmark. Lewis called the site "Camp Disappointment," because he could find no connection between the Marias and Saskatchewan rivers. From the monument, look to the north and you can see the northernmost point reached by the Lewis and Clark expedition.

As Lewis and his men left Camp Disappointment on July 26, they met eight Piegan warriors, who camped with them that night. The Piegan, who enjoyed prosperous trading with British fur companies, were concerned and challenged when the Americans told them of their alliances with the Shoshoni and Flathead—traditional enemies of the Blackfeet. The Indians were angry at the prospect that the Americans were arming the Piegan's foes. At dawn, the Piegan tried to take the Americans' arms and horses, and a fight broke out. In the melee, two warriors were killed, the only case of fatal armed conflict with Native Americans during the expedition.

Route 17: The Whoop-Up Trail

U.S. Highway 2, at Whoop-Up Trail Monument, 3 miles east of Shelby
U.S. Highway 2, at Montana Road 417 exit, 4.7 miles east of Shelby

During the 1870s, southern Alberta was wide-open country, and unscrupulous American whiskey traders took advantage of the lack of law enforcement to develop a thriving business with the Canadian Indians and the few whites in the area. These whiskey men and other traders used the Whoop-Up Trail to carry goods from Fort Benton on the Missouri to the western Canadian frontier as far north as the Oldman River at Fort Macleod, Alberta. The traders called the trail "Whoop-Up" because once they left Fort Benton, they had to "whoop it up" to the border as fast as possible.

At its peak, from 1874 to 1883, traders moved almost a third of the Fort Benton trade on the trail, allowing Montana merchants to acquire most of the riches to be made from the western Canadian frontier. Whiskey flowed freely across the

C. V. West, photographer, MHS SHPO

Whoop-Up Trail, Marias River, Montana Road 417, Chouteau County. *The Whoop-Up Trail, which connected Fort Benton and southern Alberta trading posts, was used by whiskey traders until the Royal North West Mounted Police stopped the illegal traffic in the mid 1880s.*

international boundary until the North West Mounted Police stopped most of the illegal trade in the mid 1880s.

You can follow a small section of the Whoop-Up Trail by traveling on Montana Road 417 in Toole County until it crosses the Marias River. Montana Road 417 is found by taking the Shelby exit off I-15 and traveling east on U.S. Highway 2 for about six miles to a well-marked turn-off. You can also see a fragment of the trail if you stop on U.S. Highway 2 at the highway historical marker about three miles east of Shelby.

Route 18: Buffalo Hunting Along the Marias River
Montana Road 366, at Lake Elwell
Montana Road 223, at Tiber Dam Road exit

Lake Elwell is the location of the Bootlegger Bison Kill site, which was used by Montana Indians from about 700 to 1725 A.D. The I-15 exit for the Lake Elwell Recreation Area is located about 18 miles south of Shelby at the Montana Road 366/Lake Elwell exit. Or you can leave U.S. Highway 2 at Chester and travel south on Montana Road 223 for 19 miles until you reach the turn-off for the lake.

Several years ago, archaeologists studied the area around Lake Elwell, which is now part of the Tiber Dam reservoir. During their survey, they found portions of the Bootlegger Trail, which traders had used to supply the illegal whiskey trade in Canada. They also uncovered remains of one of the most interesting bison kills in northern Montana. Prehistoric Indians probably used the Lake Elwell area as a bison kill site from late winter to early spring.

The topography of this part of the Marias River Valley had much to do with the Indians' use of it as a kill site. The south bank of the river breaks contained many gullies, the grassland was rich and often kept exposed by strong chinooks from the north, and snow never stayed on the ground for more than a few weeks. Before they acquired horses, Native Americans found this environment ideal for late winter and early spring bison hunting. The band could prepare everything necessary for a successful hunt as they waited for the large herds of bison to gather on the adjacent plains.

The communal bison kill, which provided the Indians with their major source of meat for the year, was a carefully planned operation. Some members of the band laid "drive lines," long lines of stones that gave hunters some direction as they neared the kill area, which ran from the plains to the river bluffs. Others gathered wood and stones from the riverbanks to use in the boiling pots. The hunters prepared for the kill by sharpening their arrows and spears. This activity took place over several weeks and was probably accompanied by prayers to the spirits to improve hunting and to decrease the considerable risk of failure, a failure that could jeopardize the band.

In late February or early March, when enough bison were present, hunters chased the herd into a gully and the kill began. Hundreds of bison might be slaughtered before the arrows stopped. The hunters might repeat the hunt and kill several times before the bison herds dispersed, each time repeating the preparations that marked the initial kill. Native Americans used the kill site until about mid April of each year, when they would move on, taking with them the buffalo products they would need until the fall hunting season.

Landscape 4: The Missouri River Valley

Here, on both sides of the river, the most strange forms are seen, and you may fancy that you see colonnades, small round pillars with large globes or a flat slab at the top, little towers, pulpits, organs with their pipes, old ruins, fortresses, castles, churches, with pointed towers, &c. &c., almost every mountain bearing on its summitt some similar structure.

Prince Maximilian zu Wied, 1833

These bluffs for forty or fifty miles above Fort Union, generally leave fine narrow bottoms on one, and sometimes both sides of the river, with big seams of coal in the bluffs back of them. There are some fine little prairies in these bottoms; one in particular, about a mile in diameter, was the most beautiful I have seen on the trip.

Granville Stuart, 1866

[Here was] a magnificent view of that weird and wonderful badland country. Hundreds of buttes were in sight, pyramidal, flat-topped, trunk-shaped, some of them showing only the bare earth, others grass grown, some fairly well timbered.

James Willard Schultz (Apikuni), 1901

These men seem to be describing three very different places, but they are portraying different parts of Montana's Missouri River Valley. Prince Maximilian gazed at country much like that found at the Hole in the Wall Landing Recreation Area in central Chouteau County. At the impressive Noly bridge, 11 miles south of Bainville from U.S. Highway 2, you can see the countryside that Granville Stuart described. At the Pines Recreation Area in southern Phillips County, off Montana Highway 24, or at the Hell Creek Recreation Area in northern Garfield County north of Jordan on Montana Highway 200, you can see the strange shapes that James Willard Schultz saw.

The Missouri has many natural attributes. The rich foliage of cottonwoods, aspens, and willows has provided shelter, fuel, and sometimes food for Native Americans and whites. Montanans have mined coal in the valley and have dammed the river to create additional water supplies and electrical power. The river's scenic beauty—over 100 miles of the river in southern Chouteau and Fergus counties have been designated a National Wild and Scenic River—attracts tourists in boats launched at Fort Benton.

Route 19: The Missouri River Fur Trade
Route A: U.S. Highway 87, from Fort Benton to Big Sandy
Route B: U.S. Highway 2, from Nashua to Wolf Point

Until the construction of Fort Union at the confluence of the Missouri and Yellowstone rivers in the late 1820s, American and Canadian fur trappers refused to initiate trade along the upper Missouri River. There were many fur-bearing animals, most of the river was navigable by canoe, and larger boats could travel up much of it, but the trappers were deterred by fear of the Blackfoot Confederacy.

For several decades, the Confederacy had been master of the fur trade in southern Alberta and northern Montana, and they even controlled the lucrative Three Forks region. The Confederacy would trade with the English, Americans, or Canadians, but they wanted no middlemen. Trade would be direct, with the Confederacy's warriors bringing furs to the trading posts, or there would be no trade at all.

The first substantial American trade with the Piegan took place in 1830. Kenneth McKenzie, the American Fur Company factor (or administrator) at Fort Union, ordered Jacob Berger, who spoke the Piegan language, to go west and persuade the Piegan to trade at Fort Union. Berger and his men did not meet the Piegan until they reached Badger Creek, about 450 miles west of Fort Union at a site now marked on the Blackfeet Indian Reservation on the road that connects Browning to Heart Butte. Berger was successful, and when the Piegan arrived at Fort Union, McKenzie lavished presents on them and promised to build a trading post in their territory the following season.

As you travel along the Missouri, you can see where much of the fur trade took place. The early trading houses are gone, except at Fort Benton, but the topographical setting shows why the traders built their posts in wide river bottoms with plenty of foliage nearby.

Route A: U.S. Highway 87, from Fort Benton to Big Sandy

Near Loma, along U.S. Highway 87 about 52 miles north of Great Falls, is the site of one of the American Fur Company's most important posts. From the bridge that crosses the Marias River, you can look to the south and see the confluence of the Marias and Missouri rivers. In 1831, under the guidance of the famous trader James Kipp, Fort Piegan was constructed here on the north bank of the Missouri. (A highway marker on U.S. Highway 87 just west of the bridge also roughly marks the location of Fort Piegan.) Built in less than 11 weeks from cottonwoods found nearby, the fort was enclosed by a 25-foot-high log stockade and contained three log buildings for living quarters, a warehouse, and a trading room.

After one year of trade and a harrowing episode with a group of Kainah Indians who the Hudson's Bay Company had persuaded to attack the Americans, James Kipp and other American Fur Company employees abandoned Fort Piegan. Kainah or perhaps Assiniboine warriors burned the fort soon after the Americans left.

In 1832, David D. Mitchell returned to the Loma area and built a new American Fur Company post about six miles above the mouth of the Marias River. For the next decade, Fort McKenzie served as the leading trading center in the Missouri River Valley. From Loma, you can look downriver at the rich foliage of this part of the valley and try to imagine what Fort McKenzie was like as it stood starkly in this undeveloped countryside. Prince Maximilian zu Wied described the fort this way in 1833:

> . . . it forms, a quadrangle, the sides of which are forty-five to forty-seven paces in length, and is defended by two blockhouses, with some pieces of cannon. It is much smaller than Fort Union, and worse and more slightly built. The dwellings are of one story, and low: the rooms small, generally without flooring, with a chimney, a door, a flat roof covered with green sods. . . . The flagstaff stands in the center of the courtyard. The gate is strong, double, and well-protected; when the trade with the Indians is going on the inner gate is closed: the entrance to the Indian store, between the two gates is then free, a strong guard stationed at the store.

As company profits increased, so did the size of the fort. By the early 1840s, the post factor, Alexander Culbertson, described the fort as 200 feet square with a stockade made of 18-foot-high hewn cottonwood planks.

Fort McKenzie was the scene of trial, triumph, and tragedy. In 1837, passengers on a keelboat from Fort Union broke out in smallpox, and Culbertson ordered the boat to wait at present-day Judith Landing until freezing temperatures could contain the disease. The Kainah and Piegan Indians, who were camped at Fort McKenzie waiting for trade goods, knew nothing about smallpox and did not believe Culbertson. When they angrily demanded the goods and threatened to find the boat themselves, Culbertson unwisely relented. The resulting smallpox epidemic eventually wiped out 60 to 70 per cent of the Blackfoot Confederacy and changed the course of Montana's history. Never again would the Native Americans be as powerful as they were before 1837. Ironically, the epidemic had no negative effect on the Missouri fur trade. In-

MHS Photo Archives

Fort Clagett, mouth of the Judith River, Fergus County. *Named for Territorial Delegate William H. Clagett, this trading post was one of the last built on the Missouri and operated until the late 1870s.*

dians swapped 10,000 buffalo robes that winter; and by 1841, the trade involved some 21,000 buffalo robes.

Fort McKenzie was a financial success, but because of poor management by Francois A. Chardon and Alexander Harvey, it was abandoned in the mid 1840s. Misunderstandings between some Piegan warriors and the two traders led to the murder of Chardon's black slave, and Chardon retaliated by ambushing and killing several friendly Piegan at the fort. The Indians reacted vehemently, threatening the men at Fort McKenzie with death and even harassing the traders at Fort Union, hundreds of miles to the east. Forced by the Piegan to abandon Fort McKenzie, Chardon and his employees moved to the mouth of the Judith River and constructed a smaller post, Fort Chardon.

From U.S. Highway 87 at Big Sandy, take Montana Road 236 south for 40 miles to the bridge that crosses the Missouri River at Judith Landing. Fort Chardon was located to the west toward the confluence of the Judith and Missouri rivers. The new post never became a trading center, and Indian hostility kept the post "virtually in a state of siege." Thirty years later, in 1872, near the location of Fort Chardon, fur traders would build Fort Clagett, one of the last trading posts constructed on the Missouri River. T. C. Power & Brother operated Fort Clagett until the late 1870s.

Alexander Culbertson, who had married a woman from a leading Kainah family, began to restore good relations between the American Fur Company and the Blackfoot Confederacy. In 1846, he directed the construction of Fort Lewis, about three miles upriver from present-day Fort Benton on the south bank of the Missouri. If you look west from the bridge that crosses the Missouri on Montana Highway 80, you can see the approximate location of the post. During its first year, the post received 21,000 buffalo robes in trade with the Confederacy. But the Indians did not like the fort's location on the south bank of the river; there

CHOTEAU HOUSE.

Choteau House, Fort Benton, Chouteau County, 1880. *Jerre Sullivan's Choteau House, one of Fort Benton's earliest hostelries, still graces the town's riverfront business district.*

were no easy crossings nearby and spring ice flows made trade almost impossible. In 1847, Culbertson moved the cottonwood fort three miles down the Missouri and across to the north bank, almost six miles above the mouth of the Teton River, where the Indians could camp in its richly timbered valley. Fort Clay, soon renamed Fort Benton, was the major settlement in northern Montana for the next four decades.

In 1853, Issac I. Stevens, a surveyor for the Union Pacific Railroad, wrote that Fort Benton was "smaller than Fort Union. Its front is made of wood, and the other sides of adobe or burned brick. It usually contains about a dozen men and the families of several of them." Construction at Fort Benton continued until 1854; and even though the post was designated the first Blackfeet Indian Reservation agency, these years were poor ones for the fur trade and for the American Fur Company. In 1864, the company sold Fort Benton to its rival, the Northwest Fur Company; and in 1869, the army acquired the fort and stationed a small garrison there.

The ruins of the original Fort Benton stand in a city park and mark the location of the old river front. As the town grew during the 1860s and 1870s, the center of trading activity shifted slightly to the west. Today, the site of the old fort is at the eastern boundary of Fort Benton's commercial district.

Route B: U.S. Highway 2, from Nashua to Wolf Point

During the 1860s and 1870s, the center of Missouri River fur trade shifted downriver to an area running roughly from Fort Peck to Poplar. In 1861, the

American Fur Company built Fort Charles on the north bank of the Missouri near present-day Wolf Point. In the fall of 1862, Charles Larpenteur built Fort Galpin, about 10 miles above the mouth of the Milk River, for La Barge, Harkness & Company. Two years later, traders used stands of cottonwood along the Missouri River to build Fort Copeland and Fort Kaiser, two caches for steamboat goods near Fort Galpin.

In 1867, Durfee & Peck built Fort Peck on the north bank of the Missouri about two and a half miles above the mouth of Big Dry Creek near what is now the Fort Peck Recreation Area. The site has been covered by the Fort Peck Reservoir. Located on a high bluff so that steamboats could approach the fort without difficulty, Fort Peck had a log stockade with two log bastions and log buildings for living quarters, storage, trading room, the blacksmith, and stables. The post had limited success in the buffalo robe trade, and in 1873 it became agency headquarters for the Santee Sioux and southern Assiniboine. Fort Peck was the center of the Fort Peck Indian Reservation until the agency moved to the mouth of the Poplar River in 1879.

Route 20: Steamboat Navigation on the Upper Missouri River
Route A: U.S. Highway 87, from Fort Benton to Big Sandy
Route B: Montana Highway 66, at Cow Island Recreation Area
Route C: U.S. Highway 2, from Frazer to Culbertson

When Lewis and Clark traveled through what is now Montana, they came by way of the Missouri River. For the next 75 years, travelers continued to use the Missouri as a transportation route, arriving in Montana in canoes, flatboats, mackinaws, and steamboats. Once the gold rush began in 1863, Fort Benton became the steamboat capital of Montana, and from the North Dakota border to Fort Benton steamboats puffed up and down the "Big Muddy," carrying eager prospectors and precious cargoes of gold.

Route A: U.S. Highway 87, from Fort Benton to Big Sandy

By the 1830s, St. Louis-based steamboats regularly traveled up the Missouri as far as Fort Union. Not until the late 1850s, when new broad-bottomed steamboats with twin engines and a balanced rudder were introduced on the treacherous Upper Missouri, did steamboats travel regularly beyond the fort. In 1859, the American Fur Company's *Chippewa* steamed within 15 miles of Fort Benton; and by the mid 1860s, Fort Benton was a thriving steamboat base, controlling most of the trade between eastern markets and the Montana goldfields. Designated as a National Historic Landmark, Fort Benton's fascinating array of buildings represents the town's history from the last decades of the 19th century to the 1920s. Standing on the town's historic bridge and looking toward Front Street, you can imagine the scene 100 years ago when the men and women who transformed Fort Benton from a frontier river base to a bustling trading center strolled along the riverfront.

T. C. Power of Iowa and I. G. Baker, a former American Fur Company factor, developed many of Fort Benton's leading commercial businesses. Both men operated large mercantile businesses and steamboat lines out of Fort Benton, and Power developed an extensive transportation network throughout Montana Territory. Goods arrived at his warehouses by steamboat, then stagecoaches and freighters delivered the goods to Bozeman, Virginia City, Helena, and later the Yellowstone Valley.

The Choteau House, which Power and Baker built in 1868 and rebuilt in brick in 1903, still stands on Front Street, the business strip that faces the Missouri. Next door is I. G. Baker's Fort Benton residence, tours of which can be arranged at the Fort Benton Museum.

On the north bank of the Missouri, at 1301 Front Street, is the Grand Union Hotel, an excellent example of western Italianate architecture. The original furniture, electric lights, and steam radiators for the hotel all arrived on steamboats. The hotel was built in 1882, as Fort Benton's days of glory were ending. The railroads were rapidly laying lines across the territory, diminishing the town's importance as a transshipment center. Fort Benton later became an agricultural trade and commercial center for Chouteau County and enjoyed a burst of economic expansion during the homesteading era.

The steamboats traveling the Missouri always had uncertain journeys. Traveling upriver was always a new adventure; no one could predict the location of new snags in the river or how floods had changed the river's channel. Boat captains were also kept busy searching for supplies of wood for their steam engines. From Fort Benton's historic bridge, the river looks deceptively wide, deep, and calm; but the Missouri's changing channel, sand bars, and rapids took many boats and lives before the steamboat era came to an end.

During the 19th century, Fort Benton was the center of the Missouri River transportation system, but minor bases along the river also played a part in the valley's development. Judith Landing, located at the confluence of the Missouri and Judith rivers, was one such base. In 1866, the U.S. Army constructed Camp Cooke here to protect the steamboats from potential Indian attacks. To reach Judith Landing, leave Fort Benton and travel for 38 miles east on U.S. Highway 87 to Big Sandy, then travel south on Montana Road 236 for 40 miles until you reach a bridge that crosses the Missouri River. The site of Camp Cooke is part of the Judith Landing Historic District, which is listed in the National Register of Historic Places.

In the late 1870s and early 1880s, T. C. Power and Brother moved its Fort Clagett trading post to Judith Landing and opened a ferry across the Missouri. You can see the remains of the old ferry slip a few yards east of the bridge. Power also established a stock-growing business (the Power-Norris Ranch) in this part of the valley, building his ranch headquarters on the south bank of the river, where the town of Judith Landing developed. A sandstone and granite building, which T. C. Power constructed in 1882, stands at the landing, along with the Judith Landing Post Office, made from pine logs, three of the Power-Norris ranch houses, and the town's original log schoolhouse. As you cross the bridge, you can look to the west on the river's south bank and see remnants of the Power-Norris

C. V. West, photographer, MHS SHPO

Council Island, Judith Landing, Missouri River, Chouteau County. John C. Ewers has written that the 1855 treaty negotiations between the U.S. government and several Native American tribes at Council Island were "undoubtedly the most important intertribal gathering ever held on the northwestern plains."

Ranch and the town of Judith Landing. These buildings are on private property and are not accessible to the public.

About a half mile downriver from Judith Landing and visible to the east from the Missouri River bridge is Council Island, the site of events that may have influenced the white settlement of northern Montana more than the events at Fort Benton and Judith Landing combined. The confluence of the Missouri and Judith rivers forms a wide valley that was a favorite Native American campsite. In 1846, at a meeting arranged by Father Pierre De Smet, the Piegan and Flathead Indians agreed to stop warring and band together to stop the expansion of the Crow tribe into central Montana. Nine years later, at a second council on the island, Issac I. Stevens, representing the U.S., convinced the Blackfoot Confederacy to sign "Lame Bull's Treaty," which set the boundaries of the Confederacy's territory and gave it domain over almost all of northern Montana. The treaty also established an Indian agency at Fort Benton and, most importantly, allowed white settlers to pass through and in some cases reside in the Confederacy's territory. During the negotiations, over 15,000 Native Americans camped in the valley, producing an influx of people that would never again be seen at Judith Landing.

You can reach Coalbanks Landing, another historic place associated with Montana's steamboat days, by taking the Coalbanks Landing exit from U.S. Highway 87, about eight miles west of Big Sandy. The boat landing at the Coalbanks Landing Recreation Area, which is now used by sports enthusiasts and recreational boaters, is the historic location of the Coalbanks steamboat landing. There was once a much different type of enterprise here. Steamboat captains, such as Grant Marsh, tried to use local lignite deposits to replace the cottonwoods that had already been consumed by their steam engines. But Marsh and the other captains discovered that the surface coal would only redden around the edges and would not burn. Steamboat captains also used Coalbanks Landing as a freight stop when the river was low and they could not reach Fort Benton.

Route B: Montana Highway 66, at Cow Island Recreation Area

You can reach Cow Island, another historic site of steamboat activity on the Missouri, from two different routes. You can leave Montana Highway 66 in southern Phillips County at the sign for the Cow Island Recreation Area and travel southwest for about 15 miles on an unimproved road; or you can take U.S. Highway 191 north of Lewistown for 78 miles and then take Montana Highway 66 until you reach the turn-off for the area.

By mid June of each year, navigating the Missouri from Cow Island to Fort Benton could be risky. Captains of large steamers discovered that snags, shoals, and the Bird, Dauphin, Gallatin, Deadman, Pablo, and Kipps rapids often created impassable barriers. Before 1880, huge bison herds often made boat travel very dangerous, blocking the channel, as one contemporary recalled, with "their huge, shaggy bodies," beating against the steamboat, and "blowing and pawing." Some captains transferred their cargoes and passengers to other ships; but because of treacherous river shoals at Cow Island, many large steamers stopped here and met mule packtrains that carried their goods to Fort Benton.

The Nez Perce crossed the Missouri River at Cow Island during their trek to Canada in 1877. They encountered a small group of soldiers on the island who were guarding army supplies. A skirmish broke out when the soldiers misunderstood the Indians' intentions to buy some supplies and food, and the Nez Perce finally took what they needed by force.

The recreational boat landing is the only remains of the steamboat era at Cow Island. Steamboats had no specific landing, so they tied up at the most accessible spot on the north bank of the river. From 1877 to 1880, the U.S. Army Corps of Engineers constructed a wing dam from the north bank of the Missouri, which created a calm water landing area against the bank. Today, there are no remains of this structure.

Route C: U.S. Highway 2, from Frazer to Culbertson

Steamboat travel on the Missouri River had few hazards from Cow Island to the mouth of the Yellowstone River, and knowledgeable pilots could navigate the river through most of the summer. But there were still difficulties, especially in trying to maintain supplies of firewood. Steamboats burned an average of 30 cords of cottonwood a day; and along this stretch of the Missouri, between Frazer and Culbertson on U.S. Highway 2, captains looked for "rack heaps" of driftwood piled high on sandbars and "deadenings" of standing trees near the river. At several places in the valley, you can see eroding tree trunks, places where "wood choppers" left the steamers to cut the cottonwoods for fuel. Freshly cut cottonwoods, however, were too green to produce a good fire, and some captains paid $8 a cord for dry wood to the "wood hawks" who were hardy enough to live along the Missouri River.

MHS SHPO

Fort Peck Theater, Fort Peck, Valley County. *This theater was built during the 1930s for construction workers who were working on the Fort Peck Dam.*

Route 21: The Fort Peck Dam and Reservoir
Montana Road 117 and Montana Road 24 from Nashua to Glasgow (loop-drive)

The Fort Peck Dam and Reservoir is the largest man-made alteration on the Montana landscape. Constructed during the Great Depression, it is the second largest earth-filled dam in the world, with a base 3,500 feet thick and an earthen wall 250 feet high and 50 feet wide at the top. The dam's spillway is a mile long, with a release capacity of 250,000 cubic feet per second. The power plants can generate 185,000 kilowatts of electricity. Guided tours of the dam's power-houses explain the construction and the value of the dam.

With funds from the Public Works Administration, the Corps of Engineers began building the Fort Peck Dam in October 1933 to control flooding and to improve navigation of the Missouri River. But during the 1930s, its most important contribution to Montana was the jobs that it gave to thousands of unemployed people.

In this relatively isolated section of the state, the Corps built a town for its workers. Fort Peck was Montana's first government-planned town, and the Corps designed it to be a model of urban planning. A press release bragged:

. . . the architecture will be varied and curved streets will eliminate the aspect of monotony common to the ordinary construction camps and factory towns. A pleasing color scheme has been selected for painting the exteriors of all buildings so that they will harmonize with the landscaping and lawn areas between buildings.

Fort Peck was built in a hurry. Begun in the spring of 1934, it was finished by that winter. The Corps used imaginative building techniques, specifying building materials that were readily available and having contractors prepare wooden materials on the spot. Workers built housing as if they were working a conveyor belt: they were assigned a specific task and moved from house to house to perform it.

After the dam and its electrical powerhouses were completed in the 1940s, the government removed many of the town's structures. Two decades later, the Corps built permanent buildings, including a church, a school, warehouses, a shopping center, and 77 houses. Fort Peck still contains several original buildings, including the project's administration building on Kansas Avenue and a hotel and theater on Missouri Avenue.

The Fort Peck Theater, listed in the National Register of Historic Places, is a wooden structure built in the style of a Swiss chalet. Originally designed to show movies, it seats over 1,200 people and is now used for summer theater productions. The Fort Peck Theater is the best example in Montana of the arts-and-crafts tradition that typified New Deal architecture throughout the country.

Landscape 5: The Old North Trail

You can find the remnants of Native American trails in many parts of northern Montana. The most prominent of these trails—the Old North Trail—passes through Glacier National Park and Pondera, Teton, and Lewis and Clark counties. According to North Piegan Chief Brings-Down-the-Sun, the trail began near present-day Calgary and ran "along the eastern side of the Rockies, at a uniform distance from the mountains, keeping clear of the forests, and outside the foothills. It ran close to where the city of Helena now stands and extended south into the country inhabited by a people with dark skins, and long hair [possibly Mexico]."

As you travel U.S. Highway 89, you can see the mighty peaks of the Rocky Mountains to the west and see a region of special significance to Montana Indians. Those who trod the Old North Trail created a landscape of travois ruts, hoof prints, rock cairns, and stone circles. No one uses the trail today, but its route helps define a part of northern Montana that the Native Americans considered to be very important.

Route 22: Religious Missions Among the Piegan Indians
Route A: Interstate Highway I-15, at Cascade
Route B: U.S. Highway 89, from Browning to Two Medicine
River Road

Three hundred years ago, the Blackfoot Confederacy lived on the southwestern Saskatchewan plains. During the early 1700s, the three tribes that comprised the Confederacy—the Piegan, the Kainah (the Blood), and the Siksika (the Northern Blackfoot)—lived by the Eagle Hills near the North Saskatchewan River and participated in the Canadian fur trade. As the Indians obtained iron to make arrowheads and acquired firearms, they moved westward and conquered new territory. By the 1800s, the Confederacy controlled an immense territory, including much of southern Alberta and all of northern Montana to the southern tributaries of the Missouri River.

The Blackfoot Confederacy dominated the Old North Trail, using it to extend commercial relations to tribes in the central and southern Rockies and keeping even enterprising American fur traders away. During the 1830s, the three tribes became intensely involved with *napikwan*, the white man, forming a relationship that would affect their traditional way of life.

Route A: Interstate Highway I-15, at Cascade (Mission Road)

When missionaries introduced Christianity to Confederacy Indians in the 1840s, profound changes began to take place on the landscape now divided by U.S. Highway 89. The Piegan had learned about Christianity a decade earlier from the Flathead, who saw Catholicism as a powerful war medicine. The Flathead had heard of the religion during the 1830s from a few members of the Iroquois Confederacy who had left their homes in New York, Pennsylvania, and southern Ontario and moved to western Montana. The Flathead then introduced the religion to the Small Robes band of Piegan.

The Piegan did not meet their first missionaries until 1846, when Father Nicolas Point came to Fort Lewis. Father Point traveled with several different hunting bands in the area for the next year and a half before leaving for Canada. At the urging of the federal government, Catholic priests returned to the area 12 years later in 1859. Using the trees that lined the Teton River, they built the first St. Peter's Mission near present-day Choteau on U.S. Highway 89, 73 miles south of Browning. Over the next six years, the mission changed locations three times, ending at Bird Tail Rock in western Cascade County. In 1866, the Jesuits closed St. Peter's until their return in 1874.

To reach St. Peter's Mission, take the northernmost Cascade exit off I-15 and drive west on the Mission Road for 13.5 miles. The remaining mission buildings show how Christianity changed the Confederacy's religious practices by replacing sun lodges and vision quest sites with crosses, altars, and permanent religious structures.

During its early years, the mission was quite simple. There was a small square-hewn log chapel, and the priests lived in several one-story log cabins that shared a common front porch, creating an L-shaped courtyard. In 1882, the priests built a combined residence for themselves and the mission's male students, and Ursuline nuns moved into the cabins until their permanent stone residence was completed 10 years later. The boys' school was a large stone building, dating to 1887, and the girls' school shared its quarters with the Ursuline nuns. In 1896, the mission built the "Opera House," a two-story L-shaped log structure, now covered by clapboard. In the auditorium wing, the mission held music and stage performances; the other wing was reserved for individual training in the fine arts.

Over the two decades of its construction, St. Peter's Mission evolved from a religious mission to a school for Piegan children. Its most famous resident was Louis Riel, who taught there in 1883-1884. Riel, the leader of Canadian Metis rebellions in 1870 and 1884-1885, was tried by the Canadian government for treason and executed in late 1885. By the turn of the century, the Indian school

C. V. West, photographer. MHS SHPO

Holy Family Mission, Blackfeet Indian Reservation, Glacier County. *Part of the reservation landscape, this dormitory building and church are reminders of decades of missionary activity among the Piegan.*

had closed, but St. Peter's began to build its reputation as one of the best private schools in the region.

St. Peter's Mission is listed in the National Register of Historic Places. It is on private property, so do not enter its grounds without the landowner's permission.

Route B: U.S. Highway 89, from Browning to Two Medicine River Road

The Holy Family Mission, the major Catholic mission on the Blackfeet Indian Reservation, is located about 3.5 miles east of U.S. Highway 89 on the north bank of the Two Medicine River, 11.5 miles southeast of Browning. The Jesuits founded the Holy Family Mission in 1886, and for the next 50 years the reservation's Indians were "civilized" and "Christianized" here.

The mission's priests and government officials in Helena and Washington, D.C. believed that the Piegan would not survive unless they adopted the whites' way of life by giving up hunting and stock-growing, their ancient religious beliefs, their sexual division of labor, and their notions of communal ownership. The priests at Holy Family Mission would convert the Piegan and then teach them to be successful farmers and housewives.

When it first began operations in 1886, the mission was only a crude log residence and a small log chapel. In 1890, the priests opened a large two- and one-half-story wood-frame school and dormitory, where Indian children stayed, separated from the "bad" influences of tribal life. A large sandstone boys' dormitory opened in 1895; and when the original dormitory/school burned three years later, the priests constructed another sandstone building to replace it. They also added barns, farm outbuildings, and a bakery to the mission. The Jesuits often boasted that Holy Family was largely self-sustaining and that it had made the Piegan into successful farmers. In 1937, the Jesuits replaced the mission's chapel with a new brick and concrete church.

Financial difficulties and the Indians' indifference to the mission's goals forced Holy Family to close its doors in 1940. It had never been a great success—the Jesuits' boasts had been just that—and many Piegan retained their hostility toward Catholicism and the policies of "civilizing" the Indians. Barns, the bakery, two sandstone dormitories, and the brick church still stand along Two Medicine River, symbols of the great ambitions of the Indian reformers at the beginning of the 20th century. The mission is listed in the National Register of Historic Places.

Route 23: Homesteading Along the Old North Trail
U.S. Highway 89, from Valier exit to Choteau

If you travel U.S. 89 south from Browning for 30 miles, take the Montana Highway 44 exit, and travel east for 13 miles, you will reach Valier, a town whose origin is due entirely to the Carey Act and the creation of Lake Francis. The Carey Act of 1894 provided federal land free to private individuals if they would reclaim the land by constructing and operating irrigation projects. In 1908-1909, utilizing the waters of Lake Francis and Dupuyer Creek, W. S. Cargill and other investors constructed the required irrigation head gates, canals, and ditches; and in March 1909, they established the Valier Townsite Company. A substantial town quickly developed along the banks of Lake Francis, and within five months 600 people lived in Valier.

Two important buildings from its early history still stand in Valier. To the west of the commercial district, on Montana Road 358, is Montana Western Railroad's depot, which was built in 1909. The Valier Townsite and Irrigation Project investors built the Montana Western to connect Valier to the Great Northern Railway. On the east side of town is the Valier Public School, an impressive two-story stone building that indicates the town's initial confidence in its future. It is listed in the National Register of Historic Places.

Nine miles south of the Valier exit on U.S. Highway 89 is Dupuyer, whose history is closely tied to the stock-growing industry of the late 1870s and 1880s. In 1878-1879, O. G. Cooper brought the first sheep to the Dupuyer area, and the following year W. D. Jones and Ira Brown brought their sheep herds to the land watered by Dupuyer Creek. Julian F. Burd constructed a 16- by 20-foot log store in 1882 to serve area stock-growers, but Dupuyer was not platted until 1892. Ever since, Dupuyer has remained an important trade center for the ranchers of southern Pondera and northern Teton counties.

Thirty-four miles south of Dupuyer is Choteau, the county seat of Teton County. The town is three and one-half miles south of the second Blackfeet Indian agency, constructed in 1869, and the early history of Choteau is closely tied to the reservation. In 1873, A. B. Hamilton established a trading post near the agency and enjoyed a prosperous trade with the Piegan. But in the mid 1870s, the federal government moved the agency to the north, and in 1879 Hamilton relocated his business to the present site of Choteau and served the stock-growers of the Teton River country.

Choteau was surveyed in 1883, and by the next year entrepreneurs had transformed the look of the land, as hotels, warehouses, general stores, and residences stood along the Teton River. Choteau, connected by rail to the Great Northern and the Milwaukee Road, has become an important trade center used by stock-growers throughout the Teton River and Sun River valleys.

Fort Assinniboine, U.S. Highway 87, Hill County. *Built in 1879, this post was established to guard Montana's northern frontier and to protect settlers from mostly imagined threats from roaming Metis Indians, who freely crossed the Canadian-American border. The fort, which closed in 1911, is now used as an agricultural research station.*

MHS Photo Archives

C. V. West, photographer, MHS SHPO

Old North Trail landscape, Montana Highway 17, Glacier County. *For hundreds of years, the Old North Trail was one of several primary routes used by Native Americans to travel north and south on the east side of the Continental Divide. It was part of a network of trails that extended from present-day Mexico to the arctic North.*

Judith Gap, U.S. Highway 91, Wheatland County

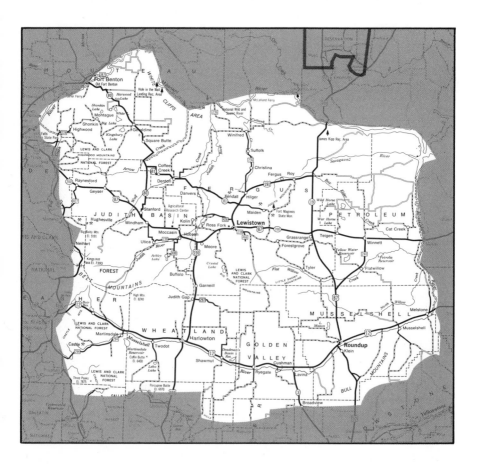

Chapter 3

The Judith Basin Country

For thousands of years, people have passed through the Judith Gap—the gap between the Little Belt and Big Snowy mountains—to exploit the natural riches of the Judith Basin. At Garneill and Judith Gap on U.S. Highway 191, you can imagine the scene 200 years ago when brightly painted Piegan and Atsina warriors moved south to battle the Crow for control of the region's abundant hunting territories.

The Native Americans were attracted to the region by the thickly grassed basins, the bison herds, and the pine forests of the Big Snowy, Little Belt, and Judith mountains. But few of the white settlers who arrived in Montana Territory during the 1860s and 1870s came to the Judith Basin. Not until 1880, when prospectors discovered gold in the Judith Mountains, did settlers, miners, stockgrowers, and entrepreneurs flood this region, lured by the possibility of sudden riches. It was not long before the Native American landscape of tipis, long lodges, and bison herds was transformed into one of log cabins, mine shafts, false-front A-frame buildings, and herds of cattle and sheep.

Fort Maginnis, constructed in the foothills of the Judith Mountains to protect the mining towns and to encourage others to settle in central Montana, was the most imposing structure on this new landscape. You can stand at the Fort Maginnis State Monument in Fergus County and imagine how the land looked when this large military post stood in the middle of the cattle range you see today.

The construction of the Chicago, Milwaukee, St. Paul & Pacific Railroad (the Milwaukee Road) through the Musselshell Valley and the extension of the Great Northern Railway through most of the Judith Basin imposed a new order on the landscape. Looking southeast and southwest from the porch of the Graves Hotel in Harlowton, located on the river bluffs overlooking the Musselshell Valley, you can see how the Milwaukee's tracks extend east and west from the town. This is part of the Milwaukee's railroad corridor of tracks, utility lines, signals, warehouses, passenger depots, and grain elevators.

The railroads brought homesteaders to the area by the tens of thousands, and dry-land farmers transformed the vast cattle ranges into a checkerboard of neatly plowed grain fields. The homesteaders named their counties Golden Valley and Wheatland, expressions of their hopes and dreams. But as you travel through this valley on U.S. Highway 12, you need merely to count the number of abandoned buildings in Ryegate and Harlowton to understand that the dreams of many homesteaders were never realized.

The Milwaukee Road declared bankruptcy in the late 1970s. In many places along the Milwaukee route, the wooden ties and steel track have been salvaged,

C. V. West, photographer, MHS SHPO

Abandoned Milwaukee roadbed, U.S. Highway 12, Golden Valley County. *Transportation routes, such as that blazed by the Milwaukee Road and U.S. Highway 12, have shaped central Montana's historical landscape.*

leaving only the roadbed and deteriorating structures. The tracks of the Milwaukee and also those of the Great Northern are now seldom used or abandoned, and the weeds covering the tracks indicate that the railroads no longer influence the landscape.

A different type of ordered landscape is also evident along U.S. Highway 12 near Martinsdale and along Montana Highway 81 east of Danvers. The uniform spaces, buildings, and structures of Hutterite colonies have produced a landscape of neat, well-arranged farms. This arrangement of space and buildings reflects the values of the Hutterite religion, which rejects much of modern culture and requires its members to live on a cooperative basis.

The Judith Basin landscape has also been shaped by modern international concerns. Along U.S. Highways 87 and 191 and on local roads, underground U.S. nuclear missile silos stand outside large towns and next to ranches. You can recognize a silo by the cyclone fence that surrounds it and the stenciled sign that identifies the silo by a letter-number code.There has never been a significant military battle fought in the Judith Basin, but World War III would probably make it into the scene of a nuclear nightmare.

Landscape 6: The Musselshell Valley

The Musselshell River, wrote Lt. John Mullan as he surveyed Montana during the 1850s, "winds through a beautiful valley, ten miles wide, covered with excellent grass." Two decades later, army surveyor William Ludlow described the Musselshell country as "level, wide, fertile, and richly grassed, with heavy clumps of timber on the low banks of the stream."

The Musselshell River flows along the eastern and southern boundaries of the Judith Basin. The only way to navigate the shallow Musselshell was in canoes and other small crafts, and even those vessels found the going difficult when the water was low. Pilots could take larger boats up the Musselshell for only a few miles above its confluence with the Missouri.

The Musselshell River Valley did not become a major transportation artery until the directors of the Milwaukee Road extended the railroad through the valley to the West Coast. Federal highway planners followed the railroad when they established the route of U.S. Highway 12 between Missoula and the lower Yellowstone Valley.

While the bottomland of the Musselshell Valley is rich, the country is dry, and successful farming is impossible without irrigation. As you travel through the valley, you can see irrigation ditches crisscrossing the valley, bringing water to farmers and ranchers.

Route 24: The Milwaukee Road
Route A: U.S. Highway 12, from Melstone to Martinsdale
Route B: Montana Road 294, from Martinsdale to U.S. Highway 89

U.S. Highway 12 from Melstone to Martinsdale parallels the tracks of the Chicago, Milwaukee, St. Paul & Pacific Railroad, better known as the Milwaukee Road. The Milwaukee declared bankruptcy in the late 1970s, but along this stretch of highway, you can still see how the railroad changed the look of the Musselshell Valley by creating towns and establishing a transportation corridor.

Route A: U.S. Highway 12, from Melstone to Martinsdale
During the early 1900s, the Milwaukee's directors decided to build their own transcontinental railroad to compete with the Northern Pacific, the Great Northern, and the Union Pacific railroads. Construction began in 1906, and the Milwaukee boasted that its large steel trestles, long tunnels, and mountain grades that ran between 1.66 to 1.8 per cent were design standards that no other Montana railroad could match. These were not idle boasts; the Milwaukee would be the most modern and efficient railroad in the state.

To build through the Musselshell Valley, the Milwaukee had to acquire the route of Richard A. Harlow's Montana Railroad Company, which ran from Lombard to Harlowton and from Harlowton to Lewistown. Hard times had forced Harlow to mortgage his "Jawbone" railroad to Great Northern magnate James J. Hill, and the Milwaukee feared that Hill would foreclose on Harlow's line, depriving the Milwaukee of its route. In 1910, the Milwaukee advanced Harlow enough money to pay off the Jawbone's mortgage, assuring its control of the Montana Railroad Company.

At Melstone, where the Milwaukee's tracks entered the Musselshell Valley, railroad officials realized that constructing the line the 85 miles west to Shawmut would be difficult and slow. There were many farms and ranches, and numerous irrigation ditches were in the way. The railroad had to destroy many irrigation systems and built new canals and head gates all over the valley. Irrigation ditches now parallel the highway between Shawmut and Harlowton. By the time the railroad left the valley at Martinsdale, the Milwaukee had accommodated the Musselshell's meandering nature by building 12 bridges over the river, many with longer spans than had been originally planned.

West of Harlowton, you can see two components of the Milwaukee's railroad corridor that do not appear on any other transcontinental railroad route in Montana: electric utility poles and transformer stations. The stations, located every 30 miles along the track, look the same along I-90 at Gold Creek, on Montana Highway 263 near Missoula, and on Montana Road 294 west of Lennep. Huge transformers in these multi-story brick buildings converted 100,000 volts of A.C. current into 3,000 volts of D.C. current. From the station, the power went to a copper cable that paralleled the railroad, where it connected with a second set of copper wires above the track.

The Milwaukee electrified its line between Harlowton and Avery, Idaho, to take advantage of the mountainous terrain. Construction began in 1914, and by the time it was completed in 1917, this part of the Milwaukee was the longest stretch of electric railway in North America. The Milwaukee saved money on this route because the electric engines could regain on the descent as much as 40 to 60 per cent of the power used for the ascent. As F. H. Johnson of the Milwaukee Road explained, the regenerative braking system on the electric engines worked simply

> by reversing the usual function of the electric motors, utilizing the momentum of the train to drive them as generators. . . . the energy that would otherwise be wasted in heating brake shoes is converted into electricity and used in pulling other trains up the hill or is returned to the Power Company and credit taken for the amount. . . . approximately 12 per cent of the entire amount drawn from the Power Company is later returned or in effect merely borrowed.

The Milwaukee Road left other physical evidence of its influence in the Musselshell Valley. At Melstone, on Highway 12 at the eastern tip of the valley, you can see a type of building found in almost every town along the Milwaukee Road: the railroad hotel. The railroad hotel was usually the town's largest and most distinctive structure, and the Antlers Hotel at Melstone is a good example. Located on the corner of Main Street and U.S. Highway 12, the Antlers Hotel faces both the railroad tracks and Melstone's main street, the center of the town's commercial district.

Roundup, the county seat of Musselshell County, is located on U.S. Highway 12 about 34 miles west of Melstone. Roundup's commercial development began

Adams Hotel, Lavina, Golden Valley County. *Painted a bright white and visible from many miles away, the Adams Hotel was a landmark in this part of Montana.*

in 1908 with the arrival of the Milwaukee Road and the railroad's decision to develop the coal mines at Klein, located two miles southwest of Roundup on U.S. Highway 87. Several hotels and rooming houses were built at Roundup for the miners and other new residents. As the Republic Coal Company's mines grew prosperous and Roundup's population increased, more permanent, architect-designed buildings replaced these unadorned wooden-plank structures. Noted Montana architects John H. Grant and Link and Haire of Billings and Butte designed some of the modern commercial buildings for the town.

If you leave U.S. Highway 12 at Roundup and travel down the town's main street, you will reach Railroad Avenue and the Milwaukee Road depot. Here you can see how changes in transportation have affected Roundup's built environment. Directly across from the depot to the north was the town's first commercial center. Today, these buildings are largely abandoned and deteriorating. The construction of U.S. Highways 12 and 87 a generation later, the increase in automobile travel, and the declining popularity of train travel caused the town's commercial district to shift away from the railroad and toward the junction of U.S. 12 and U.S. 87, which is now the center of Roundup's business district.

About 23 miles west of Roundup, just off U.S. Highway 12 on Montana Highway 3, is Lavina. Lavina's railroad hotel, the Adams, is a magnificent two-story wooden building. Louie Lehfeldt opened the hotel in 1908 and advertised it as an "elegant" hotel where each of the 22 rooms had linen sheets, down comforters, and a china bowl and pitcher. The Adams still commands attention today; and valley residents used to claim that the hotel was visible for miles, its white paint gleaming in the sunlight.

Twenty-two miles west of Lavina off U.S. Highway 12 in Golden Valley County is Barber, a ghost town from the homesteading era. A few abandoned stores re-

Grace Lutheran Church, Barber, Golden Valley County. Built in 1917, *the Grace Lutheran Church at the homesteading ghost town of Barber contains the smallest active American Lutheran congregation in the United States.*

Graves Hotel, Harlowton, Wheatland County. Built of native stone quarried *nearby, the Graves Hotel is a reminder of the prominence Harlowton once enjoyed as a leading city on the Milwaukee Road.*

main in the town, and the only remnant of the town bank is the vault. But there is also the Grace Lutheran Church, which is listed in the National Register of Historic Places. Built in 1917 by recently arrived homesteaders, the church served both Methodists and Lutherans in Barber and was the town's social center. The drought and bust of the 1920s and the Great Depression destroyed Barber's once promising future, and the town was almost completely deserted. But a Lutheran congregation, drawn from the farmers and ranchers of the Musselshell Valley, kept the church open. The church is an impressive building and an excellent example of vernacular architecture, featuring a roof of pointed arch fenestration and wooden tracery.

Twenty-four miles west of Barber on U.S. Highway 12 is Harlowton, the county seat of Wheatland County. You can see several fine examples of architect-designed railroad hotels and commercial buildings in Harlowton, and a few of the hotels are still operating, even though the Milwaukee no longer runs through the Musselshell Valley. Harlowton, located at the crossroads of U.S. 12 and U.S. 191, is still one of the transportation centers of central Montana.

Near the south end of Harlowton's Central Avenue on the bluffs above the Musselshell River and the Milwaukee tracks is the Graves Hotel, a three-story, L-shaped sandstone building. A. C. Graves and the firm of Kent & Shanley designed and built the hotel in 1908-1909, and August Pollman, a German immigrant, cut the sandstone from a bluff just west of the hotel and helped with construction.

The Graves Hotel was the first large hotel constructed in Harlowton after the town's disastrous fire of 1907, and it has served ever since as the town's finest hotel and as a social center for Wheatland County. The hotel's architectural details, particularly its wooden cornice and unique metal cupola, give it a Gothic Revival appearance. The Graves Hotel is listed in the National Register of Historic Places and is open to the public. Another prominent building is the American Theatre (now the closed State Theatre), located on Central Avenue, which was designed by the architectural firm of Link and Haire.

Harlowton was the eastern departure point for the Milwaukee Road's electric trains and a key division point for the railroad. Looking south from the porch of the Graves Hotel, you can see the roundhouses where westbound trains exchanged their steam engines for electric engines and trains going to Chicago exchanged their electric engines for steam engines. The roundhouses are closed to the public.

Route B: Montana Road 294, from Martinsdale to U.S. Highway 89

Twenty-three miles west of Harlowton, you can leave U.S. Highway 12 at Martinsdale and take Montana 294 southwest to its junction with U.S. Highway 89. About one mile south on Montana 294 is the Bair Ranch and one of the most elaborate ranch houses in Montana. (The history of the ranch is covered in Route 26.)

Along the 29 miles of Montana Road 294 between U.S. 12 and U.S. 89, there are many structures that relate to the history of the Milwaukee Road, creating an almost perfect landscape of the railroad in central Montana.

The Martinsdale depot is a good example of one of the most significant railroad architectural designs in Montana. The Milwaukee Road, whose tracks stretched from Chicago to Seattle, used several different designs for its depots. Unlike other northwestern railroads, the Milwaukee did not develop a standard building plan for small depots, except for the depots it built in the section between Evarts, South Dakota, and Butte, Montana. On the Evarts-to-Butte section, the company built its "Standard Class A Passenger Station," a utilitarian, single-story structure. The station had a passenger service area and waiting room (20 by 24 feet), an office (10 by 10 feet), and a freight room (16 by 24 feet). Its standardized interior also contained living quarters for the company agent, with a bedroom (10 by 12.5 feet), a living room (10 by 11.5 feet), and a kitchen (11.5 by 12.5 feet). Clapboard covered the station's exterior, and the only decorative details were the support brackets for the roof. One expert on the western railroad depot has described this type of depot as "the quintessence of Great Plains standardized railroad station architecture."

Lennep, a tiny village where residents have preserved an old store and where the schoolhouse is still in use, lies about 13 miles west of Martinsdale on Montana Road 294. The Trinity Lutheran Church at Lennep was built in 1910 and still serves the surrounding community. Located in the foothills of the Castle Mountains, this beautiful church is a good example of vernacular architecture.

From Martinsdale, Montana Road 294 follows the Milwaukee tracks. At several places, you can see the utility poles that supplied electricity to the trains. About five miles west of Lennep is one of the Milwaukee Road's transformer stations. This station still generates electricity and retains several original features. Transformers and transmission lines and a small storage building remain, and foundations for employee houses and offices are still evident on the landscape.

Route 25: Mining in the Musselshell Country
Route A: Montana Road 294, at Lennep (Castle Road)
Route B: U.S. Highway 87, from Roundup to Klein
The Musselshell country contains the remnants of two important mining operations. Castle, in Meagher County, is a silver camp that peaked during the 1880s and 1890s. Klein, over 100 miles to the east in Musselshell County, is the site of the old Republic Coal Company's mines.

Route A: Montana Road 294, at Lennep (Castle Road)
During the late 1880s and early 1890s, silver prices were at their peak and there were many silver boom towns in Montana. One such town was Castle, located off Montana Road 294 on a dirt road that extends seven miles northwest of Lennep in the Castle Mountains. Castle is now a ghost town, but the buildings and ruins that remain show how the streets and buildings created a haphazard pattern on the landscape. Within a few months after the first building was constructed at Castle in the spring of 1887, miners and entrepreneurs had laid out a town of tents, log cabins, and a few false-front, frame buildings. By 1891, Castle

Milwaukee Road powerhouse, Montana Road 294, Meagher County. *Located at roughly 30-mile intervals between Harlowton and Avery, Idaho, transformer stations converted A.C. current into D.C. current that the Milwaukee needed to power its electric engines.*

had over 1,000 residents, for there was plenty of work in the nearby Cumberland, Silver Star, Yellowstone, North Star, and Merimac mines.

Castle residents had great hopes for their town. They planned to build an electric street railway, provide for a railroad spur connection to the Northern Pacific Railroad, and construct an extensive waterworks project. The town's newspaper editor bragged, "the eyes of the world at present are turned toward Castle." But Castle's dreams evaporated once the demand for silver declined during the economic depression of the mid 1890s. Today, a handful of extant buildings and foundations remain in Castle from those boom years. The town is on private property; please do not enter the buildings or disturb these valuable historical remains.

Route B: U.S. Highway 87, from Roundup to Klein

The coal mines at Klein tell another kind of story about mining in the Musselshell Valley. Located in the northern foothills of the Bull Mountains immediately south of Roundup on U.S. Highway 87, the mines at Klein were developed as the Milwaukee Road built into the valley. The Republic Coal Company, a subsidiary of the Milwaukee Road, opened its first mine in 1907. Two years later, the company opened the Republic Mine No. 2, which soon became the major coal producer in the Bull Mountains.

The Republic Mine No. 2 had two shafts: one 340-foot shaft for hoisting and a second shaft to provide air and an emergency escape route. During an average day, the miners hoisted 150 cars of coal to the surface every hour. About 100 mules and horses were used to haul coal to the loading bin at the bottom of the hoisting shaft. One local historian claimed that "some of the mules were as ornery as the mule skinners and a lot smarter than some." The mules and horses

C. V. West, photographer. MHS SHPO

Miners' caves, Klein, U. S. Highway 87, Musselshell County. *In Klein's hey-day, the miners who could not find housing took advantage of the landscape by moving into these caves near town.*

were used underground until 1930, when the railroad electrified its mining operations and replaced the animals with electric locomotives.

Roundup and Klein rapidly developed near the mines, and two other mining companies were soon contributing to the towns' growth. In September 1908, the Roundup Coal Company began operations, and two years later the Davis Coal Company of Omaha, Nebraska, opened a mine two miles east of Roundup. About half of the coal produced in the area was used to fuel the Milwaukee Road's locomotives; the rest was sold to people who lived along the railroad line.

So many miners came to work in the area that the two towns could not house them all. Soon after its creation, Klein had over 1,500 residents, and those who could not find housing built dwellings with sandstone and logs in the caves surrounding the town. No one lives in the miners' caves today, but several of the caves are now shelters for animals or storage sheds. These unusual structures, located on the west side of U.S. Highway 87 at Klein, are a good example of people using natural resources in an innovative way.

With its Republic Mine No. 2 producing over 1,200 tons of coal a day by 1913, the Republic Coal Company was the major employer in Musselshell County. By 1917, there were 350 houses for miners and their families at Klein; and by 1927, 550 people worked at the mines.

In 1930, however, the mine became partially mechanized and managers cut the work force to 295 people. After the Milwaukee Road converted its engines to diesel fuel, the railroad lost interest in the property and sold the Republic Mine

No. 2 to entrepreneur A. G. Gately. One estimate is that the Republic Mine No. 2, which closed in 1956, produced over 20 million tons of coal during its lifetime.

From the Roundup depot, you can look to the southwest and see the Republic's coal chutes, warehouse, and loading area along the spur line that served the mines and parallels Railroad Avenue. The old office building for the Republic Coal Company stands on the south end of Main Street near the depot.

Landscape 7: The Judith Basin

The Judith River, which Capt. William Clark named in honor of his future wife, runs through the middle of a region bounded by the Musselshell River to the east, the Missouri River to the north, the Little Belt Mountains to the west, and the Big Snowy Mountains and Flat Willow Creek to the south. Since whites first settled in the area, the country drained by the Judith River has been called the Judith Basin.

The town of Grassrange, on U.S. Highway 87 in Fergus County, is surrounded by rolling hills and prairies covered by lush natural grasses. But if you look to the north or south, you can see snow-capped mountains, and to the northeast lie Wild Horse and War Horse lakes. The Judith Basin is a land of great diversity, with enough natural resources to support many different endeavors.

The stock-growers of the 1870s fattened their cattle on the Basin's natural grasses. Early settlers used lodgepole pines from the Judith Mountains and cottonwoods from the Judith River and its tributaries to build their houses, businesses, and ranch corrals. Deposits of gold and silver lay waiting to be discovered in the Judith Mountains, and if cared for properly the Judith Basin's topsoil was rich and productive. As one Fergus County promoter claimed in the 1920s, the Judith Basin had "an abundance of the best grass in the world, plenty of shade and where feed, both hay and grain, can be grown more successfully than in the dairy sections' of Wisconsin, Minnesota and Iowa." For wheat-growers, it was a land where "the large, level, productive bench lands of Central Montana offer unrivaled opportunities to produce the best hard red milling wheat grown on the American Continent."

Route 26: Stock-growing in Central Montana
Route A: U.S. Highway 87, from Grassrange to Montana 244
Route B: Montana Highway 200, from Lewistown to
Fort Maginnis
Route C: U.S. Highway 12, from Ryegate to Martinsdale

There is some angles to the cow bizness which you kin perdick on an' you'll not be strayin' too far off your range. You can bet a few blue chips on it, that iffen you got fat cattle, the buyers will be wantin' light, thin stuff. Iffen you got lightweight critters, the buyer'll sniff an' tell you he ain't got no outlet for nothin' but butcher stock. Iffen you got calves, he'll want steers ready to go on the block. Iffen you got dry cows, he'll want yearlins. Never

did see a buyer who didden have a ready sale for somethin' you didden have. . . .
—Greasewood Simpkins [F. Howard Sinclair], 1956

Greasewood Simpkins humorously underscored the way that many Montana stock-growers have viewed their situation. Rarely has luck seemed to be on their side. Simkins's complaints aside, the Judith Basin's open country has been home for some of the most prosperous ranches in Montana history. Four ranches in the Judith Basin represent the historical diversity of stock-growing in the area: the N-Bar and DHS ranches in Fergus County, the Sims-Garfield Ranch in Golden Valley County, and the Bair Ranch in Meagher County.

Route A: U.S. Highway 87, from Grassrange to Montana 244

The N-Bar Ranch is located about 15 miles southwest of Grassrange off U.S. Highway 87 in southern Fergus County. Situated along Flat Willow Creek, the ranch is a good example of a large stock-growing operation that survived the 19th century open-range era and prospered during the 20th century. The mixture of buildings on the N-Bar Ranch also illustrates a century of changes in technology and ranch work, from the labor-intensive open-range period to today's mechanized stock-growing business. The ranch is private property; do not enter without the permission of the landowner.

After the terrible winter of 1886-1887, wealthy Helena mine owner and banker Thomas Cruse took control of the N-Bar when he bought the Niobrara Cattle Company and acquired the N-Bar brand and 6,000 cattle. In 1913, he sold the land, 35,000 sheep, and 15,000 cattle to the A. M. Holter family; and during the homesteading era, settlers purchased large tracts of the ranch along Flat Willow Creek. Ranch owners and managers have since re-acquired much of this farmland. Today's N-Bar Ranch is diversified, with a cattle operation and several wheat fields in its upland regions.

The N-Bar Ranch is located off U.S. Highway 87, about 20 miles south of Grassrange. If you travel west on a gravel road for 19 miles along the north bank of Flat Willow Creek, nearest the road you will see the N-Bar's bunkhouse, a two-story building with a steep, gable roof and vertical board-and-batten siding. The first floor was divided into a bedroom, a living room, and a washroom; and the second floor was partitioned into four sleeping areas. About 80 feet behind the bunkhouse is the original office and storeroom, constructed in the 1890s with lumber from the ranch's own sawmill. The building has a long porch, a brick chimney, and a wood-shingle roof. The original cookhouse, of notched, square-hewn log construction, lies 80 feet to the east of the ranch office. The cookhouse has a large kitchen and dining room and sleeping quarters for the cooks. These three buildings represent an era when cowboys were essential to the stock-growing industry.

About 400 feet east of the bunkhouse is the manager's residence, a two- and one-half-story frame house constructed in the 1930s by E. B. Milburn. To the west, between the manager's residence and the original cookhouse, is the powerhouse, a rubble stone structure built during the 1930s that has always housed the ranch's electrical generator. Both the manager's residence and the powerhouse are evidence of the ranch's continuing modernization and prosperity during the 20th century. The most recent period of the N-Bar's history is represented by the new shop building of corrugated metal construction, located about 150 feet northwest of the bunkhouse.

Route B: Montana Highway 200, from Lewistown to Fort Maginnis

The DHS Ranch, another large Judith Basin open-range stock-growing operation during the 1880s, was located on Ford Creek in northeastern Fergus County. To explore the land once marked with the DHS brand, leave Montana Highway 200 at the sign for the Fort Maginnis State Monument. This gravel road will take you north to the monument, which is only a mile away from the original DHS ranch site. The site of the ranch is private property. Do not enter without the permission of the landowner.

The ranch was begun by three of the most famous men in Montana history: Andrew J. Davis, Samuel T. Hauser, and Granville Stuart. In 1879, they formed Davis, Hauser, and Company, with Stuart as manager, in the belief that quick and easy riches were assured. As Hauser commented to an associate, stock-growing was "a short and sure road to fortune." By the summer of 1880, Stuart had thousands of cattle grazing on 40 square miles of rangeland.

In 1883, Stuart bought into the company, Hauser sold part of his interest, Davis sold his share to Conrad Kohrs, the leading rancher of western Montana, and the company became Kohrs, Stuart, and Company, with Stuart as ranch manager. Selling its livestock through the Pioneer Cattle Company, the company prospered at first, but overstocking the range soon threatened the ranch's success. One of Hauser's correspondents reported that "there is actually no grass on the range." A drought, followed by the bitter winter of 1886-1887, killed about 60 per cent of the herd and devastated the company, which gradually sold its ranch assets and finally ceased operations in 1895.

Stuart had located the DHS in a favorable spot, with its headquarters along Ford Creek nestled in the shadow of the Judith Mountains. In 1880, the army had built Fort Maginnis a mile to the east of the DHS to protect local cattlemen and the Judith Mountain miners. Stuart lived on the ranch with his Native American wife, Awbonnie, and with ranch employees like his friend Reece Anderson. One historian has observed that Stuart liked the Ford Creek location

> because there was good timber and spring water handy; magnificent grass country stretched for a hundred miles in every direction; there was plenty of brush shelter—plum thickets, chokeberry trees, bullberry bushes, soil that would grow anything, and no sheep. The pine in the mountains furnished house logs and corral poles.

The accommodations at Ford Creek were rustic. Stuart wrote that the DHS contained "a log stable that would accommodate ten horses, a cabin for cowboys, and a blacksmith shop. These buildings formed two sides of a large corral." The dwellings for himself and Anderson "formed two sides of an open square," which were connected "with a bastion like those used at the early trading posts" to protect them from Indian attacks. There were also animal sheds with thatched roofs, corrals, a small cabin for Stuart's substantial library (over 3,000 volumes), and an ice house. The DHS milk house was an ingenious building, with water diverted from Ford Creek passing through it to keep it cool during the summer. Stuart and his ranch hands constructed the buildings with pine logs, using sod for the roofs.

In 1884, the DHS Ranch became the center for vigilante activity. Largely directed by Stuart, these stockmen and ranch hands hunted down and executed from 15 to 18 men in separate incidents near the Missouri River. The vigilantes claimed that each victim was a "known" horse thief or cattle rustler, although there was no proof of their guilt. The first executions took place at Fort Maginnis, with later hangings occurring along the Missouri River near the mouth of the Musselshell River.

Route C: U.S. Highway 12, from Ryegate to Martinsdale

The Sims-Garfield Ranch, a small-scale stock-growing operation that began during the open-range era, is located about one mile east of Ryegate along U.S. Highway 12. The ranch is representative of successful family ranches in Montana and is listed in the National Register of Historic Places. The ranch is on private property; do not enter without the landowner's permission.

John T. Sally built the first ranch building here in 1882 and cultivated two acres of land. But there were too many people in the valley for Sally's taste, and he sold his property to William Wilkens in 1883 and moved to Alaska. In 1885, Joseph Sims bought the ranch, and many of the buildings that he constructed can be seen from the north side of U.S. 12.

With 160 acres of prime bottomland, Sims became a prosperous stock-grower, but he sold the ranch in 1906 to a land company that hoped to profit by selling land in the Musselshell Valley to the Milwaukee Road, whose tracks would pass through the ranch. During the homesteading boom, the Victor Schaff family bought the ranch and operated it as a diversified farm until 1923, when drought and hard times cost the Schaffs their ranch. The Federal Land Bank in Spokane later acquired the property and rented it to Verne Johnson and Harry Henton. Eventually, Henton took full control, and today his descendants, Jess and Emmy Lou Garfield, operate a stock-growing business on the ranch.

There is an interesting array of buildings on the Sims-Garfield Ranch, and you can see five important historical structures from the highway. John Sally built his original log cabin in 1882 with pine logs and topped it with a sod roof, which has since been replaced with tin. Sims's six-room log house, which also dates to the 1880s, features hand-hewn log walls and corner dovetail notches. In 1910, the Schaff family constructed the modern ranch house, which has been remodeled twice and is now used by the Garfields. The log barn, one of the oldest buildings at the ranch, was constructed using the post-and-beam technique, placing two logs upright in the ground with a second set of logs placed lengthwise between them. The stone barn, which was built in the mid 1880s, features rubble stone walls and pine log roof trusses.

Over 50 miles west of the Sims-Garfield Ranch is the Bair Ranch, which includes one of the most elaborate ranch houses in Montana. You can see the ranch

W. H. Culver, photographer, MHS Photo Archives

Maiden, Fergus County, 1888. *Mining towns like Maiden developed around the mines, creating historical landscapes composed of houses, businesses, and stamp mills in the gulches and on the hillsides.*

house by leaving U.S. Highway 12 at its junction with Montana Road 294 near Martinsdale and traveling south for one mile. Charles M. Bair, the "King of Western Sheepmen," constructed this 26-room mansion in 1935. The size of the house is an indication of the riches that could be gained from stock-growing in central Montana. The ranch is private property and is not open to the public. Do not trespass.

Bair's first sheep ranch was near Lavina, about 75 miles east of Martinsdale, but in 1893 he moved south to graze his stock near the Crow Indian Reservation. During the next 10 years, Bair tried his luck in the Alaskan gold mines. When he returned to stock-growing, he expanded his holdings by leasing almost 300,000 acres of Crow Indian Reservation rangeland. By the 1910s, Bair had created a sheep empire and had become one of the leading capitalists in eastern Montana. He went on to develop coal mines near Roundup and oil fields in Wyoming, and he owned banks, irrigation companies, and real estate.

In 1910, Bair gave up his lease on the Crow Indian Reservation and moved his ranch to Martinsdale, where he controlled 120,000 acres. Bair's family still owns and operates the ranch from its headquarters at Martinsdale.

Route 27: Mining in the Judith Basin
Route A: U.S. Highway 191, from Lewistown to Hilger
Route B: Montana Highway 200, at Cat Creek

The Judith Mountains dominate the central Montana landscape, providing a striking contrast to the rolling hills, gullies, and plains of the Judith Basin. When miners entered the mountains during the 1880s and 1890s, they centered most of their activity in the gold camps at Maiden on the west side of the mountains, at Giltedge on the east side, and at Kendall, a few miles west of the Judith Mountains near Hilger.

Route A: U.S. Highway 191, from Lewistown to Hilger

Maiden is the most accessible mining town in central Montana. It is located off U.S. Highway 191 on the Warm Springs Canyon Road nine miles north of Lewistown. There is a highway historical marker about Maiden at the turn-off for the Warm Springs Canyon Road.

The discovery of the mountains' precious metals came late in Montana's mining history. Well before 1880, prospectors and adventurers had wanted to explore for gold and silver in the Judith Mountains, but fear of Native American reprisal had kept them out of that part of the territory. After Indian-white hostilities had ended in 1877-1878, Montanans began to explore the gulches in the Judith Mountains; and in May 1880, Joseph Richard "Skookum Joe" Anderson and David Jones made the first discoveries of placer gold. News of this and other placer claims spread quickly, and soon miners were rushing to the area. Within a year, Maiden was established; and by 1885, the town had 150 buildings and about 700 residents.

Jones and Anderson also discovered the Spotted Horse Mine, the most significant gold mine near Maiden. But the two miners didn't have enough money to build a stamp mill, which they needed to develop the rich quartz lode. (A stamp mill processes ore by crushing the rock with heavy steel cylinders that were usually powered by steam engines.) To finance the mill, Anderson approached Perry W. "Bud" McAdow, an old acquaintance who had once operated a mercantile business at Coulson on the Yellowstone River. Now in partnership with Charles Dexter, McAdow managed a sawmill at nearby Andersonville (the location of the present-day Big Sky Bible School) and owned a store in Maiden. In 1883, McAdow agreed to help Anderson and Jones finance the mill if they would put up the Spotted Horse as security. But even with the mill, Anderson and Jones couldn't make the mine pay, and McAdow foreclosed.

Although McAdow now had full control of the Spotted Horse, he too lacked sufficient money to develop the mine fully. His new wife, Clara Tomlinson McAdow, a shrewd and wealthy businesswoman, agreed to lend Bud $4,000 of her own money and $6,000 in borrowed funds to make the mine into a major gold producer. With Clara's money, McAdow turned the Spotted Horse into the leading money-maker in the Judith Mountains. Producing over $100,000 during the first three months, the Spotted Horse would eventually pay out over $2 million worth of precious metals.

Around 1890, the McAdows sold the Spotted Horse for $500,000 to a syndicate headed by A. M. Holter and Samuel Hauser and moved to Jackson, Michigan (near Detroit), where Clara retired to enjoy her wealth. But Perry returned to Maiden in 1891, reopened his store, and soon bought the Spotted Horse from its disenchanted owners. He extracted another million dollars in gold before selling the mine for one last time in 1893. The stone foundations for the mine's two-story stamp mill stand less than a mile east of Maiden on the Warm Springs Canyon Road.

Giltedge is about one mile west of Maiden on the Warm Springs Canyon Road on the east side of the Judith Mountains. You can also reach Giltedge by taking U.S. Highway 87/Montana 200 to the Fort Maginnis State Monument road, which

Barnes-King Gold Mine, Kendall, Fergus County, ca. 1910. *The hoist and compressor house (l.) and the cyanide mill (r.) were part of Kendall's most successful mining complex at the turn of the century.*

is about 15 miles east of Lewistown. Travel north on this gravel road until you reach its junction with the Warm Springs Canyon Road and turn left toward Maiden.

On the outskirts of Giltedge, you can see the remains of the Gold Reef Mill. In 1893, miners began to extract gold from the low-grade ore deposits at Giltedge. The Giltedge Mining Company, under the direction of R. T. Armington and T. E. Collins, tried to remove the gold by using a new and complicated method. First the ore was roasted, then crushed in a stamp mill, and finally leached in large vats where a cyanide solution separated the gold. Armington and Collins had little success, and soon they took on a new partner, Robert A. Hammond of New York. But the mining operation failed. In January 1894, the mines were closed after Hammond had sneaked out of Giltedge with $25,000 in gold bullion.

Within a short time, the town rebounded from its unfortunate beginnings and became the site of a successful mining operation. A succession of entrepreneurs operated the revived Giltedge mines until the Great Northern Mining Company gained control in 1900. The company operated the Gold Reef stamp mill until 1915, when Giltedge's heyday ended. Homesteaders removed many of the abandoned buildings to use on their own farms, and few of the town's domestic or commercial structures remain in Giltedge today.

Kendall, located in the North Moccasin Mountains, is another central Montana gold camp that boomed during the early 1900s. You can reach Kendall by leaving U.S. Highway 191 at Hilger, five miles north of the Warm Springs Canyon Road turn-off, and driving east for six miles on a dirt road. The old gold camp is now the Kendall Boy Scout Camp, but you can still see the ruins and foundations of several Kendall buildings and a reconstructed bandstand.

Montanans did not develop the gold ores of the North Moccasin Mountains until the late 1890s, when Harry Kendall opened a cyanide mill employing about 40 workers. In 1902, Kendall sold 90 per cent of his property to two Spokane businessmen who reorganized the Kendall Mining Company. You can see the remains of the Kendall mine several miles west of town on a very rough dirt road. But the town's major gold mine and mill, located at the top of Main Street, was owned by the Barnes-King Development Company, which developed the mine in 1900-1901.

Kendall's first social center was the Miners' Union Hall. The Kendall miners, who were mostly from Croatia and Bohemia, were stalwart union supporters. They often gathered at the hall to hear ministers, politicians, and socialists speak. You can still see the foundations of the hall just off the town's main street near the Barnes-King mine.

In 1911, when the Milwaukee Road created Hilger, about six miles east of Kendall, many Kendall residents and businesses moved their buildings to the new town. Large-scale mining at Kendall ended the next year, although some local mines continued to operate until 1923. From 1936 to 1941, the North Moccasin Mines Syndicate reopened several of the Kendall mines, but it had only limited success. In the mid 1980s, mining activity resumed at Kendall and continues today.

Route B: Montana Highway 200, at Cat Creek

Twenty-two miles east of Winnett on Montana Highway 200 in Petroleum County is the exit for the Cat Creek Dome, a central Montana mining location where petroleum, not precious metals, created the rush. As you drive along the gravel road, you will pass both operating and abandoned oil wells. The small town of Cat Creek dates to the winter of 1919-1920 when employees of the Frantz Corporation of Denver dug one of the first successful commercial wells in Montana. One worker, J. S. "Curley" Meek, remembered that due to a coal strike "we burned cottonwood logs for fuel. We contracted with a fellow named Bill Miller who lived down on the Missouri River. He cut the wood and delivered it to us for $8 a cord." In time, the Continental Oil Company took over the petroleum holdings in the area, and Conoco developed a small company town at Cat Creek. Conoco operates the oil wells at Cat Creek Dome today, and some of the original dwellings are still in use, reminders of Cat Creek's beginnings as a company town.

Route 28: Homesteaders in the Judith Basin Country
U.S. Highway 87/Montana Highway 200, from Stanford to U.S. 191 junction

In the spring of 1880, Perry W. McAdow wrote to Martin Maginnis, Montana's territorial delegate to the U.S. Congress, predicting that "the Judith Country is destined to be the granary of Montana a second Red River." But the transformation would not take place for well over a generation. The region's rolling hills and prairies contained a rich but thin layer of topsoil that produced lush natural grasses that were ideal for stock-growing. For the land to be cultivated, farmers had to learn dry farming techniques and rely heavily on irrigation.

The homesteading boom in the Judith Basin from 1908 to 1915 coincided with the extension of the Milwaukee Road and the Great Northern lines through the

C. V. West, photographer, MHS SHPO

Milwaukee depot, Moore, U.S. Highway 87, Fergus County. *This depot is a good example of standardized railroad architecture and is one of the few left along this now abandoned railroad line.*

region. Real estate promoters, railroad officials, and political leaders created great excitement about the potential of dry farming in the area, and the railroads brought settlers to the Basin and delivered their products to market.

Along U.S. Highway 191, Montana Highway 81, and Montana Road 236, you can see the small villages that developed along the Milwaukee Road: Coffee Creek, Denton, Danvers, Geraldine, Square Butte, and Moore. On U.S. Highways 87 and 191 are the towns along the Great Northern line: Raynesford, Geyser, Stanford, Buffalo, and Windham.

Along these highways and in these towns, you can see important buildings and places associated with the homesteading phenomenon in central Montana. But the single best route is U.S. Highway 87/Montana Highway 200 from Stanford to the U.S. 191 junction, a 28-mile-long stretch of road from which you can see the Stanford town design, the bank buildings at Benchland and Moccasin, and the Central Montana Agricultural Research Center near Moccasin.

The railroad was the most important institution in each town. Stanford, the county seat of Judith Basin County, is a classic "T-town," which was the plan adopted by many towns in the region. Several grain elevators, the Great Northern (now Burlington Northern) depot, and other railroad-related buildings make up the top of the "T," and Stanford's main street is the stem. At the bottom of the "T," away from the valuable commercial property near the railroad depot, is the Judith Basin County courthouse. This arrangement of buildings underscores the railroad's importance in Stanford and symbolically demonstrates its power in early Stanford compared to that of the local government.

C. V. West, photographer, MHS SHPO

Abandoned bank, Moccasin, Judith Basin County. *Clyde Gore of Fergus County remembered that bankers were often their own worst enemies, insisting that homesteaders follow their uninformed advice on farming. When the farmers failed, so did the banks.*

The second most important institution in these early homesteading towns was the bank, which was normally housed in the most permanent building in town. Constructed from brick, concrete, and steel, the bank was often the first substantial building in these towns, and bankers hoped that the building's sturdy appearance would bolster customer confidence. The bank buildings in these small towns are worth looking at closely. It is not difficult to find the First National Bank of Geraldine, 27 miles south of Fort Benton on Montana Highway 80; the two closed banks at Roy, 36 miles north of Lewistown on U.S. Highway 191; the closed bank at Moccasin, 27 miles west of Lewistown on U.S. Highway 87; the dilapidated state bank at Buffalo, 34 miles south of Lewistown on U.S. Highway 191; and the Farmers State Bank at Denton, 38 miles northwest of Lewistown on Montana Highway 81. The bank commanded the most prominent lot in town, often standing on the town's main corner with its front door facing the corner. A good example is in Garneill, located 39 miles south of Lewistown on U.S. Highway 191. The message was clear: everyone's business was welcome.

The banks in these towns presented a strong and stable image. Over the entrances to the banks in Moccasin, Roy, and Geraldine, there are pediments, a neoclassical architectural feature emphasizing that the banks were "solid" institutions that would last as long as ancient Greek and Italian temples.

The construction, the location, and the use of neoclassical architectural details

Abandoned bank, Buffalo, Fergus County. *When half the state's banks closed during the 1920s depression, recalled Faye Hoven, many central Montanans learned that self-sufficiency pays.*

are the three easiest ways to identify an old bank. Many of the original banks in the Judith Basin are now law offices, post offices, or churches.

The State Bank of Benchland, located about 12 miles east of Stanford on U.S. Highway 87 in Judith Basin County, does not fit this pattern. The building stands on the town's main corner, but it is made of wood and has no neoclassical architectural features. At first glance, this two-story, wooden-plank building looks like it might have been a store or a hotel, but the building was the town bank until its failure in the 1920s.

Most of Montana's financial institutions faced difficulties during the 1920s. The state had far too many banks—some said Montana was "overbanked"—when crop prices fell and a drought hit eastern and central Montana. As the agricultural depression deepened, banks began closing their doors; more than half of the state's banks failed between 1920 and 1925. Some blamed federal and state banking officials who may have chartered too many banks—every small town had at least one—and there were several cases of mismanagement. But the major reason for bank failures in the Judith Basin was the close ties the banks had with the homesteading economy; when the homesteaders failed, so did the banks.

State government played an important role in developing the Judith Basin, primarily through its promotion of dry farming. In 1908, the legislature created the Central Montana Agricultural Research Center, three miles east of Moccasin

MSU Archives, Bozeman

Central Montana Agricultural Research Center, Moccasin, Judith Basin County. *Montana aided homestead farmers through scientific studies, agricultural extension seminars, and the testing and production of hardier strains of wheat and other crops at this research center in the Judith Basin.*

on U.S. Highway 87. The government designed the center (then called the Judith Basin Substation) to teach newly arrived homesteaders about dry farming. Starting with only 160 acres of land and a two-story house, the center expanded within three years to include about 640 acres and several new houses and work buildings.

During the homesteading boom, thousands came to the center's Field Days, where state officials demonstrated the center's advanced farming techniques. After the bust hit, many state officials wanted to close the center, but the employees kept it open by developing new machines and new crops, such as crested wheatgrass, that helped local farmers improve their yields. Much of the present success of dry farming in central Montana can be attributed to the work of the Central Montana Agricultural Research Center.

From U.S. Highway 87, you can see several buildings at the research center that date to the homesteading era. The foreman's residence was the first house built on the site, and the Seed Laboratory is a two-story building that was originally the center's barn. Both of these buildings date to 1908. Seven buildings were constructed between 1910 and 1918, including a granary, two water pumphouses, a storage building, and three employee residences. Each building is a wooden-frame structure with wooden siding.

Duncan Ranch Colony, U.S. Highway 12, Wheatland County. *These balloon-frame, two-story structures with gable roofs are typical of Hutterite architecture found in the over 20 colonies located in central Montana. Hutterites live an ordered, traditional life based on a conservative theology that has its origins in 16th century Reformation Germany.*

C. V. West, photographer, MHS SHPO

Lewistown, Fergus County, ca. 1908. *Prominent in Lewistown are the stone buildings constructed by Croatian stonemasons at the turn of the century. Many of these buildings lie within the town's Courthouse Historic District.*

MHS Photo Archives

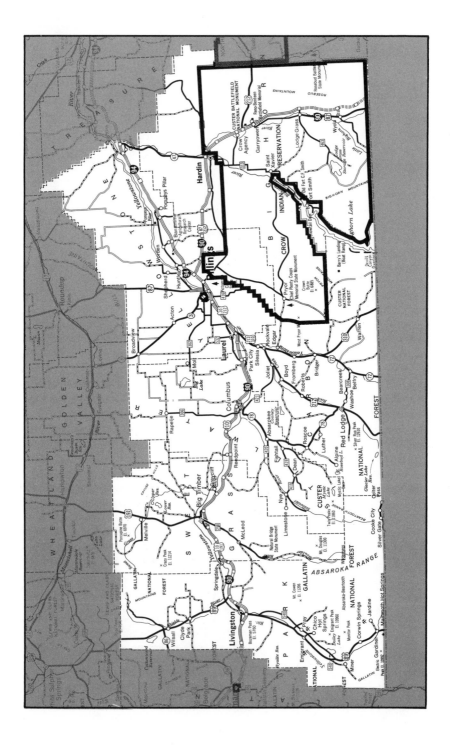

Chapter 4

The Upper Yellowstone Valley

Lush river basins, expansive forests, mighty rivers, and Montana's highest mountains dominate the upper Yellowstone Valley. This part of the Yellowstone Valley stretches from the North Entrance of Yellowstone National Park to Billings, from one of the most remote regions in Montana to the state's largest city. Looking south from the rimrocks on the Black Otter Trail Road in Billings, you can see Montana's largest urban area and the valley's productive bottomland stretching as far as the eye can see.

Some of the Yellowstone's earliest residents lived along the rimrocks and the breaks that loom above this river valley, and they left painted records of their hunts, battles, and victories at sites such as Pictograph Cave. At Sacrifice Cliffs, a part of the bluffs along the south bank of the Yellowstone, the relatives of Crow Indians who had died during the smallpox epidemic of 1837 rode off this sheer rock cliff, falling to a certain death in the Yellowstone rather than facing their grief and the disfigurement caused by the disease. You can see Sacrifice Cliffs from the bridge that crosses the river on U.S. Highway 87 east of present-day Billings.

To see other prehistorical landscapes, you must look beyond the upper Yellowstone's river valleys. Looking south from the Plenty Coups State Monument at Pryor, about 36 miles south of Billings on the Pryor Road, you can see the Pryor Mountains of Big Horn County, an area that had special significance for the Crow Indians. From the peaks of the Pryors, the site of vision quests, warriors could look out on the expansive and fertile upper Yellowstone landscape. But the Pryors delivered more than spiritual strength; the rich foliage and animals also provided important material benefits.

White Americans were first attracted to the upper Yellowstone Valley by its bountiful supply of fur-bearing animals and the gold nuggets found in its gulches. These newcomers also developed other resources in the valley. During the 1870s, for instance, Dr. Andrew J. Hunter tapped hot mineral waters found near present-day Livingston and constructed the first tourist center in the Yellowstone Valley, Hunter's Hot Springs.

A few years later, surveyors found that the valley's topography created a natural passageway and a perfect location for the tracks of the Northern Pacific Railroad. The towns of Billings and Livingston soon developed along the tracks, attracting more entrepreneurs, stock-growers, and farmers to the region.

As homesteaders came to the valley in increasing numbers, they changed the landscape. In areas where wild grasses had once fed the valley's wildlife, the farmers planted wheat, corn, barley, and oats, and irrigation ditches soon crisscrossed the land. As more farmland came into production, homesteaders made permanent homes and built communities. Some of the immigrants who came settled in small towns such as Melville, 20 miles north of Big Timber. The Melville Lutheran Church was built in 1914 by Norwegian-Americans who had come to the area in 1885. Looking to the south and east from the church, you can see the fences, plowed fields, barns, roads, and irrigation systems that have indelibly changed the upper Yellowstone landscape.

Landscape 8: The Upper Yellowstone Valley

Fur traders, miners, and settlers came to the upper Yellowstone Valley during the 19th century, but the valley had already been home to the Crow Indians for over two centuries. The words of Crow Chief Arapooish describe the valley that the whites saw. Although Native Americans left few written records about their perception of the Montana landscape, in the 1850s a fur trader recorded this sensitive explanation of why the valley was such a special place for the Crow. Arapooish told the fur trader:

The Crow country is a good country. The Great Spirit has put it exactly in the right place; when you are in it you fare well; whenever you go out of it, whichever way you travel, you fare worse.

If you go to the south, you have to wander over great barren plains; the water is warm and bad, and you meet fever and ague.

To the north it is cold; the winters are long and bitter, with no grass; you cannot keep horses there, but must travel with dogs. What is a country without horses?

On the Columbia they are poor and dirty, paddle about in canoes, and eat fish. Their teeth are worn out; they are always taking fish-bones out of their mouths. Fish is poor food.

To the east they dwell in villages; they live well; but they drink the muddy water of the Missouri—that is bad. A Crow's dog would not drink such water. About the forks of the Missouri is a fine country; good water; good grass; plenty of buffalo. In the summer it is almost as good as the Crow country; but in the winter it is cold; the grass is gone; and there is no salt weed for the horses.

The Crow country is exactly in the right place. It has snowy mountains and sunny plains; all kinds of climates, and good things for every season. When the summer heats scorch the prairies, you can draw up under the mountains, where the air is sweet and cool, the grass fresh, and the bright streams come tumbling out of the snow-banks. There you can hunt the elk, the deer, and the antelope, when their skins are fit for dressing; there you will find plenty of white bears and mountain sheep.

In the autumn when your horses are fat and strong from the mountain pastures, you can go down into the plains and hunt the buffalo, or trap beaver on the streams, and when winter comes on, you can take shelter in the woody bottoms along the rivers; there you will find buffalo meat for

F. Jay Haynes, photographer. Haynes Found. Coll., MHS Photo Archives

Emigrant Gulch and Chico City, Park County, 1905. *Miners worked the gulch for over 50 years after the first discovery in 1864. The miners altered the gulch and upland landscape by digging up the stream bed, sinking mine shafts, and building their log homes.*

yourselves, and cottonwood bark for your horses; or you may winter in the Wind River Valley, where there is salt weed in abundance.

The Crow country is exactly in the right place. Everything good is to be found there. There is no country like the Crow country.

Route 29: Mining in the Upper Yellowstone Country
Route A: U.S. Highway 89, from Gardiner to Livingston
Route B: U.S. Highway 10, from Livingston to the Cokedale Road

Much of the landscape south of Livingston on U.S. Highway 89 or west on U.S. Highway 10 and I-90 has been shaped by the back-breaking labors of miners and prospectors. These men came searching for gold in the 1860s, mined coal in the 1880s, and worked in the area's smelters and mills.

Route A: U.S. Highway 89, from Gardiner to Livingston

One of Montana's outstanding ghost towns is Jardine, located in Park County in the Gallatin National Forest. If you travel south from Livingston for 53 miles on U.S. Highway 89, you will reach Gardiner and the North Entrance to Yellowstone

Cokedale, Park County, 1890. *Today, you can see remnants of the coke ovens that stretched for over half a mile at the base of the Cokedale smelter.*

National Park. You can reach Jardine, an impressive old mining camp, by taking the Jardine road out of Gardiner for five miles up Bear Gulch.

Joe Brown first discovered placer gold in the Bear Gulch area in 1866, but the miners who came worked the diggings for only a short period of time, and there was little mining activity in the area for the next 30 years. At the turn of the century, the Jardine-Bear Gulch mining district entered a new period of prosperity when Harry Bush organized the Revenue Mining Company. The company built a 40-stamp mill, which dropped its stamps on the gold ore 90 times a minute. "With forty of them stamps going, the sound was more than noise," one old-timer remembered. "You could feel it! Felt good, though—felt just like a paycheck on Saturday night." Within a few years, the Revenue mill had recovered over $500,000 in gold. One expert has estimated that over the life of the mines $2.2 million in gold was taken from the Jardine-Bear Gulch district.

During the 1920s, prosperity again returned to Jardine when companies began mining arsenic, which had proven to be effective in fighting pests such as the boll weevil. The development and use of DDT in the 1940s, however, diminished the demand for arsenic and the mill closed in 1942. The mill reopened in 1944 to supply the military, but it closed for a final time soon after the end of World War II.

You can see the remains of the Revenue Mining Company employees' residences and the Revenue stamp mill, which is one of the best preserved concentrator mills in Montana. Please obey all trespassing notices in Jardine because of the dangerous material mined in this district.

The earliest gold mining in the valley took place at Emigrant Gulch located off U.S. Highway 89 in Park County about 31 miles north of Gardiner. Not long after Thomas Curry discovered gold at Emigrant in 1864, about 300 men rushed to the strike. Within weeks, they had put up 40 houses in what became Yellowstone City (a few miles east of present-day Emigrant). Some reported that "the ground was very deep and hard to work," and the miners had to rely on hunting to make it through the first winter.

By 1865, Yellowstone City had "about 75 log houses," and the town was still growing. Auguste Archambeau and Frank Cin opened a trading store, and John J. Tomlinson built a water-powered sawmill nine miles north of town where Mill Creek empties into the Yellowstone. W. J. Davies, on a contract with the Broad Gauge Company, a telegraph and stagecoach concern, floated lumber from Tomlinson's mill to a site just south of present-day Livingston, where he constructed a house for his family and built three ferry boats that the company used on the Bighorn, the Clark's Fork, and the Yellowstone.

By 1866, Yellowstone City had been abandoned, the victim of diminishing returns from the placers and the lure of gold strikes in other areas. All evidence of Yellowstone City has disappeared; but if you stop at the highway historical marker for Emigrant Peak, you can look up and down the Paradise Valley and imagine the prospectors trying to dig a foothold here, using pine and cottonwood trees to build their cabins, saloons, ferry boats, and general stores.

Route B: U.S. Highway 10, from Livingston to the Cokedale Road

West of Livingston and south of I-90 and U.S. Highway 10 are Park County's largest coal deposits. You can reach this old mining area by leaving I-90 at the westernmost Livingston exit (for Business I-90) and taking U.S. Highway 10 west for two miles until you reach the sign for Cokedale Road. A little over three miles past the turn-off on a gravel road is the site of Cokedale, one of the most important coke-producing areas in Montana.

Coke, a high-grade fuel for refinery smelters, is derived from placing coal in "coke ovens" where extreme temperatures burn off impurities and gases. Smelters once operated at Glentana, Wickes, and Anaconda, and there was a great demand in Montana for coke.

William Henry Williams constructed the first coke oven in the territory in 1882, and mining officials at Wickes judged the seven tons of coke it produced to be the equal of any being imported to Montana. Once this evaluation was made, Cokedale's boom began. By 1886, Sam Hauser's Livingston Coke and Coal Company had purchased Williams's holdings, and soon there were 130 coke ovens at Cokedale, stretching in a line a half-mile long. At least 100 of the brick-lined, beehive-shaped ovens, which were fired at high temperatures to burn impurities from the coal, operated constantly. All that remains are the sandstone foundations and a few remnants of the ovens, one of which can be seen at the east end of a log house on Cokedale Road. Al Olson remembered how the coke was made:

There's a big door in front where they load coal in. And that's [all] the openings there is to 'em. When they put the coal in there, they put in 7 tons in each oven. All together that's in there about 72 hours. And then, it blazes up—there's gas in the coal, and that heat in there ignites the gas and finally that's what starts the fire. They have to heat the oven to start with wood, and then after that they never have to. Then when they pull the coke out of that oven, they fill it with coal right away, so it's good and hot in there. And that's fired-brick clay, so it don't deteriorate or burn up or

anything. Lots of brick couldn't stand that heat, but that's a certain kind of
brick that they used.

The company's primary works operated until 1906.

Route 30: Settling the Upper Yellowstone Valley
Route A: Interstate Highway I-90, from Livingston to Springdale
Route B: Interstate Highway I-90, from Big Timber to Laurel
Route C: Interstate Highway I-90, at Billings

Traveling from the west on I-90, you get your first look at the upper
Yellowstone Valley when you reach the bottom of Bozeman Pass at Livingston.
For over 100 years this part of the Yellowstone Valley has been the site of events
and movements that have played an important role in Montana's economic
development. This is railroad country, and as you travel on I-90 from Livingston
to Billings, you can see landscapes shaped by the railroads in towns such as
Livingston, Big Timber, Columbus, and Laurel. The settlers who came to this area
made way for and followed the Northern Pacific as it built through the valley,
bringing economic prosperity and growth.

Route A: Interstate Highway I-90, from Livingston to Springdale

Livingston, the major railroad town in the upper Yellowstone Valley, is located
at the intersection of I-90 and U.S. Highway 89. From I-90, you can see the tracks
of the Burlington Northern Railroad and the large brick machine shops and
roundhouses that lie north of the highway and dominate the Livingston skyline.
These structures are documentation of the pivotal role that the Northern Pacific
Railroad played in the growth of Livingston.

On July 14, 1882, Joseph F. McBride of Burns & Kurtz, contractors for the
railroad, arrived in the area with orders to locate a site for a Northern Pacific supply
store. Two days later, George H. Carver arrived with 30 freight wagons loaded with
70 tons of merchandise, pitched a tent, and named the location Clark City after
Heman Clark, a Northern Pacific contractor. On August 1, business began at the
new town and for the next few weeks construction workers and entrepreneurs arrived in large numbers.

Clark City began as a tent town, with cheap frame buildings being constructed
later. Most of the people and businesses from Benson's Landing, a few miles
downriver, moved to the new settlement; and by autumn, Clark City had over
500 residents living in 130 tents and wooden buildings.

In November 1882, Robert J. Perry of the Northern Pacific arrived to plat
another townsite, which had been selected by railroad officials in the East and
would be named for Jonathan Livingston, a St. Paul railroad director. By late
December, Livingston's businesses included five hotels, four restaurants, three
general merchandise stores, two liquor stores, three drug stores, four theaters,
eleven saloons, a furniture store, a grocery, a barbershop, a blacksmith shop, a
jeweler, a lumberyard, and a newspaper office.

But Livingston's boom days did not begin until the spring of 1883. According
to one historian, its expansion "was phenomenal; it outstripped all its rivals along

Northern Pacific Depot, Livingston, Park County, 1902. The *Livingston passenger depot is among Montana's most outstanding architectural achievements and remains a symbol of the railroad's importance to the town.*

the line of the Northern Pacific." The railroad's designation of Livingston as its largest division point between Brainerd, Minnesota, and the West Coast fueled this economic growth; and the extensive machine shops brought laborers to the area and created work for hundreds of permanent employees. As one of three major division points on the line, Livingston was home to between 600 and 800 railroad workers in 1884, the largest number of permanent Northern Pacific employees in the territory.

Because of its dependence on the railroad, Livingston has suffered whenever depressions have injured the national economy. A recession in 1884 halted the town's rapid growth, but within a few years, increasing tourist traffic to Yellowstone National Park brought travelers and an economic boost to Livingston. The depression of 1893-1896 delivered another major setback, and the railroad was forced to lay off many employees. By the turn of the century, however, the Northern Pacific announced the expansion of its machine shops and the construction of a new depot. Within 10 years, the town's population more than doubled to about 7,000 people, and almost 1,200 people worked in the Northern Pacific shops. Livingston had become a major city of the upper Yellowstone Valley.

Livingston's built environment is a reflection of the town's dependence on the railroad and its boom-and-bust economic cycles. If you leave I-90 at the U.S. 89 exit and turn north on Park Street, you will find Livingston's business district. The best place to see Livingston's built environment is at the former Northern Pacific depot, about two miles north of the I-90 interchange.

At first, Livingston grew in a symmetrical fashion, with businesses and residences located on both sides of the track. On the north side were the machine shops and the homes of railroad workers; on the south side along Park

Street were the depot and the major businesses. But during the railroad-induced boom of 1883, the business district expanded to 2nd Street and Main Street, which both run perpendicular to Park Street. Among the one- and two-story brick buildings on the 100 block of North Main is the two-story Thompson Block. This structure dates to about 1883-1884 and retains much of its original architectural detailing, including transom glass over the shops' windows. This section of Livingston is part of the Livingston Historic District and is listed in the National Register of Historic Places.

The multi-story brick machine shops and the railroad depot, built in 1901-1902, are symbols of Livingston's second boom. The Northern Pacific built the new railroad depot partly to impress tourists traveling to Yellowstone National Park. Tourists disembarked from the mainline at Livingston before traveling on a Northern Pacific spur to Gardiner at the park's northern entrance. You can see the old roadbed on the west side of the road as you travel south on U.S. Highway 89 to Gardiner.

The depot, designed by Reed and Stem, an architectural firm from St. Paul that specialized in railroad architecture, cost $75,000 and "resembles an Italian villa with its curved colonnade and rich terra-cotta ornament along the track side." Burlington Northern now maintains offices in the building, and there is a cafe where the old railroad restaurant used to be. The depot is also part of the Livingston Historic District and is listed in the National Register of Historic Places. The machine shops stand northeast of the depot.

Adjacent to the machine shops is Livingston's eastside residential district. Most of the homes in this neighborhood were built during Livingston's 1900-1907 boom period; and while the houses vary in appearance, many of them have a basic four-square house plan with a simple hip roof. Contractors chose this style because its simple construction made it perfect for a rapidly growing population.

Leaving I-90 at its junction with U.S. Highway 89 about eight miles east of Livingston, stop at the bridge that crosses the Yellowstone River. To the east, where the Shields River empties into the Yellowstone, stood the few log cabins that comprised Benson's Landing, an early settlement that was the precursor to Livingston.

Benson's Landing had its beginnings in 1868 when William Lee established a ferry on the Yellowstone to connect Fort Ellis (near Bozeman) to Fort Parker, the newly created Crow Agency at the mouth of Mission Creek. The following year, Frank Williams built a cottonwood log cabin at the landing to house a saloon and trading post. After Amos Benson and Dan Naileigh built another log saloon in 1873, the place was called Benson's Landing. Later that same year, Hugo J. Hoppe opened a trading post-hotel with a saloon, and soon the settlement had its own post office and stage station.

Until the late 1870s, Bozeman merchants freighted goods (mostly foodstuffs) to Benson's Landing, floating them in mackinaw boats down the Yellowstone, where they were sold at Fort Custer (present-day Hardin) and Fort Keogh (present-day Miles City). Benson's Landing also depended on trade with the Crow Agency. When the government moved the agency to a site on the Stillwater River in 1875 (on Montana Highway 78 south of Absarokee), Benson's Landing

C. V. West, photographer. MHS SHPO

Springdale Bridge, Park County. *This pin-connected span bridge served generations of travelers until the Yellowstone's shifting current damaged it beyond repair.*

traders Horace Countryman and Hugo Hoppe moved their businesses to the mouth of the Stillwater River (near present-day Columbus). Located on the reservation's boundary, these men could maintain their business with the Crow and continue their illegal whiskey trade with both settlers and Native Americans. Despite Countryman's and Hoppe's departure, Benson's Landing remained an important trading spot until the arrival of the Northern Pacific Railroad. Only one deteriorating structure remains at the town's location, which is on private property and is not accessible to the public.

About 21 miles east of Livingston on I-90 near Springdale is Hunter's Hot Springs, where an enterprising physician developed the Yellowstone Valley's first resort. When Dr. Andrew J. Hunter traveled the Bozeman Trail during the mid 1860s, he discovered a sizable hot springs not far from the river. Returning to the upper Yellowstone with his family in 1870, Hunter built a cabin, dammed the spring, and opened Hunter's Hot Springs. Three years later, he built bathhouses, and by the end of the decade his resort had become well-known throughout the territory.

Hunter's Hot Springs burned in the mid 20th century, but you can still see its remains if you take the Springdale exit off I-90. Follow the country road north of town, cross the river, and take the first gravel road headed west. You can still see the foundations of the hotel along with several other buildings, including the remnants of the hot springs plunge. The site is on private property; stay on the road and do not enter without the landowner's permission.

Route B: Interstate Highway I-90, from Big Timber to Laurel

In 1860, an expedition party led by Lt. H. E. Maynadier reached the Yellowstone River west of Big Timber. Maynadier was part of the most significant exploration of the region that would be undertaken before whites settled here.

The exploration, which began in 1859, was led by Capt. William F. Raynolds, who was surveying the Northwest for potential wagon routes for the U.S. Army.

Guided by Jim Bridger, Raynolds entered the Yellowstone country near the Little Missouri River in far southeastern Montana and stopped at Fort Sarpy II, an American Fur Company trading post located at the mouth of Sarpy Creek near present-day Hysham. The Raynolds expedition proceeded to explore in present-day Wyoming during 1859 and split into two groups in 1860. Maynadier led his group to the upper Yellowstone country, traveling just below the foothills on the east side of the Beartooth Mountains, while Raynolds took his men over the Rockies at what would become Raynolds Pass west of present-day West Yellowstone. After reaching the river near present-day Big Timber, Maynadier surveyed the river west to the mouth of the Shields River, eight miles east of present-day Livingston.

The Civil War delayed the publication of Raynolds's and Maynadier's expedition reports until 1868, and by that time the first settlers had already arrived in the upper Yellowstone Valley. They used the Bozeman Trail, blazed in 1863 by John Bozeman and John Jacobs, which ran from the Oregon Trail north through Wyoming to the Yellowstone Valley and then west to the Montana goldfields. You can see remnants of the Bozeman Trail on Montana Highway 78 in Stillwater County south of Absarokee at the highway historical marker. Also, whenever you cross Bozeman Pass, traveling east to Bozeman on I-90 on the border of Park and Gallatin counties, you are following the route taken during the early 1860s by thousands of prospectors and homesteaders. As you travel over the pass, try to imagine the more difficult passage of those first travelers on the trail. Twenty years after Bozeman and Jacobs had developed the Bozeman Trail, the Northern Pacific built through the valley. The building of the railroad directly led to the establishment of Big Timber, Columbus, and Laurel.

Big Timber, about 35 miles east of Livingston on I-90, is the county seat of Sweetgrass County and one of the best examples on the old Northern Pacific mainline of a "T-style" railroad town. The town is also important for the masonry construction of many of its original buildings.

Columbus, about 37 miles east of Big Timber on I-90, also contains some impressive masonry buildings, especially the New Atlas Bar Building on Columbus's main street (U.S. Highway 10). Over 100 years ago, Horace Countryman operated a saloon and trading post at the mouth of the Stillwater River, the site of which is located just a few miles south of Columbus on Montana Highway 78.

The development of Laurel, 25 miles east of Columbus, is closely linked to the Northern Pacific's coal mines at Red Lodge. The Red Lodge spur line met the Northern Pacific mainline at Laurel, the former location of Canyon Creek, one of the earliest settlements in the Yellowstone Valley. Laurel is still an important railroad center, with the machine shops clearly visible from I-90. Along the highway, you can also see Laurel's newest industry, the Cenex oil refinery.

Route C: Interstate Highway I-90, at Billings

Sixteen miles east of Laurel, within the present-day Billings city limits, is the original site of Coulson. Coulson, the largest early settlement of the upper

Coulson, Yellowstone County, 1882. "*The majority of people living in the far west. . . . are here to make our pile, then we shall return and enjoy our wealth in a land of congeniality.*"—*Billings and Coulson Post*, May 20, 1882

Yellowstone Valley, pre-dated Billings, Livingston, and other railroad towns in the valley. To reach the site of the town, leave I-90 at exit 450 and turn south on 27th Street for one-tenth of a mile, then turn east on Garden Avenue for two-tenths of a mile until you reach Belknap Avenue. Follow the signs for Coulson City Park to Charlene Street and travel east for 1.4 miles to the park. There are no remnants of the town today, but the city of Billings has set aside the site as Coulson City Park.

During the late 1870s, Coulson was a social and commercial center for several families living in the Clark's Fork Bottom, an area in present-day western Yellowstone County that extends from Billings 23 miles west to Park City. There were good reasons for establishing Coulson in this fertile river basin. A ferry crossing of the Yellowstone River, which connected the U.S. Army base at Fort Custer (near present-day Hardin) with Bozeman, made Coulson a natural stage station for coaches and freighters traveling west toward Martinsdale or north to Fort Benton. But Coulson's advantageous location would have meant little if Perry W. "Bud" McAdow had not had an entrepreneurial interest in the place. In 1877, McAdow, a partner in the McAdow Brothers wholesale company of Bozeman, wrote to Montana's congressional delegate, Martin Maginnis, that "we must make an effort to save our territory from being depopulated. . . . I am satisfyed that unless we get a R. R.—that in a few years there will not be enough of us left to make a corporals guard."

In early 1877, McAdow filed a desert land claim for 640 acres in the Clark's Fork Bottom and secured economic domination of the area by constructing a sawmill (McAdow's Mill) and cultivating several types of grain—primarily oats—on his newly irrigated land. The next year, he hired a few Bozeman residents to build mackinaw boats to use in the Yellowstone River trade. With John Schock as a partner, he operated a ferry at Coulson; and in 1880, he opened a wholesale business, which served the early settlers and became an outfitting post for miners headed for the Judith Mountains. Within a year, McAdow had begun to exploit the three major natural features of the Yellowstone Valley: the land, the timber, and the river.

From 1878 to 1881, the first homesteaders settled in Coulson, where they sold produce, hay, and grain to soldiers passing through on their way to Fort Ellis or Fort Custer. The farmers also traded foodstuffs to the Crow Indians for government-issued clothing, furs, horses, and buffalo robes. It was a hard life. Henry Colwell, for example, who lived where the Montana Power Company power plant is now located along I-90, described himself as "a farmer by traid that toils for his daily Bread till early morn till the sun goes down then to the house for supper . . . the fait of a poor old Batch."

By 1880, a promotional pamphlet could boast that the Yellowstone Valley at Coulson was "level and fertile" and that the town was prosperous, with a post office, "a telegraph office, store, saw mill, ferry, and a local anomaly in the shape of a large two-story hotel." The Coulson Hotel belonged to John J. Alderson, an Englishman, and it was the first significant two-story hotel built in the upper Yellowstone Valley. Featuring a front porch and paned-glass windows, the hotel served as an overnight stop for passengers traveling on the several stages that passed through town.

In 1881, the Northern Pacific Railroad began laying track in eastern Montana, and everyone hoped that Coulson would become the railroad hub of the Yellowstone Valley. Business activity increased: McAdow built another sawmill, and John J. Alderson filed a town plan and went into the real estate business. During the winter of 1881-1882, Alderson sold the hotel to a partnership, which changed the hotel's name to the National and added a 60- by 20-foot wooden plank section to the building. By February 1882, Coulson had several saloons, a dry goods store, a jeweler, a barber, two doctors, and two dentists. During March, Coulson acquired two attorneys, a new hardware store, another sawmill, two new restaurants, a dance hall, and two book and stationery stores.

Many of these businesses and professional offices were housed in large canvas tents about 12 by 16 feet with 6-foot-high walls. Most of the wooden buildings were cheaply constructed "balloon-frame" structures, with false fronts. The balloon-frame was built of 2-by-4s nailed together, with horizontals, uprights, floor joists, and roof rafters made of thinly cut wood (2 by 6 inches) nailed so that any strain in the frame went against the wood's grain. Clapboard was the favorite covering for buildings in Coulson. Some of the farmers who lived outside town built cottonwood log cabins, but there were few log buildings in Coulson itself.

Coulson's railroad boom was short-lived. In early 1882, Northern Pacific officials decided that McAdow and Alderson wanted too much money for their property, so they created a private townsite company. Ignoring the bustling town of Coulson, the officials established their own town two miles to the north on 1,200 acres of free land made available by a fluke in the federal survey division of the Yellowstone Valley. They named the town for Frederick Billings, a Northern Pacific Railroad director from Vermont. In early April, Heman Clark of the Minnesota and Montana Land and Improvement Company came to Coulson, announced the creation of Billings, and began to organize the town. The plat filed in Miles City was for a town of 20,000 people.

Realizing that their fortune lay a couple of miles to the north, those who had led Coulson's economic boom quickly transferred their loyalty to Billings. By mid April 1882, the newspaper had changed its name to the *Billings and Coulson Post*, and six weeks later it too had moved to Billings along with other local businesses. On June 13, 1882, Coulson lost its post office. Billings soon became the economic center of the upper Yellowstone Valley, and by 1884 Coulson was a ghost town.

Route 31: Pictographs and Petroglyphs in the Yellowstone Valley

Route A: Interstate Highway I-90, at U.S. Highway 87 in Billings
Route B: Interstate Highway I-94, at Pompey's Pillar

There are two types of Native American art that can still be seen in the Yellowstone Valley: petroglyphs, which are drawings made by "pecking, rubbing or scratching rock surfaces," and pictographs, which are painted drawings.

No one knows for certain which prehistoric or historic Indian tribes are responsible for the region's pictographs and petroglyphs or when the artwork was created. It is possible that Shoshonean groups painted these figures thousands of years ago, or Hidatsa Indians traveling west may have been responsible. Some of the drawings could be attributed to visiting war parties of the Blackfoot Confederacy or the Atsina tribe. The Crow believe that spirits created the drawings, and the evidence strongly suggests that the Crow were responsible for some of the pictographs in the Yellowstone Valley. Some of the pictographs can be roughly dated to the late 18th and early 19th centuries, such as those showing guns, canoes, and horses, which were clearly done after white trade goods had become part of the Crow culture.

Pictographs and petroglyphs played an important role in Native American life. Some of these drawings had a magical role in the hunt, representing "the hunter-artist's attempt to control the real animal by attracting it, hastening its arrival, befriending it to enlist its cooperation, or perhaps reincarnating it." Drawing certain animals promised the artist good luck, and there was the belief (particularly among the Crow) that turtles, elks, and snakes possessed strong medicine. Some of the art was biographical, depicting a warrior's exploits. In this type of drawing, a shield-bearing individual followed by V-neck and stick-figure humans were common. Other popular subjects were bison, horses, bears, and mountain sheep.

The locations of pictographs and petroglyphs are among the most sacred Indian sites in Montana, and Native Americans consider them important to their religious practices. These drawings also represent a fragile art form that is disappearing from the Montana landscape. Wherever you see pictographs and petroglyphs, be extremely careful not to disturb the surrounding area or deface the drawings.

Pictograph Cave, Yellowstone County. *The best known archaeological site in Montana, Pictograph Cave contains rock art that dates to over 300 years ago.*

Route A: Interstate Highway I-90, at U.S. Highway 87 in Billings

The best place to see pictographs in Montana is the Pictograph Cave State Monument south of Billings. You can reach the monument, which is a National Historic Landmark, by leaving I-90 at the Lockwood exit west of Billings and following the signs for about five miles to the Indian caves.

At Pictograph Cave, which is about 160 feet wide and 45 feet deep, many of the drawings are of shield-bearing figures, V-necked humans, rectangular-bodied people, tipis, guns, coup sticks, and several types of animals. These drawings represent hundreds of years of Native American history, and there is some evidence that the use of the cave dates to over 10,000 years ago.

Indian artists at Pictograph Cave and the adjoining Ghost Cave usually painted with black, red, and white paint. Black paint was easily produced by mixing charcoal and animal grease; red paint was made by mixing grease and powdered hermanite or perhaps some other sort of iron oxide; and white paint may have been secured in the fur trade. Paint applicators similar to tiny brushes have been found at the two caves, but the artists used their fingers to do most of the pictographs.

Route B: Interstate Highway I-94, at Pompey's Pillar

Pompey's Pillar, located 33 miles east of Billings, is also the site of Native American petroglyphs and pictographs. Visible from I-94 in eastern Yellowstone County, this towering rock is best known as the place where explorer William Clark etched his name while traveling down the Yellowstone River in 1806. Even

L. A. Huffman, photographer, MHS Photo Archives

Pompey's Pillar, Yellowstone County, 1902. *On July 25, 1806, William Clark named "Pompey's Tower," a "remarkable rock situated in an extensive bottom" of the Yellowstone.*

at that time, Clark noticed the record of prior Indian occupation: "The nativs have ingraved on the face of this rock the figures of animals &c. near which I marked my name and the day of the month & year [July 25, 1806]." One expert believes these drawings could be the work of Shoshonean groups who lived in the area between 1200 and 1800.

Landscape 9: The Bighorn Canyon and the Pryor Mountains

To reach Bighorn Canyon, which contains some of the most desolate and the most beautiful land in Montana, you must leave the state and enter the canyon from northern Wyoming. Seventy-six miles south of Laurel on U.S. Highway 310 is Lovell, Wyoming. The exit for the Bighorn Canyon National Recreation Area is located just east of Lovell on U.S. Highway 14A.

Prehistoric people saw the canyon as part of a larger landscape, which included the Pryor Mountains to the west. There are centuries of history attached to this "confusion of hills and cliffs of red sandstone, some peaked and angular, some round, some broken into crags and precipices, and piled up in fantastic masses." The Indians learned to exploit the region's resources, its forests, caves, and mountain streams; and from many places in the recreation area you can imagine how they built a secure way of life on this land.

You can stop at any of the roadside overlooks in the Bighorn and see breathtaking scenery. For thousands of years, the Bighorn River flowed through southern Montana and northern Wyoming, forming a canyon of great depth and beauty. But in 1968, the look of the land changed dramatically when the federal government dammed the Bighorn River, created Bighorn Lake, and established the Bighorn Canyon National Recreation Area with camping sites, boat landings, and hiking trails.

C. V. West, photographer. MHS SHPO

Milk house, Hillsboro, Bighorn Canyon National Recreation Area, Carbon County. *William Barry built this milk house as part of his ranch in about* 1915.

Route 32: Living in the Bighorn Canyon
Montana Road 37, at the Bighorn Canyon National Recreation Area

You can see the prehistoric landscape of the canyon as soon as you cross the Montana/Wyoming state line traveling north on Montana Road 37 from Lovell, Wyoming. For the next 6.5 miles, the park road parallels Bad Pass Trail, one of the most important Native American sites in Montana. Hundreds of rock cairns and travois ruts still mark the trail, which is listed in the National Register of Historic Places. Bad Pass Trail connected the grasslands and high plains of central and eastern Montana with the Great Basin of Wyoming.

Two miles north of the Montana line is the roadside stop for Devils Canyon, where the steep and colorful cliffs are almost overwhelming. If you look carefully at these sheer rock cliffs, you can see many caves and crevices in which archaeologists have discovered information about the Native Americans who once lived in this country.

Archaeologists have also discovered information about the people who first occupied Bottleneck Cave, located near the canyon's entrance just south of the Montana line. In around 6000 B.C., people who used the cave hunted deer, antelope, bison, bighorn sheep, foxes, rabbits, and rodents. About 4,000 years later, the diet of the cave's residents included coyotes, pack rats, mice, and catfish. In about 500 A.D., another group of Indians hunted bobcats, porcupines, and toads. And just a few hundred years ago, the last Indians to live in Bottleneck Cave added other kinds of fish and mink to their diets.

C. V. West, photographer, MHS SHPO

Near Barry's Landing, Bighorn Canyon National Recreation Area, Carbon County. *Caroline Lockhart, a Bighorn Canyon homesteader, discovered that much of her land was "so hard that the digging of post holes required blasting sometimes."*

The Pretty Creek archaeological site is located 4.5 miles north of the Devils Canyon Overlook and is next to the Hough Creek Ranger Station. For 8,000 years, prehistoric groups used the Pretty Creek site as a campground because it was near Bad Pass Trail and had a plentiful supply of water from Hough Creek. It was also a good place to hunt both small and large animals. There is some evidence that the Pretty Creek archaeological site was a place of worship; the area contains remains of vision quests, where Indians sought an individual relationship with the spirits. The Pretty Creek site is listed in the National Register of Historic Places.

The Hough Creek Ranger Station, which is also listed in the National Register of Historic Places, was originally a homesteader's dwelling. Although the country around the station is sparsely vegetated—hardly land suitable for home-steading—several hardy ranchers settled in the canyon area during the 1890s. Erastus T. Ewing began ranching here after he failed to discover gold in the canyon or in the Pryor Mountains. His ranch was the post office until 1906, and in 1947 the ranch shop became the local schoolhouse. The ranch also had a corral, a root cellar, an irrigation system, sheds, and a privy. Today, Ewing's original one-story home, which features a hipped roof and lap-joint log construction with a front gable end, is the ranger headquarters.

Caroline Lockhart, the first woman reporter for the *Boston Post* and a well-regarded western writer, also built a ranch in this area. You can see the ranch site by leaving Montana Road 37 at the Barry Landing turnoff, 2.4 miles north of the Hough Creek Ranger Station, and by traveling the gravel road north for the next

2.5 miles to the ranch's parking area. From there you can hike a few hundred yards to the ranch. The Lockhart ranch has 2 wooden-frame buildings, 16 log structures, a bridge, and a corral.

Lockhart and her partner, Lou T. Ketcham, lived here during the Great Depression; but when the two women submitted final proof for their canyon homestead, the government rejected the claim, maintaining that the women had done nothing to improve the homestead. Not until a lengthy court fight in 1936 clearly established that Lockhart and Ketcham had been successful homesteaders did the women receive title to their land.

From the Lockhart Ranch, you can return to Montana Road 37 and take the turnoff for Hillsboro and Barry's Landing, two other places associated with the early settlement of the Bighorn Canyon. About a mile east of the turnoff, there is a road to the Hillsboro parking area. From there, it is a mile or so round-trip hike to the site of Hillsboro (1915-1945). Over 80 years ago, William Barry built a barn and corral, a chicken house, a rock-walled milk house, a root cellar, and cabins on this site. Remains of these structures and the abandoned Hillsboro post office still stand in this ghost town.

Barry came to the canyon in 1903 to try placer mining along Trail Creek. When his efforts didn't produce, he tried horse ranching at Hillsboro; but his Embar Horse Company, which marketed English Hackneys, made little money. Finally, Barry established the Cedarvale Dude Ranch, where he found success entertaining tourists who had come to enjoy the scenic wonders of the Bighorn Canyon.

From Hillsboro, return to the paved road and continue until you reach a dead end at Barry's Landing. Barry originally developed this recreational spot as a starting point for motorboat tours of the canyon, which he began giving in about 1905, and it is still a popular boat landing.

Route 33: Living in the Pryor Mountains
Montana Road 37, at Bighorn Canyon National Recreation Area
Pryor Road, from Montana Road 37 to the Crow Indian Reservation

At any place on Montana Road 37 through the southern portion of the Bighorn Canyon National Recreation Area, you can look to the west and see the pine-covered peaks of the Pryor Mountains. During the summer, you can travel along the Pryor Gap Road south from the town of Pryor on the Crow Indian Reservation and see rugged countryside that has an important history. Like the Bighorn Canyon, at first glance this land appears to be inhospitable, but the Pryors have provided a home for people for thousands of years.

The record of human history in this area begins 10,000 years ago at False Cougar Cave, a small cavern located near the top of the Pryors that was home to prehistoric hunters who lived on deer, bison, and mountain sheep. About 4,000 years ago, the Indians who lived here subsisted on smaller creatures, such as marmots, grouse, rabbits, and squirrels, perhaps as a result of a temporary change to a warmer and drier climate.

On the mountains' highest peaks, the Crow Indians built vision quests "by piling rocks to a height of one or two feet, although some have [used wood] in the construction," usually creating a U-shaped structure "with the opening facing the rising sun." During the vision quest, which might last for several days, a warrior developed a personal relationship with the spirit world and sought good luck in battle and material success in life. Big-Ox, a Crow shaman or medicine man, recorded a vision quest:

I slept on a mountain and chopped off a joint of my little finger. I saw a bird, which made me a chief. The birds sat round me; they had human heads. Five balls of different color were in front of me, one of them pure white. I sat there and some of the birds vanished without my knowing it until only one sat by me. This last one told me I should be a great chief and that he would not forget me. "We shall constantly watch you." He repeated this twice. He flew away without my seeing him go.

For a mile along Pryor Gap, over 60 rock cairns line this pass through the northwestern section of the mountains, which begins about four miles south of Pryor. When traveling through the Pryor Gap, the Crow left offerings at the cairns, hoping their journey would be safe and successful. Many Crow Indians will still spit on a rock or a coin and toss it on top of the mounds for good luck.

The Crow call Pryor Canyon "Hits-with-the-Arrows." According to tribal tradition, a "very dwarfish people" once lived in the canyon. They had no fire and hunted with bows made of deer antler and flint arrowheads. These little people "were so powerful that they could carry buffalo on their backs." Crow tradition tells how the little people once saved the tribe. A Crow child, who had been lost in the canyon and had been taken care of by the little people for many years, returned to his tribe to aid them in a time of trouble. The Crow were facing starvation, and the little people allowed the young man to return to tell his kinsmen where to find food. In tribute to the little people's generosity, the Crow began a tradition of shooting arrows at the ledge where the little people lived.

Although stock-growing dominates the agricultural landscape of the Pryors today, homesteaders settled here just after the turn of the century. In 1906, the government allowed homesteaders 160 acres in the national forests. Most of the homesteading ranches had log or frame structures, built with Douglas fir or lodgepole pine trees. Ranchers also built stables of both log and wooden-frame construction.

The homesteaders found that 160 acres could not sustain a homestead in the rugged Pryor environment. One forest ranger remarked that some homesteaders claimed land "where it would be impossible for anybody to maintain a winter residence altho to hear of some of the applicants talk, one would think that Pryor Mountain contained the biggest part of the Banana Belt and that pineapple grew wild."

In 1955, the discovery of uranium spurred a mining rush and brought industry to the Pryor Mountains. Bulldozers cut shallow mines throughout the mountains, making especially large excavations at Old Glory and Sandra on the eastern side of Red Pryor Mountain. By the late 1950s, mining had ceased, leaving behind tons of machinery and scars on the land.

When you look at the forbidding environment of the Bighorn Canyon and the Pryor Mountains, think about how Native Americans and whites have used the area's resources and how the landscape has changed over the last 200 years.

Route 34: Warfare in the Bighorn Canyon
Montana Road 313, from Fort Smith to the Yellowtail Dam

The only access to the Bighorn Canyon National Recreation Area in Montana is on Montana Road 313 from Hardin, which will take you to the area's northern section. Leave I-94 at Hardin and take Montana Road 313 south for 43 miles to the town of Fort Smith. A few miles north of town is the site of old Fort C. F. Smith, which was built by the army in 1866 to defend the Bozeman Trail from attacks by Sioux and Cheyenne warriors. Remnants of the Bozeman Trail, which cut through present-day Wyoming and linked the Yellowstone Valley to the Oregon Trail, can be seen about 10 miles west of Wyola on Montana Road 418. The Sioux destroyed Fort Smith in 1868 after waging two years of intermittent warfare against the U.S. Army along the Bozeman Trail.

As you travel the few miles from Fort Smith to the Yellowtail Dam Visitor Center, look to the west at the drainage of Grapevine Creek. Along those cliffs lie the remnants of seven Native American fortifications, including one fortified cave. According to Crow history, during the 1830s the Crow and Piegan fought a major battle at one of those fortifications.

With the abundant game in the Bighorn Canyon and the Pryor Mountains, it is not surprising that tribes battled for control of the region's bounty; but the appearance of the Piegan in the canyon was unusual. The Piegan's homeland lay hundreds of miles to the north, from present-day Browning to Calgary, Alberta, and it was very risky for them to travel in Crow country, so far from their own people.

If fur trapper Zenas Leonard's journal is correct, luck was not on the side of a group of Piegan warriors traveling on the northern section of the Bad Pass Trail in 1834. Leonard's account of that bloody battle between the Crow and Piegan paints a vivid picture of what warfare in the Bighorn Canyon was like. According to Leonard, once the Piegan learned they had been spotted, they moved to the high ground near Grapevine Creek.

> . . . the Blackfeet had chosen a most fortunate spot to defend themselves, and by a little labor found themselves in a fort that might have done credit to an army of frontier regulars. It was situated on the brow of a hill, in a circle of rocks shaped similar to a horseshoe, with a ledge of rocks from three to four feet high on either side, and about ten feet, on the part reaching to the brink of the hill, with a very creditable piece of breastwork built in front, composed of logs, brush, and stones.

The Crow repeatedly failed to overrun the fortress. A black member of the tribe, probably Edward Rose, warned that if the Crow failed to kill the Piegan "the Blackfeet would go home and tell their people that three thousand Crows could not take a handful of them." The Crow were enraged, and they risked life and limb in one final assault against the fortification. Leonard reported:

Here now was a scene of no common occurrence. . . . A space of ground about the size of an acre, completely crowded with hostile Indians fighting for life, with guns, bows and arrows, knives, and clubs, yelling and screaming until the hair seemed to lift the caps from our heads. As soon as most of the Crows got into the fort, the Blackfeet began to make their escape out of the opposite side, over the rocks about ten feet high. Here they found themselves no better off, as they were immediately surrounded and hemmed in on all sides by overwhelming numbers. . . . When the Blackfeet found there was no chance of escape, and knowing that there was no prospect of mercy at the hands of their perplexed and aggravated, but victorious enemy, they fought with more than human desperation. From the time they left their fort, they kept themselves in regular order, moving forward in a solid breast, cutting their way through with their knives, until the last man fell, pierced, perhaps, with an hundred wounds.

With the battle over, the female relatives of the 30 Crow warriors who had died exhibited "the most excruciating anguish that any human being could suffer." The surviving warriors avenged the dead by torturing the Piegan who had been wounded in the fight. They cut off the Piegan's "ears, nose, hands, and feet, pluck out their eyes, pull out their hair, cut them open and take out part of their insides, piercing them with sharp sticks—in short, every method of inflicting pain was resorted to." Yet, not one Piegan would "acknowledge themselves prisoners in the Crow village. Death they preferred to this, and death with indescribable horrors did they receive." The Crow eventually beheaded their victims, the heads of "which were hoisted on the ends of poles and carried about, and afterwards [they] dashed them against the trees, rocks, &c., leaving them on the plain to be devoured by wild beasts."

To understand the ferocity of battle, the emotion of the mourning, and the brutality of the revenge, it is necessary to know about the nature of Indian warfare in the 19th century. Throughout the prehistoric period, the Indians had always tried to avoid bloodshed, believing that nothing was worth the lives of more than a few warriors. But during the 19th century, after fur traders had introduced firearms to the Indians, the rules changed. The ferocity of warfare increased dramatically, and the larger number of casualties led to massive social dislocation. Because the tribe lost so many warriors in battles, revenge for additional losses was swift and sure, serving as a psychological release and allowing the Crow to continue with their lives despite the painful loss of family. The vengeance carried out after the battle at Grapevine Creek allowed the surviving Crow to deal with decades of death caused by the bitter warfare of the fur-trade era.

Route 35: Crow Country
Route A: Interstate Highway I-90, from Crow Agency to Hardin
Route B: Montana Road 313, from Hardin to St. Xavier

Cutting a winding path through south central Montana, the Bighorn River and its tributary, the Little Bighorn, were the scene of some of the most important events in Montana history.You can consider how one battle in June of 1876

Custer Battlefield National Monument, Crow Indian Reservation, Bighorn County. *Northern Cheyenne chief Brave Wolf said of the battle: "It was hard fighting... I have been in many hard fights, but I never saw such brave men."*

changed the history of southern Montana when you stop at the Custer Battlefield National Monument at Crow Agency, 15 miles south of Hardin on I-90. You can see where Catholics established a mission in the 1880s to teach Crow people white ways when you stop at St. Xavier, 23 miles south of Hardin on Montana 313. And you can think about how the arrival of the Burlington Route line in the early 20th century dramatically changed the landscape of the Bighorn country when you stop at the former Burlington railroad depot at the end of Center Street in Hardin.

Route A: Interstate Highway I-90, from Crow Agency to Hardin

On grassland bluffs overlooking the Bighorn River, about 15 miles south of Hardin and visible from I-90, is the Custer Battlefield National Monument, the scene of one of the most crucial events in the history of Montana Indians. Here, on June 25, 1876, George A. Custer lost his entire command when he was trapped by Sioux and Northern Cheyenne warriors. The topography of the area afforded the soldiers little protection, and the Indians attacked and counterattacked until all of Custer's men were dead. The monument is open year-round and park rangers can give you an interpretation of the events of the battle.

The Sioux and the Northern Cheyenne won a decisive victory on June 25, 1876, but Custer's defeat galvanized the nation and the government reaffirmed its commitment to "solve the Indian problem." With new vigor, the army resumed its relentless pursuit of the Native Americans. Within months, the Sioux and Northern Cheyenne had given up their armed struggle and agreed to cease hostilities.

Custer's defeat at the Little Bighorn also hastened changes on the Crow Indian Reservation. A month before the Custer battle, Congress had approved the funding for a Bighorn army post. Near the present location of the Big Horn County Museum in Hardin, about 15 miles north of the Custer Battlefield on I-90, the army built Fort Custer in the summer and fall of 1877. The soldiers originally built some of the fort's barracks out of the tipi poles that the Sioux and Northern Cheyenne had abandoned when they fled the Little Bighorn battlefield. First named Big Horn Post, Fort Custer became the most modern cavalry post in the Northwest.

The army withdrew its soldiers from Fort Custer in late 1897, and the Indian Service eventually took over the post. In 1903, the government allocated funds to dismantle and salvage Fort Custer and today there are no remains of the fort. Information about the post can be obtained at the Big Horn County Museum in Hardin.

About 15 miles south of Hardin on I-90 is Crow Agency, the major Indian settlement of the Bighorn country. The agency for the Crow Indian Reservation, which had previously been located in two other places in the Yellowstone Valley, was moved here in 1878. The town has a variety of government buildings, tribal offices, modern Native American dwellings, churches, and commercial and industrial structures. A carpet factory is the most visible industry and represents a recent attempt to bring new jobs to the reservation.

In 1904, the federal government forced the Crow to give up a huge area of the reservation, from the Yellowstone River to today's northern reservation boundaries. In exchange, the Crow were to receive individual allotments of land. The Chicago, Burlington & Quincy Railroad (the Burlington Route) also played an important role in the history of the Crow Indian Reservation. In a scheme hatched by officials of the Burlington Route, the Lincoln Land Company, and the Indian Service, the land at the confluence of the Bighorn and Little Bighorn rivers was allotted to deceased Indians and then purchased from the relatives. Here is where the Lincoln Land Company platted Hardin in 1907.

Hardin, located 43 miles southeast of Billings on I-90, was the major city in the area established by the Burlington. The railroad began laying tracks in the 1890s, and I-90 basically follows the old Burlington Route from the Wyoming line to Huntley on the Yellowstone River. Two buildings have a special significance to Hardin's history. The old Holly Sugar Company sugar beet refinery is located just east of Montana Highway 47 off I-90 and is visible for miles. Established in 1936, the Holly refinery made it possible for farmers to process their sugar beet crops locally. At its peak, the Holly refinery employed 250 seasonal workers. The second historically significant building is the Becker Hotel. Located across from the Burlington Route depot at 200 N. Center Street in downtown Hardin, the hotel was constructed in 1908 and was expanded in 1917 to meet the needs of arriving homesteaders. The hotel represents the importance of both the railroad and homesteaders to the development of Hardin. Designed by Curtis C. Oehme, this three-story red brick hotel is among Hardin's most distinctive buildings.

Hardin's original residential district also contains homes with some interesting architectural features. The many Craftsman-style homes you can see in these neighborhoods are characterized by "the use of machine-made, mass-produced materials and decorative elements to create a picturesque, rustic effect." The Craftsman-style house became popular with middle-class Montanans during the 1910s and early 1920s.

St. Xavier Mission Chapel, Crow Indian Reservation, Bighorn County. In 1888, St. Xavier's founder, Father Peter Paul Prando, supervised the construction of this wooden-frame chapel where mass is still celebrated.

Route B: Montana Road 313, from Hardin to St. Xavier

St. Xavier, located about 23 miles south of Hardin on Montana Road 313, is another important settlement on the Crow Indian Reservation. Here, along the Bighorn River in 1887-1888, Jesuit missionaries established the St. Xavier Mission. The priests initially built a simple wooden-plank chapel, which is still used for worship services, and a boarding school for 20 children. The school, now named the Pretty Eagle Indian School, stands next to the mission chapel and continues to hold classes for students from the reservation.

If you travel west from St. Xavier for about 35 miles on a paved road you will reach Pryor, a former stop on a Burlington Route spur line. (You can also reach Pryor by traveling south from Billings on the Pryor Road.) Two miles south of Pryor is the Chief Plenty Coups Memorial State Monument. Plenty Coups (Allek-chear-ahoosh) was a Crow chief who lived from 1848 to 1932. At the monument, you can see his original reservation cabin and his more elaborate two-story home, structures that indicate the significant changes that the Crow Indians have endured. Plenty Coups was probably born in a tipi and lived in tipis throughout his early adult years. Later, he moved into a log cabin with dirt floors, and he finally accommodated himself to reservation life and the white man's ways by living in a two-story home with wooden floors and a staircase. Chief Plenty Coups's grave is a few yards behind the two houses.

Landscape 10: The Beartooth Mountain Range

The Beartooth Mountain Range contains Montana's highest peaks: Granite Peak at 12,779 feet, Silver Run Peak at 12,610 feet, and Mt. Rearguard at 12,350 feet. During the 1930s, the federal government constructed the Beartooth

Cooke City, Park County, ca. 1900. *Cooke City developed in the heart of the New World Mining District. During the 1880s, miners brought in equipment and took out ore on a crude wagon road that snaked across the northern portion of Yellowstone National Park.*

Highway (U.S. Highway 212), linking Red Lodge to Cooke City. A true engineering marvel, this two-lane road crosses the Rockies at almost 11,000 feet, offering travelers the dazzling scenery of the Beartooth Mountains. Because of winter snow, the road is open only during the summer. During the late 19th century, these mountains attracted miners, looking for gold, silver, and coal in the rock outcroppings and gulches you can see along U.S. Highway 212. How Montanans developed these mineral resources is largely the history of the Beartooth Mountain Range.

Route 36: Mining the Beartooth Country

Route A: U.S. Highway 212, from Cooke City to Red Lodge
Route B: Montana Road 308, from Red Lodge to Belfry

The first mining in the Beartooth country was for gold and silver, discovered by prospectors who roamed the many gulches of the Beartooth Mountains. During the 1880s, however, coal became the region's most important resource; and hundreds of miners went to work in coalfields near Red Lodge, which became the county seat of Carbon County.

Route A: U.S. Highway 212, from Cooke City to Red Lodge

The first miners who dug in the Beartooth Mountains near present-day Cooke City, 69 miles south of Red Lodge on U.S. Highway 212, did so illegally. The Bear-

Beartooth Highway, Park County, ca. 1955. *One of America's most dramatic scenic routes, the Beartooth Highway connects the Northeast Entrance of Yellowstone National Park with Red Lodge in Carbon County.*

tooths were then part of the Crow Indian Reservation and were off-limits to mineral exploration. Nevertheless, miners uncovered several rich veins during the 1870s, working them haphazardly at least partly because they had no legal title to the claims.

In 1880, Jay Cooke, Jr., the son of a founder of the Northern Pacific Railroad and for whom Cooke City was named, inspected these first mines and decided to invest. Because of the mining activity the federal government negotiated another treaty with the Crow, forcing them to give up the land. In April 1882, the government opened the country around Cooke City to settlement, beginning the first mining boom in the Beartooths.

Cooke City grew rapidly during that first summer, and soon there were 135 pine log huts with dirt roofs and many tents perched on the mountainside. By 1883, the town had two smelters, two sawmills, two hotels, two stables, and three general stores. One newspaper reported that "the houses were dirt-covered shacks, that indicate the lack of building material instead of poverty of purse and mild architectural ambitions rather than indifference to comfort." Settlers built few frame structures until the following year.

In 1888, almost 20 years after gold was first discovered in the area, the Homestake Mine opened on Henderson Mountain. The mining was difficult at the complex, which would become one of the largest in the New World (Cooke City) Mining District. At the Homestake mining complex, you can see the two-mile-long tramway and the remains of a steam generating plant and other mine buildings.

The country's heavy winter snowfalls and extremely low temperatures limited the typical mining "season" to only a few months, but the major impediment to developing the district's mines was poor transportation. The mountain topography made building major eastern and northern highways impossible, and Congress refused to approve a railroad connection through Yellowstone National Park to Cooke City. Without adequate transportation, the mines foundered; by the early 1900s, the district's fortunes had fallen. By the 1930s, every large-scale operation, including the Homestake, had closed. Ironically, it was during that same period that the government completed the Beartooth Highway and made Cooke City a tourist center, a gateway to Yellowstone National Park and the Beartooth Pass.

Red Lodge, about 65 miles northeast of Cooke City at the eastern end of the Beartooth Highway, was a commercial center for a prosperous coal-mining area for 60 years. In 1888, the Northern Pacific Railroad built a branch line from Billings to the coalfields along the northeastern flank of the Beartooth Mountains. The Rocky Fork Railroad—named after Rock Creek, a tributary of the Clark's Fork of the Yellowstone—carried coal to fuel the Northern Pacific's steam engines. The construction of the railroad and the opening of the mines of the Rocky Fork Coal Company led to the establishment of Red Lodge in the late 1880s.

Although the Northern Pacific was active in both the mines and the town's commercial development, Red Lodge was not a classic company town. Many smaller coal-mining companies had an interest in the town, and the Rocky Fork Coal Company did not enforce its own rule that employees live in company-owned boarding houses and duplexes. From the beginning, Red Lodge developed its own character, and the town's large immigrant population made it even less likely to look like a company town. By 1910, half of Red Lodge's population were immigrants, with 25 per cent coming from Finland and many others from eastern European countries.

Many of the one- and two-story brick and masonry buildings that were constructed at the height of the area's mining activity still line U.S. Highway 212 (Broadway) in downtown Red Lodge. Most of these buildings were constructed with local materials, such as wood, brick, and sandstone, and are excellent examples of the unpretentious vernacular architecture often found in western commercial centers of the late 19th and early 20th centuries.

The Red Lodge Commercial Historic District, which is listed in the National Register of Historic Places, includes several outstanding buildings. Along Broadway, you can see the Labor Temple, a three-story brick building constructed in 1909, and the Savoy Hotel, a two-story concrete building with a metal cornice that dates to 1910. On Billings Avenue are the Talmage Building, a two-story masonry structure built in 1905, and the two-story brick Carbon County Bank, constructed in 1899.

Route B: Montana Road 308, from Red Lodge to Belfry

Seven miles east of Red Lodge on Montana Road 308 are the old coal-mining towns of Washoe and Bearcreek, and a highway historical sign near Bearcreek marks the remains of the Smith Mine, the scene of one of Montana's greatest mining disasters.

Coal mining began in the Bearcreek-Washoe area around the turn of the century. George Lamport operated the first large mines in the district and

MHS Photo Archives

Smith Mine, Washoe, Montana Road 308, Carbon County. *Frank DeVille remembered that before the underground explosion at the Smith Mine, Bearcreek Coal Company officials ignored the recommendations of safety officials. The disaster killed 74 men and ended over four decades of coal mining in the Washoe district.*

transported his coal via freight teams to Red Lodge. By 1907, the Bearcreek Coal Company employed 175 miners, who pulled almost 500 tons of coal a day out of the mines. Smaller mines in the district also consistently produced, and one state mining official bragged that the Bearcreek-Washoe district had enough coal to keep miners busy for the next 500 years.

During the 1920s and 1930s, however, Americans increasingly turned to oil, natural gas, and electricity for heating, and the demand for Bearcreek coal diminished. Then on February 27, 1943, the mining era at Bearcreek came to a thundering, sickening halt. An underground explosion at the Smith Mine released poisonous gases, killing 74 miners and forcing the mines to close. Aside from a few small "wagon" mines, the days of the Bearcreek-Washoe district were over.

From the highway historical marker on Montana Road 308, you can see the remnants of the Smith Mine. As you travel on this road, you can see many other structures and mine openings that are excellent examples of how coal mining changed the look of the land.

Sacrifice Cliffs, Billings, Yellowstone County. *These rimrocks on the south side of the Yellowstone River near Billings were the scene of suicidal leaps by Crow Indians who mourned those who had perished from smallpox during the 1830s.*

Melville Lutheran Church, U.S. Highway 191, Sweetgrass County. *Lutheran immigrants settled in Melville in 1885 and built this church in 1914 when this was a prominent sheep-growing region. Montana writer Spike Van Cleve, who wrote about his experiences as a dude rancher, lived north of Melville on a ranch at the base of the Crazy Mountains.*

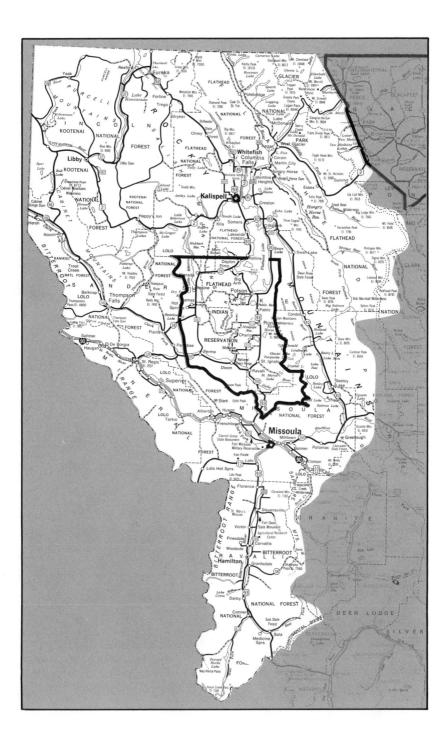

Chapter 5

The Western Valleys

Western Montana is rugged country, a place of dense forests, challenging mountain passes, and treacherous waters. You can stop at the turnoff for Kootenai Falls on U.S. Highway 2 five miles west of Libby and see where forests, steep river cliffs, and the Kootenai River's rapids and falls combine to create a landscape of unmistakable beauty. This is also a landscape that holds profound religious significance for the Kootenai people, for here their ancestors camped, built religious shrines, and worshipped their gods.

No matter where you travel in western Montana, you cannot escape the forests' commanding physical presence. At the turnoff for Libby Dam, about 13 miles east of Libby on Montana Highway 37, you can imagine when the forest contained "open, park-like" areas where the Kootenai Indians burned sections of the undercover every year, enabling them to travel quickly through the woods and making hunting small animals much easier.

Western Montana is also home to two of the state's most historic valleys: the Flathead and the Bitterroot. South of Kalispell on U.S. Highway 93 is the Flathead Valley, a vast basin dominated by beautiful Flathead Lake, one of the largest freshwater lakes in North America. Both the lake and the valley are named for the Flathead Indians, who have lived here for hundreds of years. The first whites to enter this country were Canadian and American fur traders; and near the St. Ignatius Mission, about 80 miles south of Kalispell on U.S. Highway 93, you can see the remains of Fort Connah, a Hudson's Bay Company trading post.

Leaving the Flathead Valley at Ravalli, you can travel south on U.S. Highway 93 for 35 miles to Missoula, the largest city in western Montana and the gateway to the Bitterroot Valley. Over 140 years ago, white missionaries and farmers settled in this fertile valley; and at St. Mary's Mission in Stevensville, about 28 miles south of Missoula on U.S. 93, you can see where Catholic missionaries established the first mission in present-day Montana. Within a few decades, whites had settled in the Bitterroot Valley, using the valley's resources and changing the landscape.

Concern about conserving the region's natural resources came rather late to western Montana. At DeBorgia, 71 miles west of Missoula on I-90, a firestorm in 1910 destroyed everything except the town's school. The fire consumed much of the timber in western Montana, leaving logging camps, railroad structures, and towns in ruins. In the aftermath, the forest service built lookouts in the region in an attempt to prevent future catastrophes.

Montanans have used the vast resources of western Montana in many different ways since the turn of the century. Dams generate hydroelectric power, orchards and Christmas tree farms flourish, and the mountains, lakes, and streams attract hundreds of thousands of tourists each year. Sawmills and ranches are also part of the western Montana landscape. Throughout the region's history, each group and occupation has left an indelible mark on the land.

Landscape 11: The Kootenai River

The Kootenai River, with its headwaters in the Canadian Rockies, runs through the forests of the northwestern corner of Montana. The river took its name from the Indians who lived in southeastern British Columbia and north-western Montana. When you stop at one of the turn-outs on Montana Highway 37 between Libby and Rexford, you can look out across Lake Koocanusa (the dammed Kootenai River) and consider how the river has provided life-sustaining resources for centuries.

David Thompson, an employee of the North West Company, a Canadian fur-trading firm, recognized most of the Kootenai's resources when he traveled the river during the spring of 1808. It had in places "very fine woods of Larch, Red Fir, Alder, Plane, and other woods," and one larch tree he found had a "thirteen feet girth and one hundred and fifty feet clean growth, and then a fine head." In looking at hundreds of similar trees, Thompson couldn't help but think "what fine Timber for the Navy in these forests. . . . The other Woods [are] fine Red Fir, Pine, Cypress, white Cedar, Poplars, Aspins, Alders, Plane, and Willows."

You can see the same spectacular landscape that Thompson saw about 180 years ago if you stop at the turnoff for Kootenai Falls, five miles west of Libby on U.S. Highway 2. Thompson also noticed the river's power. Thompson recorded: "the River had steep banks of Rocks, and only thirty yards in width; this space was full of violent eddies, which threatened us with destruction and wherever the river contracted the case was always the same, the current was swift, yet to look at the surface the eddies make it appear to move as much backward as forward." Thompson accurately predicted that the river would become a transportation route, a source of valuable lumber, and a source of power.

Route 37: The Kootenai Indians
U.S. Highway 2, from Libby to the Idaho state line

The Kootenai River created a natural border between the areas inhabited by the Upper and Lower Kootenai people. Although the Upper and Lower Kootenai saw themselves as one people, with the Kootenai River being the "thread" that held them together, the two groups lived in different sections of the region and each tribe developed its own language and cultural traditions. Along U.S. Highway 2 from Libby to the Idaho line, you can see the historical landscape of the Lower Kootenai tribe and that of the Agiyinik band of the Upper Kootenai who lived around Jennings.

Before they acquired horses, the Lower Kootenai and the Agiyinik Kootenai built their way of life around the resources that could be found in the region.

C. V. West, photographer, MHS SHPO

Kootenai Falls, U.S. Highway 2, Lincoln County. *The most prominent natural feature in the Kootenai River, Kootenai Falls was revered by Native Americans and was an obstacle to explorers who traveled upriver.*

Using "sturgeon-nose" canoes, the Kootenai used both traps and individual fishing tools; and during the winter, they trapped small animals by chasing them into snowbanks. Each year, the Kootenai burned the forest underbrush to make it easier to hunt blacktail and whitetail deer, mountain goats, and sheep. During the spring and summer, they gathered plants, particularly camas root, bitterroot, and berries.

During the mid 1700s, the use of horses revolutionized the Kootenai's culture, making the Indians less dependent on the area's fish and fowl and more dependent on bison and caribou. Having horses also increased the number of areas where they could gather plants. Each May, the Kootenai collected camas root at a prairie northeast of present-day Columbia Falls, about 104 miles east of Libby on U.S. 2. Later in May, they dug and prepared bitterroot near Elmo, now a small village on the Flathead Indian Reservation 50 miles south of Columbia Falls. They also cultivated tobacco along the east bank of the Flathead on Lone Pine Prairie, at the junction of Spotted Bear Creek and the south fork of the Flathead about 50 miles southeast of Columbia Falls, and between Bull Lake and the Clark Fork River far to the west along Montana Highway 56 south of Troy. The horses also allowed the Kootenai to join their kinfolk to the north in bison hunts on the plains of northern Montana and southern Alberta.

Bison hunting improved the Kootenai's standard of living, giving them more meat and the many things that could be made from the bison's hide and bones. But this better life also brought them the enmity of the Blackfoot Confederacy. The Confederacy attempted to dominate bison hunting on the high plains and its military power forced the Lower Kootenai into an alliance with the Kalispell Indians. To further the alliance, they left their winter homeland on the Kootenai River and moved to new winter quarters near the northern end of Flathead Lake. The Kootenai now live on the Flathead Indian Reservation.

Between Libby and Troy on U.S. 2, you can see an important landscape in the Kootenai Indians' history. About five miles west of Libby is the turn-off for Kootenai Falls, a place that holds special religious significance for the Kootenai Indians.

On the north side of the river, you can see traces of an old trail that prehistoric Indians and the Kootenai used to portage around the falls. Along the trail are several rock cairns, made from a nearby outcropping of hard shale. One expert speculates that the cairns were constructed to ensure that the builder would stay "in the good graces of the many spirits which inhabited the land." Jerome Hewankorn, a Kootenai Indian, thinks that the cairns may have been built to give good luck to travelers who took the risky portage route. Offerings to the traveler's guardian spirit would be placed on the cairn to "insure the success of one's journey."

The Kootenai considered it very important for each tribal member to have a supernatural guardian or spirit, which they called *nupika*. The Indians had "a deep and abiding affection for the spirits, a feeling of loving dependence on them, implicit faith in their wisdom and benevolence, and a will to do all one can to make the spirits happy." Tribal members regularly sought visions at several places along the river canyon, including the falls area. The song they learned, the warning they heard, and the exhortation they received from their guardian spirits remained a secret. Only the spouse could know the mate's secret power.

At the falls, you can see where the Kootenai camped along the river, most of them for long periods of time. Here men prepared nets for fishing and arrows for hunting, and women processed animal bones and readied roots and berries for storage. At one 200-year-old campsite, there is evidence that the Indians hunted and ate deer, elk, and black bears in the Kootenai Canyon that overlooks the falls.

Route 38: The Kootenai River in the 20th Century
Route A: U.S. Highway 2, from Libby to the Idaho state line
Route B: Montana Road 508, at Sylvanite
Route C: U.S. Highway 93, from Eureka to Olney
West of Libby on U.S. Highway 2, between Libby and Eureka on Montana Highway 37, and on U.S. Highway 93 south of Eureka, you can see how the Kootenai River region developed from the first explorations of fur traders to the modern lumber industry. Historical markers at several places along Montana 37 explain some of the developments on the Kootenai River.

Route A: U.S. Highway 2, from Libby to the Idaho state line
The Kootenai Falls overlook, five miles west of Libby on U.S. Highway 2, is one of the best places to look at the river and consider its history. Here, in 1808,

C. V. West, photographer, MHS SHPO

Abandoned farm, U.S. Highway 2, Lincoln County. *Homesteaders in the Lincoln County area altered the historical landscape by carving farms out of the forests. Most built their log homes and shingled barns using heavy post-and-beam construction techniques.*

explorer and fur trader David Thompson became the first white man to visit Kootenai Falls and the first to use the Indian portage trail around the falls. A few months later, Finian McDonald of the British North West Company built the region's first fur trading post on the river's north bank just above the falls. In 1811, the company established a permanent trading post several miles upriver. There are no visible remains of either post.

The old portage trail that Thompson had used in 1808 was essential to the fur traders. The trail remained the only route between Libby and Troy, except for the railroad, until 1915. Until that year, people in Troy had to travel to Libby or move their wagonloads or automobiles on the Great Northern Railway. Lincoln County's growing population demanded a better and cheaper alternative. So, the Old Libby-Troy Road (sometimes called the Highline Road) was constructed, connecting the people in western Lincoln County to Spokane and to the county seat in Libby. Looking south from Kootenai Falls, you can see the remains of this road, especially the old concrete retaining wall cut into the bedrock above the river.

Most residents found it difficult to travel on the road: the grades were steep, the curves were treacherous, and it was only one lane wide. One couple remembered that when driving at night the husband drove the car while the wife stood in front, peering around the sharp corners to make certain that no one else was on the road. Tourists traveling between Spokane and Glacier National Park used the road more than did local residents.

C. V. West, photographer, MHS SHPO

Keystone Mill, Montana Road 508, Sylvanite, Lincoln County. *During the 1890s, prospectors discovered sylvanite ore—a gold-silver telluride—-in Lincoln County near the Yaak River.*

By 1934, U.S. Highway 2 skirted the treacherous canyon, running through the Kootenai River Valley near the tracks of the Great Northern Railway. Until U.S. 2 was completed, travel through the Kootenai Falls region was almost as dangerous during the early 20th century as it had been during David Thompson's time.

One hundred years ago, eager prospectors looked for gold and silver in the mountains you see as you travel west from Libby on U.S. 2 to the Idaho state line. From the 1860s to the 1880s, prospectors found only a little placer gold; but by the 1880s, significant quartz deposits had been discovered in the Kootenai country. By the turn of the century, several mines operated between Libby and Troy. The Snowshoe Mine south of Libby produced over $1 million in gold, silver, and lead. Prospectors discovered the Banner and Bangle mines near Troy during the 1880s, but the mines were not developed until the late 1910s when the Snowstorm Mining Company was organized. The mine closed in 1927. These mining sites are closed to the public, but you can see the heavily forested and mountainous terrain they occupied by traveling on U.S. 2 from Libby to Troy.

To reach the ASARCO mine, the largest operating mine in the Kootenai region, turn off U.S. 2 three miles east of Troy and travel seven miles south on Montana Highway 56 to the mine complex. One of area's largest employers, ASARCO Inc., built this large silver and copper mining complex in 1979 and began production in the summer of 1981. The mine employs about 350 people, and each year it produces 20,000 tons of copper and 4,200,000 ounces of silver.

Fifteen miles east of the U.S. 2/Montana 56 junction is Libby, the county seat of Lincoln County. Libby lies at the heart of the timber-producing region in northwestern Montana. The St. Regis paper mill has been Libby's leading employer for decades, and sawmills and logging operations are important to many local economies in Lincoln County. From 1906 to 1916, timber companies built plants along the Kootenai River at Troy, Libby, Warland, and Eureka. Since 1914, when the Libby Lumber Company produced 41.5 million board feet and the Eureka Lumber Company produced 21.5 million board feet, Lincoln County has steadily grown into one of the major lumber producers in the country.

There is a very different historical landscape along U.S. Highway 2 beginning 14 miles east of Libby. For the next 16 miles, you can see a series of farms and ranches that reflect the homesteading history of Lincoln County. Many of these farms contain original homestead structures, built between 1900 and 1920. Some of the buildings are now abandoned, but most are still part of multi-generational farms and many have distinctive architectural features.

Most of these homestead buildings have roofs made of cedar shakes or shingles and are usually in the gable style. Homesteaders built with logs, using several different types of notching to connect the logs at the corners. Some followed the practice of saddle-end and V-notching, so popular in the Northwest, but others used squared logs, either with tenon laps or British Columbia laps. A few of the buildings have stone foundations, but most used the heavy post-and-beam construction technique.

There are also a few "salt-box" buildings, a style of New England colonial architecture that features a large chimney and a gable roof extending in the rear to create another room. These simple buildings also have dormer windows in the front that have gable roofs of their own.

Route B: Montana Road 508, at Sylvanite

About 13 miles west of Troy on U.S. Highway 2 is the exit for Montana Road 508 (the Yaak Road). In the Kootenai National Forest about 20 miles to the north is the ghost town of Sylvanite and the remains of its Keystone Mine. With the Keystone concentrator still standing by the road and several old residences nearby, this is one of the best places to see Lincoln County's mining past.

During the early 1890s, Bill Lemley and Pete Berg made the first claims in the area, mistaking the gold ore for sylvanite ore, but the claims had little value. In 1895, two Spokane businessmen built a 10-stamp mill at the Keystone Mine, and the next year Sylvanite boomed. The owners of the Goldflint Mine built a 20-stamp mill. A sawmill cut lumber for frame buildings from trees that had been stripped from the surrounding countryside. The town prospered, and by 1900 about 500 people lived in Sylvanite, which had three general stores, three hotels, a post office, a drug store, and several saloons. But the easily accessible ore was soon played out and no one would invest more money in the district. Sylvanite entered a period of decline and most people moved away. In 1910, a mining company reopened the Keystone but failed to uncover substantial deposits of ore. By the end of the decade, all was quiet along the banks of the Yaak River.

F. Jay Haynes, photographer. Haynes Found. Coll. MHS Photo Archives

Thompson Falls, Sanders County, 1884. *Thompson Falls was the site of explorer David Thompson's fur post, Saleesh House, in 1809.*

Route C: U.S. Highway 93, from Eureka to Olney

Federal and state governments have played a large part in the history of Lincoln County's forests. The many forest service ranger stations and lookouts scattered throughout the Kootenai National Forest provide evidence of Montana's commitment to forest management. Lincoln County residents have moved one lookout to the Pioneer Village in Eureka, 69 miles north of Libby on U.S. 93. At the Stillwater State Forest Headquarters near Olney, 33 miles south of Eureka on U.S. 93, there are several original buildings dating to the 1920s.

The Stillwater Forest was established in the late 1910s, the result of a land swap between state and federal governments. In exchange for a 60,000-acre block of forest along the Whitefish and Stillwater river drainages, the state gave up 60,000 acres of land in several national forests. State forester Robert McLaughlin directed the construction of the headquarters' first building in 1922. After the disastrous fire of 1926 destroyed almost 40,000 acres of timber, the state built a permanent year-round ranger station and a warehouse for fire equipment, inaugurating a new era in Montana's forest management.

Landscape 12: The Clark Fork River

From its headwaters high in the Rocky Mountains, the Clark Fork River flows through the middle of western Montana on its way to the Columbia River. David Thompson, probably the first person to record a description of this area, noted the river's narrowness, its wide and beautiful meadow (at Plains along Montana Highway 200 in Sanders County), and the difficulty in navigating it. Although Thompson had to portage around the river's numerous rapids and falls, he thought that the river basin would be the ideal location for a fur-trading post. At Thompson Falls, on Montana 200 in Sanders County, you can see the river bottomland and rich foliage that first attracted Thompson almost 200 years ago.

The Clark Fork was also popular with the Kootenai Indians, who dug camas root along the riverbanks and used the river bluffs as a natural fortification. They also used the river as a travel corridor through the Rocky Mountains.

The Clark Fork continued to serve as a major transportation route during the 19th and 20th centuries. John Mullan followed the river when he built the first military road (the Mullan Road) through Montana during the late 1850s. More than 30 years later, the Northern Pacific Railroad followed the river's northern fork to the Idaho state line, and two decades later the Milwaukee Road followed Mullan's route across the Rocky Mountains. When you travel on I-90 from Missoula to St. Regis, you follow the historic transportation routes created by the Clark Fork River.

Route 39: Canadian Fur Traders on the Clark Fork River

Route A: Montana Highway 200, from Thompson Falls to Plains
Route B: U.S. Highway 93, at Fort Connah historical marker in Lake County

The first fur traders who came to present-day Montana traded in the state's northwestern corner, hundreds of miles from the more famous fur trapping areas on the Missouri and Yellowstone rivers. It was in the Clark Fork country that fur companies first tried to develop a trading relationship with the Indians in the region. Canadian fur companies dominated the trade, primarily because of geographer and trader David Thompson. "I know of no man," wrote one historian,

> whose intimate acquaintance with Indians covered so wide a territory, or included more tribal variations. Inside the territory bounded by Fort Churchill, Sault Ste. Marie, the Mississippi River, the mouth of the Columbia, Peace River Landing, and Fort Chipewyan, on Lake Athabasca, are about a million and half square miles of land, within which he knew the Indians better than any other fur trader.

At Thompson Falls, 50 miles east of the Idaho line on Montana 200, you can stop at the monuments above the Clark Fork River and see the area where Thompson and Canadian fur traders developed the region's fur trade.

Fort Connah, U.S. Highway 93, Lake County. A *visitor to Fort Connah during the 1850s noted that its buildings were "barely habitable," worth no more than "twelve hundred dollars."*

Route A: Montana Highway 200, from Thompson Falls to Plains

Before coming to the Clark Fork River in 1809, David Thompson had established two trading posts west of the Continental Divide: at Kootenae House on the Columbia River near Lake Windermere, and at a second house on the eastern end of Pend d'Oreille Lake in Idaho. In late November 1809, when Thompson was camped very close to present-day Thompson Falls, a Flathead warrior invited him to trade. The large band of Flathead Indians had plenty to trade, since they were returning from a successful hunt in the bison country east of the Continental Divide. Thompson selected a site for a new trading post near where the city of Thompson Falls now stands, but Thompson and his men were so weak from hunger that they delayed construction for five days while they waited for new supplies of dried meat. They built Saleesh House about three miles below the confluence of the Thompson and Clark Fork rivers on the Clark Fork's northern bank. At the time, the trading post was surrounded by a clump of trees, but the site is now clear and covered only by grass.

There are no remnants of the post and archaeologists have been unable to determine the exact location of the buildings, but Thompson's journals and the observations of early travelers provide some clues to its appearance. Saleesh House was not a fortified trading post; it had no protective walls around it. There were three log buildings, each with a stone and mud chimney and gable roofs covered by grass and foliage. The traders used animal skins to stop the leaks in the roofs, and paper windows kept out the elements.

Thompson and his men lived in these rather drab quarters the entire winter, trading with Flathead, Kootenai, and Kalispell Indians and to a limited extent with a group of Nez Perce. The traders hired Native American hunters to supply them with meat until mid April, when the trading season ended. Then the Indians left to begin gathering plants, and the traders returned to Canada.

Thompson returned to Saleesh House in November 1811 to repair the post's buildings and construct new ones. It was a difficult time. Thompson recorded in his diary on Christmas Day that the only thing to eat was "Berries and a little fat." North West Company employees occupied the post during the trading seasons of 1812 through 1814.

The post probably changed in appearance several times from 1809 to the early 1820s. A traveler passing by the remains of Saleesh House during the 1830s observed that "this establishment formerly consisted of seven hewn log buildings." It is not clear when these additional buildings were constructed.

During the early 1820s, the Canadian traders abandoned Saleesh House and moved to Flathead Post, a new trading post about 10 miles up the north bank of the Clark Fork River at the mouth of Swamp Creek (about 13 miles east of Thompson Falls on Montana 200). From 1823 to 1846, Flathead Post was the major Montana post of the Hudson's Bay Company, which had taken control of the Canadian fur trade by buying out its rival, the North West Company, in 1821.

Route B: U.S. Highway 93, at Fort Connah historical marker in Lake County

You can see the site of the Hudson's Bay Company's last post in Montana if you travel east on Montana Highway 200 until you reach its junction with U.S. Highway 93 at Ravalli. About 11 miles north on U.S. 93 is the highway historical marker for Fort Connah, which is listed in the National Register of Historic Places.

Responding to competition from Americans for the western Montana fur trade, in 1846 Neil McArthur moved the Hudson's Bay Company's operations from the Clark Fork River to a new post, Fort Connah, on Post Creek in present-day Lake County. One company employee recorded that the location of the new post had many advantages "as it is much nearer the road the Indians pass than at the old House." He also reported that "a small farm is now cultivated, the Soil is capital, and may expect in a year Or two to raise sufficient Grain, so as to enable us to live without making it necessary the expense of transporting flour hence."

The new post opened for the 1847 season after Angus McDonald had finished the last building. Like the other Canadian posts in Montana, Fort Connah's buildings were unadorned and had no palisade (a wall of pointed logs that protected forts from intruders). Unlike their American counterparts, the Canadian traders never considered heavily palisaded forts to be necessary for they saw the Native Americans as important and trustworthy allies in their fur-trade enterprise.

According to one visitor during the 1850s, there were five basic structures at the post: "a wooden building, about twenty-four by sixteen feet, of one story, with a bark roof; one wooden bastion, about fourteen feet square; and two store-rooms, each ten feet square; also a log corral, about sixty feet square."

You can see one of Fort Connah's buildings from the highway historical marker on U.S. 93. The structure, measuring 24 by 16 feet with 8-foot-high walls, is a single-story hewn-log building featuring the Manitoba style of construction. It dates to the late 1840s and was probably the traders' original residence.

Through trade at Fort Connah, the Hudson's Bay Company was able to acquire goods that were unavailable at its other posts, including horse accoutrements, parfleches, rawhide, bison hair cords, skins, and other bison products. This trade made it possible for the company to operate its more prosperous northern Canadian trading posts. Even though American settlement increased after the 1850s, Fort Connah remained in business as a Canadian fur post until 1871.

Route 40: Developing the Clark Fork Country

Route A: Montana Highway 263, in Missoula
Route B: Interstate Highway I-90, from Frenchtown to the Idaho state line
Route C: Montana Highway 200, from Paradise to Trout Creek

For the last 100 years, the Clark Fork country has provided northwestern Montanans with a transportation corridor through the Rocky Mountains and access to the region's gold and silver deposits. When you travel on I-90 and Montana Highway 200, you can see how people have used the varied resources of the Clark Fork.

Route A: Montana Highway 263, in Missoula

In 1855, at a clearing on the north bank of the Clark Fork River a few miles west of Missoula on Montana Highway 263 (the Mullan Road), the U.S. government signed a treaty with the Flathead, Kalispell, Pend d'Oreille, and Kootenai Indians. The Council Grove State Monument, which commemorates the site, is accessible by gravel road off Montana 263 about seven miles west of Missoula. The treaty officially established the Flathead Indian Reservation, which would be shared by the four tribes. In exchange for a railroad right-of-way and territory for white settlers, the Native Americans received $120,000 plus $500 a year for each of the tribal leaders for the next 20 years. Called the Hellgate Treaty of 1855, the agreement opened the door for whites to develop the Clark Fork country.

Missoula, the county seat of Missoula County, has long been the transportation center of the Clark Fork country. The Mullan Road was built near Missoula in the early 1860s. Both the Northern Pacific and Milwaukee Road built lines through the city and constructed passenger depots. The Northern Pacific's depot (at Railroad and Higgins) and the Milwaukee Road's depot (at 250 Station Drive) are listed in the National Register of Historic Places. Missoula is also home to the University of Montana and several important historic buildings, including the old Carnegie Public Library, now the Missoula Museum of the Arts, on 335 North Pattee Street, the Higgins Block on 202 North Higgins, and Fort Missoula, located off Reserve Street. Each of these sites is listed in the National Register of Historic Places.

Route B: Interstate Highway I-90, from Frenchtown to the Idaho state line

In 1859, the U.S. Army ordered Capt. John Mullan to build a wagon road between Fort Benton, Montana, and Fort Walla Walla, Washington. You can trace the route of the Mullan Road by traveling from Missoula to Frenchtown on Montana Highway 263, then following I-90 for 90 miles from Frenchtown to the Idaho state line.

Beginning at Fort Benton in the summer of 1859, Mullan and his soldiers reached the Bitterroot country by September. They built the road along the Clark Fork River until they reached the mouth of the St. Regis River, which they followed until crossing into present-day Idaho at St. Regis Pass. The road was not completed until 1862.

The road challenged the army's road-building capabilities. One of the most difficult sections to build was the 33-mile stretch between St. Regis and the Idaho line. You can drive part of this route, the "Camelhump Road," by leaving I-90 at St. Regis and taking U.S. 10 to its junction with I-90 about three miles east of DeBorgia. Along this section of the highway, you can get some idea of how difficult it was to blaze a road through these forests. Mullan's men had to contend with a narrow river valley, a particularly dense forest, and fallen trees that made travel by land almost impossible. They worked from dawn to dusk for weeks before completing this section of the road. "Justice cannot be done to the industry and fortitude of the men while mastering this wilderness section," Mullan reported.

Settlers began moving into the region while the Mullan Road was being built. One group of French-Canadians moved into the Clark Fork Valley northwest of Missoula during the late 1850s; and within 10 years, 50 French-Canadian families, many from New Brunswick and Quebec, had settled in Frenchtown, 18 miles west of Missoula on I-90.

You can still see the French-Canadian influence in the style of barns the Frenchtown settlers built. Constructed of hand-hewn logs and joined by dovetail notching, the structures are good examples of *en pieces* construction, a French-Canadian building style that dates to 1698. None of the barns have a stone foundation, and all of them have gable roofs and rectangular floor plans. By the turn of the century, however, farmers were building or refurbishing barns that exhibited little French-Canadian influence. They used milled lumber that was sometimes placed over the old *en pieces* construction as an improvement.

Fifteen miles west of Frenchtown on I-90 is Alberton, which was originally established in 1907 as a division point for the Milwaukee Road. The railroad built a roundhouse, a depot, employee housing, and railroad shops; and by 1916, over 400 people lived in Alberton. Most of the adults worked for the railroad or provided services for passengers, but within a year the Milwaukee electrified its western Montana route and closed intermediate division points like Alberton. Many families left, and the town entered an era of economic stagnation that continues to the present. From I-90, you can see the recently restored Milwaukee depot, a symbol of Alberton's founding and its economic development and decline.

Superior, the Clark Fork's mining center for many years, is located 28 miles west of Alberton on I-90. From 1869 to 1873, 3,000 miners worked in the mines in the Cedar Creek Mining District near present-day Superior; and small towns like Cedar Creek, Cayuse, Louisville, Oregon Gulch, Amador, Forest City, old

Alberton, Missoula County, ca. 1917. *This view shows Alberton when it was a division point on the Milwaukee Road, not long after the railroad converted to electricity.*

Superior, Junction, and Charter quickly appeared to serve their needs. Except for Superior, these boom towns disappeared once the placers played out during the early 1870s.

During the late 1880s and 1890s, there was a second boom in the Superior area. From 1888 to 1896, the Iron Mountain Mine, a silver, gold, and lead operation north of Superior at Pardee, enjoyed its best years. Smaller-scale mining continued during the first decades of the 20th century, and a few buildings from this later activity remain at Pardee.

There was also some excitement at Keystone, a quartz mining town just north of Superior, when prospectors discovered gold there in 1895. The boom was over by 1900, but the mines reopened 10 years later, and with a new stamp mill the town came back. Miners lived in the town's original buildings while they built new ones. But the second boom came to a halt when the Great Fire of 1910 destroyed millions of acres in Idaho and Montana and roared through Keystone leaving behind nothing but cinders. The community rebuilt in 1911—the buildings at Keystone date to that time—but the mines never prospered as many people had hoped.

The Clark Fork River turns north at St. Regis, 14 miles west of Superior. You can continue to follow the river if you leave I-90 at St. Regis, take Montana Highway 135 north for 21 miles, and then take Montana 200 to the Idaho line.

Route C: Montana Highway 200, from Paradise to Trout Creek

Montana Highway 200 follows the route of the Northern Pacific, the first railroad to build through northwestern Montana. Paradise, three miles west of the junction of Montana Highways 135 and 200, was an important water supply stop, and the railroad owned the town's water system into the 1980s. The one-story, unadorned brick depot in Paradise indicates how important the town was to the Northern Pacific. Only in one other small Montana town—in Garrison, Powell County, a key railroad junction—did the railroad build a brick depot.

Eight miles west of Paradise is Plains. Located in a wide, well-grassed section of the valley where wild horses once grazed, Plains was called Horse Plains until 1884. The Wild Horse Plains School (located on Montana 200) and the Horse Plains Jail (located in the middle of town) remain from those early years. In 1883, the Northern Pacific built through the settlement, creating a corridor with important buildings on both sides of the tracks. The Grange Hall, the newspaper office, and grain elevators stand on the south side of the tracks, and the McGowan Block (a commercial enterprise established in 1883), the Odd Fellows Hall, and the town's schools are on the north side.

The Northern Pacific had to pass through a narrow section of the valley at the town of Thompson Falls, 26 miles west of Plains on Montana 200. The railroad solved the problem by following the high ground between the river's bottomland and bluffs, which would neatly divide the future town of Thompson Falls. On terraces above the railroad and the Clark Fork River are houses, community centers, and churches, which comprise a large part of the city's residential district. Below the tracks, near the banks of the river, are the commercial district, the Sanders County courthouse, the old jail, and more houses.

The history of Thompson Falls has been one of brief economic booms and long periods of stagnation. After the railroad passed through the valley in 1883, the town became an important outfitting stop for prospectors headed for the Idaho gold mines, but the town was largely abandoned when the Idaho rush faded. The town again prospered during the early 1900s, when Thompson Falls was named the county seat in 1906 and the Thompson Falls Dam and Powerhouse was constructed from 1913 to 1915. The powerhouse, which is now owned by the Montana Power Company, originally supplied electricity to the Milwaukee Road. Once the construction crews left town, Thompson Falls entered another period of economic stagnation, and today only about 1,500 people live in the town.

Trout Creek, some 15 miles west of Thompson Falls on Montana 200, was the community center for the farm families who lived in northern Sanders County. Most community events took place at the Grange Hall, a wooden structure built in 1937-1938. The Grange members met at the hall to listen to extension agents talk about agricultural issues and government officials explain rural electric co-ops and soil conservation. The hall was also the scene of card parties, box socials, basket socials, teenage dances, and square dances, and is now the Trout Creek Senior Citizens building.

Landscape 13: The Flathead Valley

The Flathead Valley is one of the most beautiful valleys in Montana. From the upper Flathead Valley at Columbia Falls on U.S. Highway 2, you can see the peaks of Glacier National Park to the east. At Somers, 25 miles south of Columbia Falls, you can see Flathead Lake, the largest natural lake in the state. On the other end of this 30-mile-long lake at Polson, the valley widens and the Mission Mountains dominate the landscape to the east.

Flathead River, Flathead County. *Railroads in western Montana followed river courses through the mountains, creating new historical landscapes.*

At the beginning of the 20th century, the influence of Native Americans was still evident on the landscape south of Flathead Lake. Flathead Indian Paul Charlot remembered, "I could go anywhere and see the cattle and the horses all over the reservation. The cattle were plentiful. They were everywhere you looked [and] there was Indian horses mixed up with the cattle. Over at the [St. Ignatius] Mission, in Camas Prairie—wherever the Indians lived—it was just the same. They even had buffaloes, and they were the Indian's buffaloes."

The landscape changed quickly once the reservation was opened to homesteaders in 1910. The bison were confined to the National Bison Range at Moiese, northwest of Ravalli; the Flathead River was regulated by the Kerr Dam, a few miles south of Flathead Lake; irrigation ditches were dug; and resort areas were developed on Flathead Lake.

Route 41: The Flathead Indian Reservation

Route A: Montana Road 212, from Dixon to Two Eagle River School
Route B: U.S. Highway 93, from St. Ignatius to Pablo

The Flathead Indian Reservation, which has been occupied longer than any other reservation in Montana, extends from Flathead Lake south to the Jocko River Valley. The reservation was created in 1855 for the Flathead, Kootenai, Kalispell, and Pend d'Oreille Indians.

The Flathead tribe, the largest and most powerful on the reservation, is part of the Salish, six linguistically related tribes who live in the Northwest. Ethnographers often call these people the Interior Salish to distinguish them from their kinfolk who lived on the West Coast. During the 18th century, the

Spokan lived in an area that extended from the Spokane River to near the Idaho line. The Kalispell Indians lived in present-day Montana and Idaho, along the Clark Fork River and Pend d'Oreille Lake; the Pend d'Oreille resided in the Bitterroot and Flathead valleys; the Salish Tunaxe occupied the area of the Dearborn and the Sun rivers; and the Salish Semtayuse lived along the Big Blackfoot and Little Blackfoot rivers and in parts of the Deerlodge Valley. Intertribal warfare and smallpox wiped out the Semtayuse and the Tunaxe, and little is known about these people. The Flathead Indians claimed an immense homeland, with settlements located as far south as the Prickly Pear Valley, present-day Butte, and the Big Hole Valley.

During the late 17th and early 18th centuries, the Flathead Indians amicably shared their Montana domain with the Shoshoni, but things changed after the Blackfoot Confederacy obtained horses and guns during the mid 1700s. The Confederacy challenged the Flathead and Shoshoni for control of the territory east of the Continental Divide. Before the end of the century, the Confederacy had pushed the Salish tribes, including the Flathead, west of the Divide and had chased the Shoshoni into the southwestern corner of Montana.

In their new location, the Flathead Indians had to place more importance on gathering camas roots, bitterroot, and berries for food. They still crossed the Rockies to hunt bison on the eastern plains, but they became less dependent on bison and hunted more small animals in the western Montana valleys.

The seasons and available resources set a pattern for the Flathead Indians' way of life. In May and June, they lived where they could harvest camas root, bitterroot bulbs, and wild onions. They found camas fields near present-day Hot Springs and Camas, on Montana Highway 28 about 65 miles south of Kalispell, and bitterroot near Philipsburg and in the "grass valley" between Frenchtown and Missoula. It was important to harvest the bitterroot bulbs on time, for if the plant was gathered late, it was difficult to remove the bitter-tasting outer layer. During the summer, they gathered huckleberries, chokecherries, raspberries, gooseberries, and serviceberries. Near the end of the summer, the Flathead gathered wild carrots and parsnips.

According to Father Nicolas Point, when the Flathead hunted bison in the summer and the fall some small groups traveled as far east as present-day Billings. When hunting deer and elk nearer their homeland in the western mountains, two or three men would drive a herd of animals to a concealed place where other men waited in ambush. During the fall, the Flathead prepared furs for trading and meat for the winter months, when they would divide into smaller bands and live along the rivers and lakes until spring.

The government created the reservation in 1855, but some Flathead Indians refused to move there for almost 40 years. Chief Victor's band continued to follow its traditional way of life in the Bitterroot Valley until large numbers of settlers arrived. After Victor's death, the tribe remained in the valley with his son Charlot. In 1872, Gen. James A. Garfield claimed that Charlot had signed a treaty exchanging the Bitterroot Valley for $50,000, log cabins, some farming equipment, and some vegetables. The signature on the treaty was fraudulent, but Garfield persuaded minor chiefs Arlee and Adlof to sign the treaty and ordered

Charlot and his followers out of the Bitterroot Valley. Charlot refused to budge until 1891, when the government evicted him and his followers from the Bitterroot. Charlot told government officials: "My young men are becoming bad; they have no place to hunt. My women are hungry. For their sake I will go. I do not want the land you promise. I do not believe your promises. All I want is enough ground for my grave. We will go over [to the Flathead Indian Reservation]."

According to Charlot's son, Martin, the government kept few of the promises it made in 1891. But after the Flathead re-united with their kinfolk, the Pend d'Oreille and Kalispell, and their allies, the Kootenai, they discovered that working together they could become prosperous in the Flathead Valley. "After the irrigation system was in," Martin Charlot recalled, "many more people started farming. They were successful in farming both sides of the Jocko River. In time, we even had a threshing machine. . . . All in all, we made a good living." But this brief period of prosperity ended when the homesteaders arrived during the 1910s. No longer did the Native Americans control the reservation's land and resources.

Route A: Montana Road 212, from Dixon to Two Eagle River School

The Two Eagle River Indian School, located on Montana Road 212 where it crosses the Jocko River about two miles north of Dixon, is the original location of the Jocko Agency, the government headquarters for the Flathead Indian Reservation from the late 19th through the early 20th centuries. Many of the agency buildings are still in good condition, especially the employees' houses. The agency's main street was lined with these hip-roof, wooden-plank buildings with front porches, which contrasted sharply with the log cabins, tipis, and hewn-log homes owned by many of the Native Americans. Today, school officials use these buildings for classrooms, residences, and offices.

Route B: U.S. Highway 93, from St. Ignatius to Pablo

Thirteen miles east of the Two Eagle River School on U.S. Highway 93 is the St. Ignatius Mission, another important reservation center in the early 20th century. Located in a beautiful meadow at the base of the Mission Mountains 26 miles south of Polson, this National Historic Landmark is a reminder of the 150-year-old relationship between the Catholic religion and many Flathead Indians.

In 1844, Father Pierre De Smet established the St. Ignatius Mission along the Pend d'Oreille River in present-day Washington state, but the Flathead Indians asked the Jesuits to move the mission eastward so it would be closer to their homeland. In 1854, the priests moved the mission to its present location, about 70 miles north of St. Mary's Mission, which had been abandoned four years earlier. During that year, the Jesuits built a cabin, a blacksmith shop, a carpentry shop, and a chapel, which the priests used as a residence. The original wooden chapel still stands next to the present-day church at St. Ignatius. Ten years later, the priests supervised the construction of a flour mill (which still stands to the

St. Ignatius Mission, Flathead Indian Reservation, Lake County. *Constructed in 1891 at a cost of $28,000, St. Ignatius was built with hundreds of thousands of bricks fired at a nearby kiln.*

north of the mission) and a sawmill and began to teach the Indians who resided near the mission how to cultivate crops.

From 1888 to 1896, the mission experienced its greatest activity and a second period of expansion. In 1888, the Jesuits opened a school for boys, and two years later the Ursuline nuns started a nursery school. At its peak during the early 1890s, the boys' school had 320 pupils. In 1891, workers built a large church, which became a landmark in the Flathead Valley. They constructed the 120- by 60-foot church using bricks made from local materials and fired on the spot, and they added a belfry that is almost 100 feet high. Inside the church, a series of spectacular murals executed by Brother Joseph Carignano depict the biblical history of man.

The Flathead Indians' fortunes changed dramatically from 1909 to 1912, when the federal government used the Dawes Act of 1887 to open the reservation to settlers and homesteaders. You can see how the homesteaders changed the landscape by traveling north on U.S. Highway 93 from St. Ignatius to Pablo. Sophie Moeise remembered that "before the reservation was opened it was easy for the people to get rich. It was not fenced and they had free pasture and they had lots of cattle and lots of horses." Paul Charlot concluded that when the government "threw the reservation open we all went broke and the stock disappeared. They had too much stock and they could not take care of it on the allotments that they got [usually 160 acres], so the Indian just gave up his ambition and sold their stock and got poor."

At several places in northwestern Montana, you can still see evidence of the Native Americans' past domination of the region. Before whites settled in this area, the Indians burned the forests every fall to aid hunting and create new areas for horse grazing. The fires would transform thick forests into "open, park-like" areas and would increase berry production by eliminating old, low-yield bushes. The fires also produced clearings for campsites, killed insects and inhibited the spread of disease, and limited the danger of natural wildfires. The Native American landscape of 100 years ago is evident in the large stands of ponderosa pine trees in the Ninemile Valley west of Missoula, along the west fork of the Bitterroot River near Darby (U.S. Highway 93), in the area west of Elmo (Montana 28), along Indian Creek near Thompson Falls (Montana 200), near Wolf Creek east of Libby (U.S. 2), along the west fork of the Fisher River, and in the Tenmile Creek drainage of Lincoln County. Once the Indians stopped setting the fires at these northwestern Montana locations, the Douglas fir began to dominate the forests, which became overgrown with vegetation and made overland traffic through the forests difficult.

Route 42: Settling the Flathead Valley

Route A: U.S. Highway 2, from Marias Pass to Kalispell
Route B: U.S. Highway 93, from Whitefish to Polson
Route C: Interstate Highway I-90, at Bonner and Milltown

The settlement history of the Flathead Valley is closely tied to the construction of the Great Northern Railway through the upper Flathead Valley in 1891 and the opening of the Flathead Indian Reservation to homesteaders during the early 20th century. On U.S. Highway 2 from West Glacier to Kalispell and on U.S. Highway 93 from Whitefish to Polson, you can see some of the important places associated with the settlement of the Flathead Valley.

Route A: U.S. Highway 2, from Marias Pass to Kalispell

In 1891, the Great Northern Railway crossed the Continental Divide at Marias Pass, the lowest major pass over the Divide (at 5,216 feet) and the last one to be discovered in Montana. Great Northern surveyor John F. Stevens mapped the route in December 1889. You can see evidence of the early settlement of the area by taking U.S. 2, which follows the route of the Great Northern across the pass and into the upper Flathead Valley.

Twelve miles west of Marias Pass, U.S. 2 crosses into Glacier National Park, which was established in 1910. James J. Hill, president of the Great Northern Railway, lobbied heavily for the park, believing that it would become a major tourist attraction along his line. During the 1910s, the railroad built several of Glacier's first hotels and chalets. The Many Glacier Hotel, the Glacier Park Hotel, and the Sperry and Granite chalets are from that era and are listed in the National Register of Historic Places. The Great Northern dominated travel to Glacier and centered much of its publicity on the park. When tourists began using Going-to-the-Sun Road, which the federal government had constructed through the park in the 1930s, the Great Northern's domination of Glacier's tourism industry diminished. Going-to-the-Sun Road, which is also listed in the National Register of Historic Places, links St. Mary on the eastern side of Glacier with the park's western entrance at West Glacier.

As you leave West Glacier, you will enter the upper Flathead Valley. In the farms along U.S. Highway 2 from Columbia Falls to Kalispell and along the secondary roads in Flathead County, you can see three important patterns. First, many newcomers built their homes on small rises, exposed to the elements. This seemingly strange location was actually very logical, for the rocky rises provided good building foundations and put settlers' dwellings above the insect-infested lowlands and on the least valuable land they owned. The second pattern is the number of multi-generational farms that still contain original structures. Farmers constructed these solid, heavy, unadorned log buildings low to the ground. You can see the third pattern in the hay sheds situated throughout the Flathead Valley. While the open sides of the sheds left the hay somewhat unprotected, the design allowed the hay to breathe, an essential compromise in the relatively humid climate of the upper Flathead Valley.

A major town in the upper Flathead Valley is Columbia Falls, 15 miles west of West Glacier on U.S. 2. At one time, the town's leading employer was the Anaconda Company's smelting plant, but over the last few decades the tourist industry has become an important part of the local economy. One of the more important buildings in Columbia Falls is St. Richard's Church, which is located at 505 4th Avenue West and is listed in the National Register of Historic Places.

Kalispell, the county seat of Flathead County, is 15 miles south of Columbia Falls on U.S. 2. Established in 1891 as a Great Northern division point, Kalispell became the trade center for farmers and ranchers in the upper Flathead Valley. By the time the Great Northern changed its route in 1904 and moved its division point to Whitefish, 14 miles to the north, agriculture had become the leading industry in the area. As a result, Kalispell suffered only a slight economic downturn, and major roads still connect Kalispell to the rest of Montana.

You can see how the changes in transportation routes have affected Kalispell's built environment. The town was originally a textbook example of a "T" town, with the Great Northern depot (now the Chamber of Commerce building), grain elevators, and warehouses forming the top of the "T" to the north and the commercial blocks running south from the depot forming the stem. At the base of the "T" at the south end of town was the Flathead County courthouse.

Kalispell is still a "T" town, even without the railroad's presence. Modern highway construction has imposed a modified "T"-town look to the city, with U.S. 2, which is a few hundred yards north of the depot, forming the new top of the "T" and U.S. 93 forming the stem to the south. Kalispell's major shopping centers, hotels and motels, and the county fairgrounds lie along these two highways. Kalispell is also home to the impressive shingle-style mansion of the town's founder, Charles E. Conrad. Located at 313 6th Avenue East, the house is listed in the National Register of Historic Places.

Route B: U.S. Highway 93, from Whitefish to Polson

Whitefish, 14 miles north of Kalispell on U.S. Highway 93, is located on the Great Northern mainline and is still very much a railroad town. Its two-story Swiss chalet-style depot, built in 1927, is one of the most prominent on the Great

Great Northern depot, Whitefish, Flathead County, 1953. A *division point on the railroad after 1904, Whitefish relied on the lumber industry and the Great Northern for its economic base.*

Northern Railway. Thomas McMahon designed the depot to match the appearance of the railroad's chalets in Glacier National Park.

About 22 miles south of Whitefish, on U.S. Highway 93, is the town of Somers, the center of the timber products industry in the upper Flathead Valley. Here, in 1901, on the northwestern corner of Flathead Lake, John O'Brien established the O'Brien Lumber Company. Hoping to supply lumber to the Great Northern Railway, he constructed a sawmill and a railroad-tie mill. The company, which was later called the Somers Lumber Company, established a town for its workers with 120 dwellings and used Flathead Lake as the holding area for the freshly cut logs. The company stayed in business until the late 1940s when it was acquired by the Great Northern Railway, which continued to produce railroad ties at the plant into the 1980s. Overlooking Somers, the mill, and the lake is John O'Brien's mansion. This house is privately owned and closed to the public. You can also still see many of the original company houses in the town.

The development of the lower Flathead Valley took place after the government opened the Flathead Indian Reservation to settlers in the early 20th century. You can see the landscape created by the homesteaders at Polson, 45 miles south of Somers on U.S. Highway 93. Polson became a commercial center for the newly arrived farmers and ranchers. In time, a spur line connected both Polson and Ronan (12 miles south on U.S. Highway 93) to the mainline of the Northern Pacific. By 1923, there was sufficient white population in the lower Flathead Valley to create Lake County, with Polson as the seat of government. Only in

MHS Photo Archives

ACM Bonner Lumber Co., Montana Highway 200, Missoula County, 1953.
The Bonner mill has been operating on the banks of the Blackfoot River for over a century.
Originally built by the Anaconda Company, it is now owned by Champion International.

isolated areas of the Flathead Valley did the countryside retain its pre-20th century appearance.

Route C: Interstate Highway I-90, at Bonner and Milltown

Timber from the Flathead country is still processed at mills at Bonner and Milltown. You can reach this large mill complex by taking I-90 for five miles east from Missoula to the exit for Bonner.

The Bonner milling operations began as part of Eddy, Hammond and Company, the most important timber concern in northwestern Montana. In 1881, the company agreed to supply the Northern Pacific Railroad with its timber needs, and it built several new mills in Hell Gate Canyon, one in O'Keefe Canyon, another along the Clark Fork River at Clinton, and later one at Bonner on the Big Blackfoot River.

During the summer of 1882, Eddy, Hammond and other investors, including the Northern Pacific Railroad, established the Montana Improvement Company to provide the railroad with timber. The Montana Improvement Company cut timber from the Northern Pacific's land grant timberlands and from public land. The Northern Pacific gave the Montana Improvement Company very low freight rates, which helped the company become one of Montana Territory's economic powers.

In 1885, the federal government charged that the Montana Improvement Company had systematically and deliberately cut timber from thousands of acres of federally owned land. But the lawsuit, which the company eventually won, did not impede the company's expansion. In 1886, it constructed a permanent mill at Bonner on the Big Blackfoot River, an ideal place for rafting logs downriver to the sawmill.

In 1898, Marcus Daly's Anaconda Copper Mining Company acquired controlling interest in the Bonner mill in order to secure an inexpensive source of timber for its ever-expanding mining empire. A few months later, Daly purchased the Northern Pacific's forest land, providing the Bonner mill with all the timber it could handle. When it purchased all of the property of the Montana Improvement Company in 1910, the Anaconda Company gained complete control of the Bonner mill, which it operated for the next 50 years as the Lumber Department of the Anaconda Copper Mining Company. The company sold the mill and timber holdings to Champion International Corporation in the early 1970s.

Many of the buildings at Bonner are of recent origin. In the early 1960s, Anaconda built a new "pushbutton" mill that cost several million dollars. "The size of the operation," wrote a local historian, "was hard to visualize as huge buildings painted a light green dominated by the planner storage structure covered seven acres—the size of seven football fields." For much of its history, Bonner has been a company town, and you can see the company houses on both sides of Montana Highway 200 near the mill complex. These unadorned frame dwellings are reminders of Bonner's beginnings.

Landscape 14: The Bitterroot Valley

In 1884, writer and publicist E. V. Smalley calculated that the Bitterroot Valley was about 90 miles long and in some places 7 miles across, with mountains to both the east and west. He reported that the country "has the reputation of being the best agricultural valley of Montana, its comparatively low altitude (four thousand feet) favoring the raising of fruit and Indian corn, as well as of wheat, oats, and barley." Both whites and Flathead Indians lived in the valley, creating a built environment rarely seen in the U.S. Smalley reported:

The Indians lands are scattered through the valley among the farms of the whites, and their owners occupy log-cabins in winter, but prefer the canvas-covered teepee for their summer dwellings. As a rule, the houses of the white settlers are of hewn logs—a material preferred to sawn lumber because it makes thick walls that are warm in winter and cool in summer. If well built, there is no better dwelling for a mountain country than a log-house, and a little trouble will deck its walls with vines and make it as pretty as it is substantial.

Irrigation, Smalley suggested, accounted for the high crop yields in the Bitterroot, "and abundant water is supplied by the streams which leap out of the mountain gorges, full-fed by springs and melting snows." Furthermore, the valley's foliage was undeniably rich. "Wild roses," he observed, "grew in thickets along the margin of the cool, swift stream [the Bitterroot River]; bluebells,

Tincup and Como Peaks, Bitterroot Valley, Ravalli County, ca. 1910. *In September 1844, Father Hoecken found the Bitterroot Valley to be ''a beautiful region, evidently fertile, uniting a useful as well as a pleasing variety of woodland, prairie, lake and river.''*

geraniums, and many varieties of golden compositae abounded; and there were multitudes of strange, nameless flowers peculiar to Montana."

When Smalley wrote his description of the Bitterroot Valley in 1884, he included nearly all of the area's natural resources: water from the Bitterroot River and the many mountain creeks, rich soil, beautiful scenery, and plentiful forests. You can see how people have used these resources by traveling from Sula to Missoula on U.S. Highway 93.

Route 43: Lewis and Clark in the Bitterroot Valley

Route A: U.S. Highway 93, from the Idaho state line to Lolo
Route B: U.S. Highway 12, from Lolo to Lolo Pass

On September 4, 1805, the Lewis and Clark expedition entered western Montana's Bitterroot Valley, one of the most critical sections of their journey. As you travel on U.S. Highways 93 and 12, you can see many historic sites associated with the expedition.

Route A: U.S. Highway 93, from the Idaho state line to Lolo

Thirteen miles north of Lost Trail Pass, which is located on the Montana-Idaho state line on U.S. Highway 93, the Lewis and Clark expedition met a party of 400 Flathead Indians. The meeting place was a beautiful cove on the east fork of the Bitterroot River, now known as Ross' Hole (named for the Hudson's Bay Company's Alexander Ross who camped here in the winter of 1824). The Indians were friendly and willing to trade with the Americans, who needed more horses for their overland journey across the valley and into the Bitterroot Mountains.

The Americans traveled north along the Bitterroot River for three days, finding rich plant life but few animals to hunt. Lewis wrote in his journal: "the country in the valley . . . is generally a prairie and from 5 to 6 miles wide the growth is almost altogether pine principally of the long-leafed kind, with some spruce and a kind of furr resembling the scotch furr." Along the small streams, Lewis noted

MHS Photo Archives

"a small proportion of the narrow leafed cottonwood; some redwood honeysuckle and rosebushes." On September 9, Lewis and his men stopped at Travelers' Rest along Lolo Creek near present-day Lolo. This site is a National Historic Landmark, and a highway historical marker on U.S. 93 shows the approximate location.

Route B: U.S. Highway 12, from Lolo to Lolo Pass

From Travelers' Rest, the expedition began the most difficult part of its journey, during which expedition leaders feared for their men because they could not find food in the high mountains. It would take them 11 grueling days to cross the Bitterroot Mountains on the Lolo Trail, an Indian trail that the Nez Perce used to travel eastward into Montana for annual bison hunts. U.S. Highway 12, from Lolo to the Lolo Pass on the Montana-Idaho line, roughly follows the first part of this old Indian trail, which is a National Historic Landmark.

The Americans left Travelers' Rest on September 11 and spent the next two days negotiating a trail that was often blocked by fallen trees. The party reached Lolo Hot Springs on September 13, continued the few additional miles to the pass, and began the long, fearful trek across the mountains to the tributaries of the Columbia River and on to the Pacific Ocean. It was the longest section of the expedition route that did not follow a major river course.

The Lewis and Clark expedition was again at Travelers' Rest in late June 1806 on its return from the Pacific Ocean to St. Louis. While at Travelers' Rest, the two expedition leaders divided the group. Lewis led one contingent to explore the Marias River drainage north and west of the Great Falls of the Missouri, and Clark led the rest south to the Big Hole River Valley and then down the Yellowstone River.

Route 44: Settlements in the Bitterroot Valley
U.S. Highway 93, from Stevensville to Darby

U.S. Highway 93 from Stevensville to Darby takes you through the region of the earliest white settlements in Montana. During the 1840s and 1850s, Jesuit priests built the first Catholic mission in present-day Montana and white settlers established farms here in the Bitterroot Valley.

St. Mary's Mission is about 28 miles south of Missoula in Stevensville. In 1841, Father Pierre De Smet established the mission at the request of Flathead Indians who believed that the rituals of Christianity brought good luck in battle.

St. Mary's Mission was built of cottonwood logs cut from the banks of the Bitterroot River, which flows nearby. As De Smet reported to his superior, the priests began "with what appeared to be the most urgent. We enclosed the field destined to become God's portion of the settlement. We started the buildings intended to be hereafter dependencies of the farm, but serving temporarily for a church and residence." With the assistance of Flathead Indians, who cut from 2,000 to 3,000 wooden stakes, in a very short time the priests, "with no other tools than the axe, saw and auger, constructed a chapel with pediment, colonnade and gallery, balustrade, choir, seats, &c." Within a few years, the priests had constructed 12 frame houses and had diverted the course of Burnt Creek, creating a mill race that operated a small flour mill and sawmill.

The mission was the first place that whites cultivated Montana's soil over an extended period of time. The priests grew their own vegetables and their own grain for the flour mill, and by 1846 they were harvesting wheat, oats, and potatoes.

The first St. Mary's Mission was located less than a mile north of its present site. You can see the mission's second location a few blocks west of Montana Highway 269 as it passes through downtown Stevensville (look for the sign). Father Anthony Ravalli built the church and adjacent pharmacy in 1866, using logs from the original St. Mary's church. The 1866 church, which is listed in the National Register of Historic Places, is a small structure with an unadorned frame belfry and a white frame front.

In 1850, the Catholics abandoned St. Mary's Mission and sold the land to John Owen for $250. Owen, who had arrived in the West via the Oregon Trail, wanted to build a trading post. At the Fort Owen State Monument in Stevensville, you can still see the east barracks of Fort Owen, including John Owen's combination office and library, bedrooms, and dormitory rooms. You can reach Fort Owen by following the highway signs from U.S. Highway 93 to the fort's location on the northern outskirts of Stevensville. Fort Owen is listed in the National Register of Historic Places, and an interpretation of the site is available at the monument.

Owen spent eight years building the fort. In 1852, he fenced the mission's adobe brickyard and began to build the fort's huge adobe walls, which extended about a foot above the buildings and were wide enough at the top that a person could run on them. But most of the construction of Fort Owen took place between 1857 and 1860, after Owen had been named the agent for the Flathead Indian Reservation and his fort became the agency headquarters. By mid June 1857, Owen and his employees had finished much of the fort's adobe foundation, and within a few weeks they had built two adobe bastions at the fort's southeast and southwest corners. The buildings had thick adobe walls, plank floors, and large fireplaces, and the interiors were lined with hewn lath and plaster. They also built other adobe buildings, a root cellar, and a well, and they refurbished the mission's grist mill and sawmill. By 1860, when Owen completed the fort, it was the most substantial group of structures in the Bitterroot Valley.

During the 1860s and 1870s, Fort Owen became less important as profits from the fur trade and Owen's agricultural enterprises declined. Owen became ill and was hospitalized in Helena in 1872. He left Montana five years later and died in 1889 in Pennsylvania.

Fifteen miles south of Stevensville is Corvallis and the Western Agricultural Research Center, which was established by the state legislature in 1907. An important contributor to the Bitterroot's agricultural history, the research center played a key role in transforming the valley's small, 30-year-old apple business into the major agricultural industry in the Bitterroot.

During the homesteading era, the agricultural research center and promoters created an "apple boom" in the Bitterroot. During the early 1910s, valley residents joined a group of Chicago-based capitalists to create the Bitterroot Irrigation Company. The company constructed a 75-mile-long canal along the east side of the valley. From 1910 to 1916, farmers roughly tripled the number of apple trees planted in the valley, covering thousands of acres. But despite the new irrigation system and the best efforts of the research center's employees, the apple "boom" suddenly "burst" in 1917. There was not enough nitrogen in the valley's soil for a high-yield apple crop, and there was not enough water to irrigate a million trees.

By 1920, apple growers had abandoned over 75 per cent of the valley's apple orchards, and by the 1930s the industry was dead. Only the research center at Corvallis and a few orchards in the valley remind us of the Bitterroot's experiment with fruit growing. At the research center, you can see the buildings constructed during the 1920s, a cottage-style residence for the center's manager built in 1910, and a 30-foot-high frame barn built in 1911 to store the center's equipment.

Corvallis is also home to Marcus Daly's 20,000-acre Bitterroot Stock Farm. You can see the entrance leading to Daly's ranch house, which many consider to be the most beautiful mansion in Montana, by taking Montana Highway 269 two miles north of Corvallis. The ranch is private property and is not open to the public. Do not trespass.

The history of Hamilton, located four miles south of Corvallis on U.S. Highway 93, is closely tied to the fortunes of Butte copper magnate Marcus Daly. In 1890, two years after establishing a sawmill at present-day Hamilton, Daly decided to expand his investment in the Bitterroot area by creating a town near the southern terminus of the Northern Pacific's Missoula-to-Grantsdale spur line. Hamilton is named for James Hamilton, a Daly employee who surveyed the town and designed the town plan. The Hamilton City Hall, at 175 S. 3rd Street, is listed in the National Register of Historic Places.

Hamilton quickly became the leading trade center in the Bitterroot Valley, and in 1898 it was named the seat of government for Ravalli County. The original county courthouse, at 225 Bedford, is listed in the National Register of Historic Places. One of the town's most imposing landmarks is an 85-foot-high smokestack, clearly visible from U.S. Highway 93 on Hamilton's northern outskirts. In 1916-1917, the Montana-Utah Sugar Company planned to build a sugar beet processing factory at Hamilton; but the company declared bankruptcy before the factory was completed, leaving the useless smokestack towering over the city. Another building that has been important to Hamilton is the Rocky Mountain Research Lab, a government medical center whose scientists developed antidotes for tick fever. This discovery helped to open several areas in the valley that had been considered uninhabitable because of tick infestation.

Darby, 17 miles south of Hamilton, is a major logging center in the Bitterroot. From 1890 until the turn of the century, large numbers of settlers moved into the Darby area and made timber claims, which they promptly sold to Bitterroot sawmills. By the 1940s, 50 years of "cut-and-run" logging practices had seriously depleted the timber reserves of the area; but conservation measures taken since that time have allowed local sawmills to re-open. Logging is still Darby's leading industry.

East entrance, Daly Mansion, Hamilton, Ravalli County. *Butte copper magnate Marcus Daly owned this magnificent mansion and ranch in the Bitterroot Valley, which he named the Bitterroot Stock Farm.*

Richard A. Smith, photographer, MHS Photo Archives

St. Mary's Mission, Stevensville, Ravalli County. *St. Mary's Mission was first established in 1841 and then abandoned in 1850. In 1866, the Jesuits returned to the mission and built this church, which has recently been restored.*

C. V. West, photographer, MHS SHPO

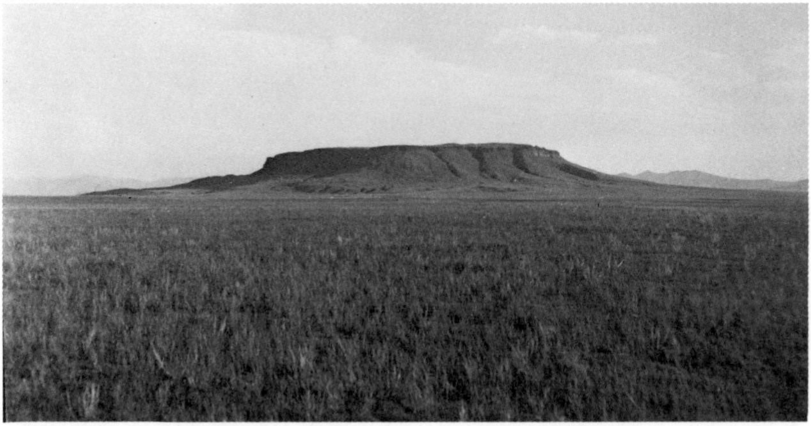

MHS Photo Archives

Square Butte, northwest of Cascade, Cascade County

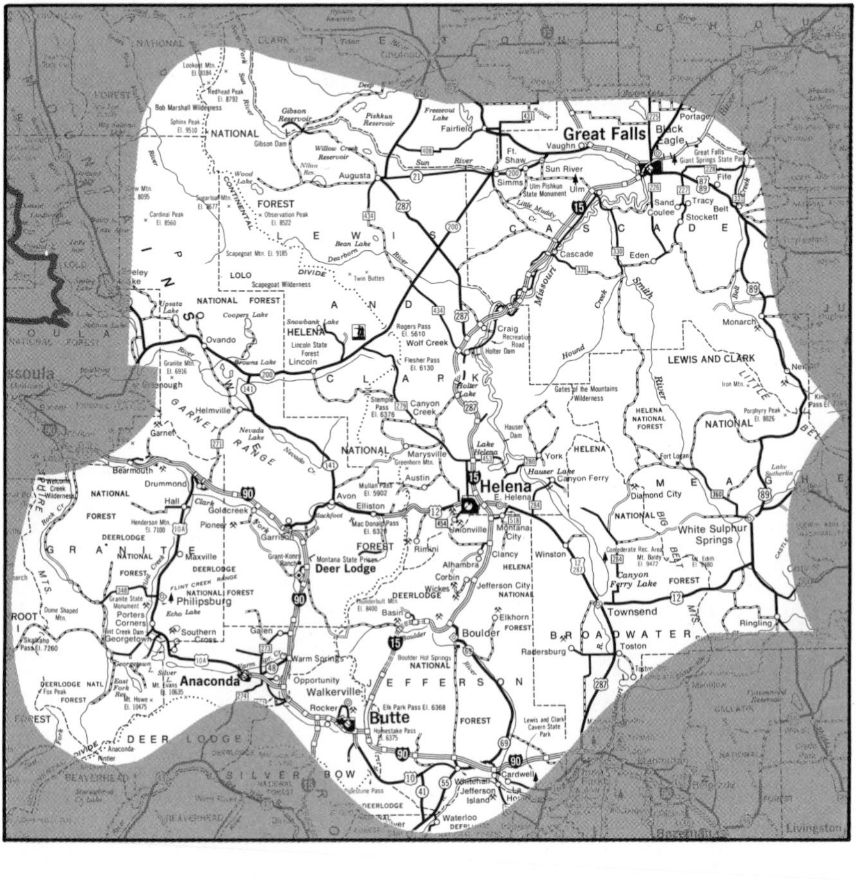

Chapter 6

The Continental Divide Country

The land lying on both sides of the Continental Divide contains prairies, mountains, and river basins, topographical features that make this area of Montana one of the most beautiful in the state. At Cascade, 26 miles south of Great Falls on I-15, you can see a landscape created by the mighty Missouri River, which flows through country studded with buttes and framed by picturesque mountains. Many different Native American peoples have lived in this region over the centuries, hunting the animals that once roamed the prairie.

At the Gates of the Mountains, located off I-15 in the Missouri River Canyon 45 miles south of Cascade, you can see where members of the Lewis and Clark expedition navigated their boats between towering sheer rock cliffs almost 180 years ago. Within a few years, fur traders and mountain men were exploring the Missouri and its rich tributaries for valuable fur-bearing animals.

About 15 miles farther south is Helena, Montana's capital city. In 1864, four prospectors found gold at Last Chance Gulch, beginning a rush that drew miners, entrepreneurs, and capitalists to the new town of Helena. The influences of those people and Helena's wealth would be felt throughout Montana. Evidence of Montana's mining past can be found in almost every gulch in the mountains of this part of Montana. Along I-15 between Helena and Boulder, you can see large piles of mine tailings on the hillsides, mounds of gravel from dredging in the creek bottoms, and mine entrances that were bored into the mountainsides. No matter how pristine the landscape may appear, you can be certain that 19th century prospectors and miners were there.

Some 60 miles south of Helena, in the Rocky Mountains at Elk Park Pass, you cross the Continental Divide before dropping down into the city of Butte, the site of the "Richest Hill on Earth." The mining frenzy at Butte and at many other places in the region transformed Montana's landscape as nothing else had. Miners dug into hillsides, changed hills into vast empty pits, altered stream courses, polluted the air, and left a clutter of tools and machinery.

Much of the land west of the Continental Divide has been shaped by the mining industry. About 26 miles west of Butte on I-90, at the southern end of the Deerlodge Valley, is Anaconda, where the giant Washoe smelter stack dominates the town and the surrounding countryside. The stack and the Berkeley Pit in Butte are symbols of the industrial might of the copper industry and its influence on the state's economy, landscape, and politics. At Philipsburg, about 30 miles west of Anaconda on U.S. Highway 10A, you can still see the twin smokestacks of the Bi-Metallic Mill, which processed the silver and gold ore taken from Granite Mountain.

But mining is not the only activity that has affected the landscape in this part of the state. As early as 1859, stock-growers and farmers settled in the Deerlodge Valley; and during the late 19th and early 20th centuries, others settled in the Prickly Pear, the Missouri, the Broadwater, and the Boulder valleys. These farmers and ranchers found ready markets for their produce and beef in Montana's mining camps, and many prospered. But others found that the land had its limits, and the failed homesteads that you see on the landscape are reminders that agricultural life was not without great risk.

During the last two decades, Montanans have discovered that there are also limits to the region's mineral wealth. Compared to 50 years ago, there are few mines operating in this area. Even in the hills around Butte—where the ore once seemed endless—the mines have shut down. When the Anaconda Company turned off its pumps in the spring of 1982, allowing water to fill its mine shafts and eventually the Berkeley open-pit copper mine, an important era in the mining history of the American West came to an end.

Landscape 15: Mining Along the Continental Divide

Along the interstate highways and on secondary roads, you can see the rims, rock outcroppings, and gulches where valuable minerals were found a century and more ago. You can also see mine tailings, the residue of some of Montana's most productive mines. The operation of both large and small mines, many owned by such industrial magnates as Marcus Daly, William A. Clark, and Samuel T. Hauser, had a powerful and visible effect on the landscape.

There are three parts to this mining landscape. The first includes mining operations in Cascade and Lewis and Clark counties and the route of I-15 from Great Falls to Helena, which follows the tracks of the old Montana Central Railroad. One writer described this route as it passes through the Missouri River Canyon as "a blending of the weird, the grand and the picturesque."

The second section, from Helena to the Continental Divide at Elk Park Pass, is rugged and mountainous. During the 1870s, prospectors found some of Montana's richest silver veins in the hills south of Helena. Important discoveries were also made on the eastern and western slopes of the Boulder Valley, some 35 miles south of Helena.

The third section, from the Continental Divide to Anaconda, includes the "Richest Hill on Earth," the site of the Butte copper mines. One early 20th century writer described the mining activity at Butte:

... shafts were sunk, smelters arose, clouds of sulpher [sic] smoke killed the
last bud and sprig, and the hills stood naked, lean and stripped. . . . [and]
beneath, swimming in a palpitating sea of smoke which filled the bowl of
the valley with opal waves, lay the likeness of the Inferno itself, there tall
chimneys were capped with points of flame; long, lurid, crawling streams
of molten slag burned the heavy darkness into a crimson glow, and, occa-

The Richest Hill on Earth, Butte, Silver Bow County, ca. 1905. *Copper mining in Butte, Montana's most ethnically diverse city, created an industrial landscape with mills, smelters, headframes, and slag dumps.*

N. A. Forsyth, photographer, MHS Photo Archives

sionally, a bright flare of red light, when the slag was dumped, completed a scene of picturesque horror.

From the "weird, the grand and picturesque" to the flames of Hell, this Montana landscape is largely the result of the demands of mining technology.

Route 45: Railroads to the Mines

Route A: Interstate Highway I-15, from Great Falls to Butte
Route B: Interstate Highway I-90, from Butte to Anaconda

During the late 19th century, Montana capitalists were instrumental in building railroads to serve the territory's burgeoning mining industry. The two most important railroads were the Montana Central, which ran from Great Falls to Butte, and the Butte, Anaconda & Pacific, which ran from Butte to Anaconda. You can still see where these railroads cut through the countryside and how miners shaped the landscape.

Route A: Interstate Highway I-15, from Great Falls to Butte

Between Great Falls and Butte on I-15, you can see the route of the Montana Central Railroad, which closely parallels much of the interstate highway. In early 1886, Montana friends of James J. Hill organized the Montana Central, a branch line of the Great Northern, to connect Great Falls with mining and smelting operations at Helena, Wickes, and Butte. The new railroad would also connect with the Utah and Northern Railroad at Butte, giving the Great Northern access to markets in Oregon and California. Marcus Daly, president of the prosperous Anaconda Gold and Silver Mining Company (which would become the Anaconda Mining Company in 1891 and the Anaconda Copper Mining Company in 1895),

C. V. West, photographer, MHS SHPO

Montana Central roadbed, near Basin, Jefferson County. James J. Hill built
Montana Central through difficult terrain, linking Great Falls to Butte. As he told Marcus Daly in 1884, the line will "furnish you all the transportation you want. . . ."

also supported the new line, believing that a new railroad in the Butte market
would increase competition and lower freight rates on the Utah and Northern.

By late 1887, the Montana Central had built from Great Falls to Helena along
the Missouri River. Construction crews had little difficulty building the line until
they reached the Missouri River Canyon, where they had to follow the river's
twisting course and blast several tunnels. The Burlington Northern still uses the
tracks on this part of the route. The Helena-to-Butte portion, however, took the
railroad's crews into more difficult terrain. I-15 between Helena and Butte
follows this section of the Montana Central's line, and you can still see several
railroad tunnels near Basin and the railroad's roadbed, which often appears to
be a gravel road paralleling the highway.

Route B: Interstate Highway I-90, from Butte to Anaconda

In 1892, Marcus Daly closed his mines in Butte and shut down the copper
smelter at Anaconda to dramatize his frustration with the high freight rates he
was forced to pay the Utah and Northern, a branch of the Union Pacific Railroad.

In September of that year, Daly incorporated the Butte, Anaconda & Pacific Railroad; and by New Year's Day 1894, Daly had completed the new line to connect his copper mine at Butte to his Washoe smelter 26 miles to the west at Anaconda. You can follow the route of Daly's line by traveling west from Butte on I-90 for 20 miles to the turnoff for U.S. 10A.

The railroad's primary function was to carry copper ore between Butte and the Washoe smelter, but Daly also used it to carry freight and passengers. In 1913, John Ryan, president of the Anaconda Copper Mining Company, converted the line from steam to electric power, "being the first steam road operating both freight and passenger schedules to electrify its lines purely for reasons of economy." During the 1960s, the Anaconda Company opened a copper ore concentrator near its Berkeley Pit in Butte, and the need for the railroad decreased. In 1967, with less freight on its rails, the railroad switched from electric engines to a few diesel-powered trains.

You can still see the depots built for the Butte, Anaconda & Pacific in Anaconda (at 300 W. Commercial), in Butte (at 823 Utah Avenue), and in Rocker (seven miles west of Butte on I-90). In Anaconda, you can also see the railroad's roundhouses, machine shops, and offices along U.S. Highway 10A.

Route 46: Mining in Cascade County
Route A: U.S. Highway 87/89, at Belt
Route B: Montana Road 227, from U.S. 87/89 to Stockett
Route C: U.S. Highway 89, from Neihart to Monarch
Route D: Montana Road 498 (River Drive), in Great Falls

Cascade County's major coal-mining region is located east of Great Falls along U.S. Highway 87/89 and Montana Road 227. The country between Great Falls and Belt is the beginning of the eastern Montana prairies. On the landscape in this area, you can see many ravines and coulees that hold significant reserves of lignite coal.

Route A: U.S. Highway 87/89, at Belt

Cascade County's most important coal-mining center was the town of Belt, 21 miles east of Great Falls on U.S. Highway 87/89. Coal mining began in Belt in 1876 when John K. Castner opened the first lignite coal mine along Belt Creek, which was named for the visible belt of colored rocks that ran above the creek. He freighted coal in mule-drawn wagons to the steamboats at Fort Benton, a three-day trip in good weather. In 1879, H. W. Millard built the first coke ovens in the vicinity of Belt. During the 1880s, T. C. Power and other businessmen established the Castner Coal and Coke Company in the Belt area; but because of insufficient demand for coal or coke, Power and his partners did not develop the Belt mines.

In the 1890s, agents of Marcus Daly acquired control of the mines, and the high quality of Belt coal convinced Daly to develop the mines as a wholly owned subsidiary of the Anaconda Copper Mining Company. At nearby Belt Creek, the

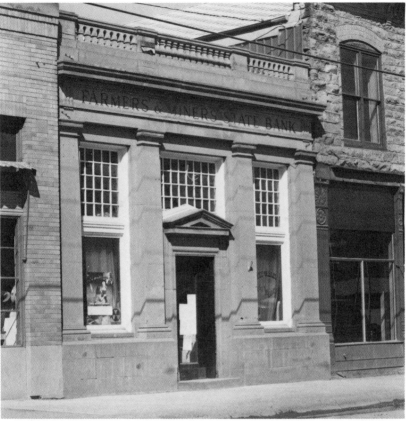

Farmers' & Miners' State Bank, Belt, Cascade County. *When established in 1914, the neoclassical Farmers' and Miners' State Bank in Belt was the only financial institution in the country with this distinctive name.*

company built 100 coke ovens and a large coal washhouse, where powerful streams of water washed away the coal's impurities before it was fired in the ovens. During the process, the heavier impurities would sink to the bottom and the crushed coal would rise to the top, where it could be separated by machine and drained. After it was fired in the ovens, the coke would be shipped on Great Northern branch lines to the mainline and to other mining operations.

Belt developed rapidly during the coal boom. During 1894-1895, over 200 carpenters constructed many of the town's buildings; and by the turn of the century, Belt was Cascade County's second largest city and the Anaconda Copper Mining Company employed about 1,000 workers. Each day, the company shipped over 1,500 tons of coal to its smelters in Anaconda and Great Falls.

The boom ended when Anaconda began buying coal from the rich mines in Wyoming, British Columbia, and Utah. Coal production at Belt declined, even though the mines continued to supply coal for home heating and for the Great

Sand Coulee coal mine, Cascade County. *Part of the reason that Hill decided to build his railroad to Great Falls was because of significant coal deposits found to the east in Sand Coulee and Stockett.*

Northern's engines. In 1913, competition from the Sand Coulee mines further threatened operations at Belt; and aside from a brief boom during World War I, coal mining was no longer the lifeblood of the town. During the 1910s, the homesteading boom brought many farmers to the Belt area, and the town soon became a commercial center for area miners, grain farmers, and cattle ranchers.

The town jail, which is listed in the National Register of Historic Places, is one of the few buildings that remain from Belt's boom years. Built in about 1895 and located near the railroad depot on Castner Street, the 28- by 30-foot jail is a stone structure that now houses a local museum. There are several stone masonry buildings in Belt's small downtown district that were built during the early 20th century. The Farmers' & Miners' State Bank, built in 1914, represents the town's transition from a mining to an agricultural trade center.

Route B: Montana Road 227 from U.S. 87/89 to Stockett

The old coal-mining towns of Sand Coulee and Stockett are located a few miles off U.S. Highway 87/89 on Montana Road 227, five miles west of Great Falls. Along Montana Road 227, you can still see many remnants of the mining era, including coal depressions, filled mine shafts, and deteriorating wooden support structures. In several places, you can also see outcroppings of lignite coal.

The Great Northern Railway developed the Sand Coulee coal mines to provide fuel for its locomotives. Great Northern President James J. Hill, convinced by geological reports that predicted the presence of large coal reserves, claimed the Sand Coulee coal beds and soon constructed a spur to the mines. By the 20th century, the Nelson and the Gerber coal companies were operating at Sand Coulee and the Cottonwood Coal Company had opened mines at Stockett. These

Anaconda Smelter, Great Falls, Cascade County, 1901. *Paris Gibson's vision of an industrial town on the Missouri River was realized when the Anaconda Company built a major smelting works in Great Falls. Hydroelectric power from a dam across the river, the availability of inexpensive coal from nearby mines, and rail connections to national markets made this a premier industrial site.*

Ruins of stack and flume, Anaconda Smelter, Great Falls, Cascade County, 1984. *In 1984, a year after Anaconda closed its smelter at Great Falls, a salvage company destroyed the smelter's enormous smokestack, instantly changing an industrial landscape that had stood as a landmark in Great Falls for over 80 years.*

companies prospered for several years, but changes in technology and the increased use of electric power, diesel fuel, and natural gas made the Sand Coulee and Stockett mines uneconomical to operate. The mines closed during the 1920s and 1930s.

Many original houses and commercial structures remain in Sand Coulee and Stockett, and some are still in use. The old stone jail at Sand Coulee, for example, has been converted into the community's fire hall. There are also some remnants of the railroad tracks that once served this bustling mining area, and local residents still use several of the mines as "wagon" mines, digging out the coal and carrying it home by wagon or truck.

Route C: U.S. Highway 89, from Neihart to Monarch

Some of the coal from Cascade County was shipped to Neihart and Monarch, gold and silver camps nestled high in the Little Belt Mountains. The silver mining center of Neihart, located 36 miles south of Belt on U.S. 89, was founded in 1881-1882. The town and surrounding mines developed slowly, but by 1885 there were about 75 buildings at the camp. "Dwellings are of a primitive nature, small log houses covered with poles and dirt," a reporter noted, "and the place looks for all the world like a new placer camp." There are still some small mines operating in the Neihart area, and you can also see abandoned mine adits, shafts, and headframes.

During 1885-1886, the Hudson Mining Company constructed a large concentrator and smelter at Neihart, fueled with coal from the Belt and Sand Coulee mines. After several lean years, the Neihart mines were infused with new life when a Great Northern branch line was constructed in 1891. The town prospered until silver prices collapsed in 1893. Except for companies who worked the old silver tailings for zinc and lead during World War I, there have been no major operations in Neihart for almost a century.

Monarch, 13 miles north of Neihart on U.S. Highway 89, began as a processing center for the mines in the Little Belt Mountains. Workers at Monarch operated a stone charcoal kiln to produce fuel for smelting operations. After the Great Northern built a branch line to the town in 1890, Monarch became the region's major transportation center. The railroad brought in supplies and coal and coke for the local smelters, and Monarch became a commercial center for the area's miners. With its fortunes so closely tied to the mining industry, Monarch slid into a long period of economic decline after the silver crash of 1893. Today, few buildings remain in Monarch to remind you of its importance in the region's history.

Route D: Montana Road 498 (River Drive), in Great Falls

In 1908, the Anaconda Copper Mining Company built a large reduction works along the Missouri River at Great Falls. The smelter stack was 506 feet high and over 50 feet wide at the top. You can still see the buildings and structures of the Great Falls Reduction Works at the highway historical marker for Black Eagle Falls on Montana Road 498 (River Drive) in Great Falls. You can see the electrolytic zinc plant, the copper wire mill buildings, and the Black Eagle Falls Dam and Powerhouse, which supplied electricity to the industrial complex. The company demolished the smelter stack in the early 1980s, and a salvage company is slowly tearing down the buildings. Most smelter workers lived at Black Eagle, directly northwest of the smelter. Here you can see many of the original company houses, which are now privately owned.

Route 47: Gold and Silver Mining

Route A: Montana Road 279, to Marysville
Route B: Interstate Highway I-15, from Helena to Jefferson City
Route C: Montana Highway 69, from Boulder to Elkhorn
Route D: Interstate Highway I-15, at Basin

Marysville, Wickes and Corbin, Elkhorn, and Basin are four of the region's most important hard-rock mining districts. Revolutionary changes in mining technology that occurred during the 1870s made the mining in these districts a profitable and efficient proposition. The first improvement was compressed air or pneumatic drills, which "sounded like demented woodpeckers" and allowed miners to dig faster and handle dense material. While the new drills increased mine production and the owners' profits, their use affected both the number of miners employed and their health. There were fewer miners working the mines, and those who did often contracted "miner's consumption," caused by the fine silica dust that the new drills pounded out of the ground. During the 1890s, the water-flushed drill was developed, which abated the silica dust hazard.

The second technological innovation was a new explosive, nitroglycerine, which was used to make dynamite. The use of pneumatic drills and dynamite increased production, allowing miners to open new mountain mining areas and making it possible for them to extract relatively low-grade silver and gold ore.

The most important machine at any hard-rock mining complex was the stamp mill. After the Blake crusher had crushed the rocks from the mine into the size of corn kernels, the ore was passed to the stamp mill, which smashed the ore further by dropping heavy metal cylindrical stamps on it. The mills could contain from as few as 5 to 50 stamps or more. The smaller mills were easy and inexpensive to build, easy to repair, and easy to move—perfect for Montana miners. Many mills also had a concentrator, located on a hillside, which separated minerals from the ore by using gravity and water pressure on low-grade mill screenings and stamped ore. Miners used a Frue vanner to concentrate the ore even further before it was sent to the smelters.

At the smelters, which were located in districts that had abundant and high quality ore, the crushed and concentrated ore was fired at very high temperatures that reduced it to molten metal for casting into gold and silver bars. A smelter's most distinguishing feature was its high stack, which made it possible to use the draft caused by prevailing winds to create an extremely hot fire. You can see the remains of smelting complexes at Great Falls, Wickes, Basin, and Anaconda. The smelter in East Helena, part of which was originally built in 1887, is still in operation.

Abandoned stores, Marysville, Lewis and Clark County. *Architectural details on brick buildings in Marysville document the town's boom years—1885-1910—when it was the county's second largest settlement and area mines produced millions of dollars in gold.*

John Smart, photographer, MHS Photo Archives

Route A: Montana Road 279, to Marysville

You can reach Marysville by taking the Lincoln Road exit off I-15 eight miles north of Helena, traveling west on Montana 279 for about seven miles, and then taking a gravel road south for seven more miles. While not a true ghost town—several families still live here—Marysville retains much of the flavor of its mining heyday in an interesting array of residences, commercial buildings, community centers, and mining remnants.

Prospectors first discovered gold along Silver Creek, northeast of Marysville, in the early 1860s and eventually realized over $3 million in gold from these early placer claims. At the Silver Creek diggings, the mining camp of Silver City developed. In later years, after the placers were no longer producing, miners dredged along Silver and Trinity creeks. The tailings from the dredging on Trinity Creek can be seen to the left of the road on the way to Marysville. The discoveries of rich quartz lodes were made on the slopes of the Divide near present-day Marysville.

In 1876, Thomas Cruse staked a claim at what would become the richest mine in the district, the Drumlummon, on the mountainside just east of Marysville. Cruse lacked the capital for a full-scale mining enterprise, so he developed his mine slowly and did not mill ore from the Drumlummon until 1880. Cruse's mill had only five stamps, too few to process the mine's valuable deposits. In 1884, the Montana Company of London, England, purchased the Drumlummon for $1.6 million, and Cruse wisely retained a one-sixth interest in the mine.

Drumlummon Mine, Marysville, Lewis and Clark County, 1894. *The Drumlummon, named by discoverer Thomas Cruse for his native town in Ireland, became the largest gold mine in the Helena area.*

The Montana Company dramatically increased production soon after the purchase when it built a 50-stamp mill, whose stamps weighed 900 pounds each and could strike over 100 blows per minute. A fire in 1971 destroyed the mill, but you can still see its massive foundations to the left off the Marysville Road just before you enter the town. To supply the mill with water, the Montana Company also constructed a large ditch, which roughly parallels the Marysville Road.

By the late 1890s, the Drumlummon's best years were over. By 1909, the Montana Company had sold its property, but the new owners were unable to operate the mine at full capacity, signaling an end to Marysville's mining era.

Marysville's commercial district served not only the Drumlummon workers but miners at Penobscot, Belmont, Gloster, Empire, Shannon, Bell Boy, and Bald Butte mines, which were located along the Divide near the town. Residents built log, wooden-frame, brick, and stone dwellings and shops, and in 1887 the town had over 50 commercial establishments. Today, you can still see the deteriorating hulks of brick, masonry, and frame buildings where miners and townspeople lived and worked. The only business now operated in Marysville is a tavern, which was once the Silver City passenger depot.

Eight miles south of the Lincoln Road exit on I-15 is Helena, Montana's capital city. Located at the center of the western Montana mining landscape, Helena was important to miners, politicians, and merchants as a commercial center. First established in 1864 as a typical boom camp consisting of tents and shacks, Helena had at least 188 businesses by 1866. Today, you can walk along Last Chance Gulch in downtown Helena and see imposing 19th century commercial

Original Governor's Mansion, Helena, Lewis and Clark County. *Built in 1888 as a private residence, the Mansion was the official residence for Montana's governors from 1913 to 1959. In 1981, it became a museum under the care of the Montana Historical Society.*

blocks like the Atlas Block and the Power Block. This section of Helena's downtown is part of the Helena Historic District, which is listed in the National Register of Historic Places. About a mile south of Last Chance Gulch is the Grizzly Gulch Road, which takes you to the ruins of the Grizzly Gulch kilns, a reminder that Helena was an important mining center throughout the 19th century.

Route B: Interstate Highway I-15, from Helena to Jefferson City

Between Helena and Jefferson City on I-15, you can see one of the earliest and most important mining landscapes in Montana. In 1863-1864, the area's first gold rush took place in Montana City, six miles southwest of Helena on Montana Road 518; and in 1865, prospectors struck gold at Clancy, 10 miles south of Helena on I-15. A mile south of Clancy on the east side of I-15, entrepreneurs established the Alhambra Hot Springs in 1865. Alhambra was a popular hot springs resort until 1959, when fire destroyed it and local residents were able to save only "a piano and a little beer." The Hillbrook Nursing Home now stands at the site of the resort.

About six miles south of Clancy is Jefferson City, which was established in 1864 by four prospectors. Nathaniel Merriman, John Radcliff, Allen Axe, and Phil Sheenan were on their way from Virginia City to the new boom town of Helena

Remains of concentrator, Corbin, Jefferson County. *The heart of the mining complex at Corbin was a sizable concentrator that processed ore from nearby mines. The concentrator burned down in 1900.*

when they discovered the rich Gregory lode, and soon their camp experienced a boom of its own. West of Jefferson City, you can see placer mine tailings from the Gregory and other mines in the area.

Silver mining began at Wickes in 1877 when a group of capitalists, led by William W. Wickes of New York City, formed the Montana Company and constructed a mining complex about four miles southwest of Jefferson City. Soon thereafter, a disastrous fire at the reduction plant crippled the company's operations, and Samuel T. Hauser, who owned the Helena Mining and Reduction Company, purchased both the Montana Company's and other companies' mines and processing machinery in the Wickes district.

One of the stacks that was built in 1881 still stands at the site of the smelter reduction works at Wickes. When Hauser's company moved a large part of the complex to East Helena in 1889, it left behind three smokestacks, one of which you can still see at Wickes. You can also see the remains of the charcoal kilns that once produced the smelter's fuel. Stone foundations for one of the two concentrators of the Helena Mining and Reduction Company stand along the road that connects Wickes and Corbin. The concentrator no longer exists, but the location of the foundations indicates that it was gravity-based. The "works on the side of the hill are very advantageous for the purposes for which they are employed," the *Helena Weekly Herald* reported in 1884, "as offering descents by gravity, and at the end of the operation almost every trace of the mineral has been eliminated" from the stamped ore. The concentrator handled 125 tons of ore every day. In 1888, the Montana Central built a high, wooden trestle at Corbin and a 3,481-foot-long tunnel with heavy iron doors at Wickes as part of the line that would connect Great Falls and Butte. In 1902, the railroad built a new steel trestle, which the Burlington Northern used until 1982.

Northeast of Wickes is the Alta Mine, which produced most of the silver and lead for the Helena Mining and Reduction Company. Connected to the smelter at Wickes and the concentrators at Corbin by a Northern Pacific spur line, the Alta Mine produced over 350,000 tons of ore before it was closed in 1957. Northwest of Wickes is the Gregory Mine complex. First discovered during the 1860s, the claim was not fully developed until Hauser's Helena Mining and Reduction Company gained control of the property. The Gregory is considered to be the first silver mine in the territory, and Montana's second oldest smelter was built there in 1867. In 1884, Hauser built a concentrator near the mine to increase production; and in 1886, its top production year, miners extracted over half a million dollars worth of silver from the Gregory.

The 1893 depression shut down most of the mines in the Wickes-Corbin district. Smaller companies have attempted to revive the mines over the years, but none have met with success.

Route C: Montana Highway 69, from Boulder to Elkhorn

Boulder, located 11 miles south of Jefferson City on I-15, began as a mining camp in 1862. Boulder is the county seat of Jefferson County, and two important buildings survive from its early years: the 1889 courthouse and the Old Administration Building at the Montana Deaf and Dumb Asylum (now known as the Boulder River School and Hospital). John Paulsen, a German-trained architect who lived in Helena and was famous for his "richly textured, skillfully ornamented structures," designed both buildings, which are listed in the National Register of Historic Places.

Three miles south of Boulder on Montana Highway 69 is the Boulder Hot Springs Hotel, another Jefferson County building listed in the National Register of Historic Places. The hotel dates to 1883 and represents an early period of the tourism industry in Montana. Over the past century, the hotel's various owners have adopted new architectural styles to maintain the resort's appeal to tourists, so the building's appearance has been changed several times. From 1888 to 1891, a new wooden-frame building with a stone masonry foundation replaced the original hotel. Built in the Queen Anne architectural style and covered with white clapboard siding, the new hot springs hotel was L-shaped and featured gable roofs and many double-hung sash windows. The northwest corner of the structure contained a four-story bell tower with a spire, and a balcony extending from nearly every window of the tower. Balconies were also prominent on the hotel's second and third floors, and a long veranda surrounded the first floor.

During 1909-1910, the veranda was extended to connect a second addition to the main part of the hotel. By this time, Queen Anne architecture was no longer in vogue, and the owners remodeled the hotel in the Spanish Colonial Revival style. They added curved dormer windows and placed pressed-iron coping on the end walls. The hotel's massive, castle-like appearance is the result of these modifications. During this remodeling, workers added stucco to the outside walls and a balloon roof to the bell tower, giving the building an overwhelming facade. The Boulder Hot Springs Hotel is one of the best examples of Spanish Colonial Revival architecture in Montana.

Lambert Florin, photographer, MHS Photo Archives

Elkhorn, Jefferson County. *The silver-mining boom at Elkhorn attracted thousands of workers: Irish miners, Italian and Austrian smelter workers, and Norwegian and French wood-cutters.*

If you travel 3.5 miles south of Boulder Hot Springs on Montana Highway 69 and then 12 miles north on the Elkhorn Road, you will reach Elkhorn, a mining ghost town. The road is often impassable during the winter, so stop in Boulder and ask about road conditions.

In 1872, Anton Holter, a Helena merchant who had formed the Elkhorn Mining Company, purchased the area's first claims, which were discovered by Peter Wys in the late 1860s. Holter built a five-stamp wet crushing mill nearby and laid out the Elkhorn town. For 10 years, Elkhorn miners extracted as much silver ore as the mill could handle. In 1883, after production had increased dramatically, Holter reorganized the company, acquired new capital, and built a 10-stamp mill. In that year alone, the mines produced almost $200,000 in silver bullion.

Six years later, a group of English capitalists bought the Elkhorn property, and the mine had its best years from then until the collapse of the silver market in 1893. A government official estimated that over $14 million in silver was removed from the mines before the silver bust. Soon after, the English investors sold their interest in the Elkhorn property. There have been several more recent attempts to reopen the district, but none have succeeded.

You can still see several significant historic structures at Elkhorn. On the northern outskirts of the town, you can see the remains of the Elkhorn stamp mill. Signs identify several extant buildings and the locations of commercial buildings that have been razed. The two most prominent buildings that remain are Gillian Hall and Fraternity Hall. The first floor of Gillian Hall was a saloon, and dances were held on the second floor. Fraternity Hall, which is listed in the National Register of Historic Places, was Elkhorn's social and architectural showplace and one of the best examples in the West of a neoclassical-style facade on a mining building. Constructed in the early 1890s, this balloon-frame building measures about 28 by 72 feet and has a stone foundation.

The buildings and other remnants of mining operations at Elkhorn and at other mining camps are very fragile. Do not enter the buildings or mining adits. It is often very dangerous, and in many cases it is illegal. People walking through such historic structures have unknowingly destroyed many of Montana's priceless artifacts.

Route D: Interstate Highway I-15, at Basin

You can find the town of Basin by taking the Basin exit nine miles southwest of Boulder on I-15. As in Marysville, placer miners were the first to work the Basin district, and among the earliest miners were Granville Stuart, James Stuart, and Reece Anderson who worked claims along Cataract Creek, a tributary of the Boulder River.

The first quartz claim in the area was made in 1864, but no one hit a paying claim until 1877 when Michael O'Donnell discovered the Katie and Hope mines. O'Donnell developed the mines over the next two years, and Basin's mining boom began. In 1880, John Allport developed placer mines along Basin Creek, and in 1881 William H. Nichols laid out a town plan. Soon a stagecoach line connected the bustling community to Butte, and developers moved a 20-stamp mill from Montana City to process Basin's ore.

Basin grew slowly during the 1880s and survived the silver bust of 1893. By the turn of the century, Basin began to develop into an urban landscape in an isolated mining setting. The town's businesses supplied local miners with the commercial services of a modern city; and when the Montana Central Railroad built through in the late 1880s, Basin had the benefit of rail connections. You can see the Montana Central's roadbed west of the interstate highway.

Several buildings constructed at the turn of the century remain in Basin. In the middle of town is the Sockerson Block, a two-story, red brick structure built in 1896 that has been a rooming house, a bar, and a barber shop. The grade school, built in 1895 and located a few blocks north of Main Street, is a two-story wooden-plank building with Victorian architectural influences. This building is one of the more impressive small-town schools in the state. Near the center of town is the jail, a stone building with a wood and tin roof that was built from local materials in 1899. The railroad delivered the jail's iron bars from Baltimore.

In 1903, a fire destroyed two-thirds of the town, so most of the buildings you see today in Basin were built after that time. The Masonic Hall, which prominently displays the Masonic symbol on its facade, is a two-story brick building constructed in 1903. The Merry Widow Mine headquarters, built in 1913, is a good example of wooden false-front architecture. The rebuilt town served a thriving mining industry until the 1920s.

On both sides of I-15, you can see the mine shafts and adits of several mining operations. Overlooking Basin on a hillside to the north are the remains of the Glass Brothers' smelter, which was constructed in 1903. This red brick smelter still dominates the countryside, just as it did 80 years ago.

Located in the mountains that surround Basin is a complex of three mines: the Comet, the Gray Eagle, and the Morning Glory. These mines kept Basin an active commercial center throughout the first half of the 20th century. All three sites are on private property, and mining is still being done at Comet. These mines are not open to the public. Do not trespass.

Route 48: Copper Mining in Butte and Anaconda
Interstate Highway I-90, from Butte to Anaconda

Butte, nestled in the Rockies at an altitude of 5,767 feet, is perhaps the best place to explore Montana's mining past. Located 29 miles south of Basin on I-15, the city had its beginnings in placer strikes during the 1860s and silver mining during the 1870s. But copper mining has really shaped this landscape. If you look to your right as you descend into the valley on I-15 from the north, you will see the Berkeley open-pit mine, a massive excavation carved out of the mountains at the city's east end.

Butte's copper era began in 1880-1881 when Marcus Daly purchased the Anaconda Mine for $30,000. With backing from a group of San Francisco capitalists, Daly began mining the Anaconda in 1881, and his workers began building the 8- by 20-foot shaft into what would eventually become the "Richest Hill on Earth."

At first, the Anaconda produced silver, but after drilling for 300 feet, the miners struck copper—lots of rich copper sulphide ore. With more money from his San Francisco backers, Daly purchased the surrounding mines, the St. Lawrence and the Neversweat. From 1882 to 1884, Daly shipped 37,000 tons of copper ore (some of it with over 50 per cent copper) to eastern and foreign smelters. Shipping costs were high, so in 1884 Daly decided to build a smelter nearby. About 25 miles northwest of Butte, Daly constructed his reduction works along Warm Springs Creek in adjacent Deer Lodge County. He then designed the town of Anaconda to house the construction workers and future employees of the smelter.

When the Anaconda Reduction Works began operations in 1884, it was considered to be one of the most magnificent structures of the western mining landscape. It had the territory's largest concentrator and the world's largest copper smelter, which could handle about 500 tons of copper ore a day. The ruins of the original Anaconda smelter, which contained 60 reverberatory roasting and matte furnaces along with two 70-ton blast furnaces, is located along Warm Springs Creek on the north side of the town.

The reduction works created significant air pollution in southern Deer Lodge County, where the smelter's smoke hung in the air, killing nearby foliage and damaging agricultural land. When the company decided to build the Washoe smelter in 1902, it chose a site on the other side of Warm Springs Creek on the south side of Anaconda, where the prevailing winds from the west could better disperse the smoke. But the company negated the benefit of the new location by constructing a 225-foot-high stack, which increased the volume of smoke released into the atmosphere. The noxious smelter dust and residues worsened

Washoe Stack, Anaconda, Deer Lodge County. *Tom Dickson remembered his work at the smelter: "you wore rubber gloves and a gauze mask, because of the fumes [of] hydrogen [but] there had to be something else in there, because it would corrode your teeth. Would eat your teeth out."*

and severely affected the livestock and agriculture of southern Deer Lodge County. The Deer Lodge Farmer's Association reported that thousands of animals died in 1902-1903 because of the poisonous smoke.

In 1903, Anaconda increased the height of the Washoe smelter stack to 300 feet, which again increased the level of pollution in the southern Deerlodge Valley. Area farmers lacked the financial means to contest the mighty copper company, and even the urgings of the federal government and the personal intervention of President Theodore Roosevelt failed to halt the smelter's continued pollution. By this time, the pollution had adversely affected hundreds of acres of national forest land.

In 1918, the Alphonis Custodis Chimney Construction Company built the smelter stack that you see today at Anaconda. The stack is 585 feet high, 60 feet wide at the top, and has an interior diameter at the base of 75 feet. The stack has the largest volume of any in the world; and when it was in full operation, it released three to four million cubic feet of gas per minute. Anaconda claimed that the new stack would solve the air pollution problems; but even with sophisticated pollution control devices, the stack never met federal or state clean air standards. During the 1920s and early 1930s, Anaconda officials negotiated transfers of adjacent federal lands for company property in other sections of the state, and it bought out most of the ranches and farms that had suffered pollution damage.

F. J. Haynes, photog., Haynes Fdn. Coll., MHS

W. A. Clark Mansion, Butte, Silver Bow County, 1890. *Copper Baron William A. Clark built this 30-room, 3-story brick mansion in 1888 at a cost of $260,000. The mansion is now a museum open to the public.*

C. V. West, photographer

Berkeley Pit, Butte, Silver Bow County. *The Anaconda Company developed its enormous open-pit mine on the site of Meaderville, an Italian community east of Butte that was noted for its entertainment district. Mining has ceased in the pit, and toxic water from Butte's deep mines is now filling this 1,800-foot-deep gash on the Butte landscape.*

You can still see the effects of years of pollution in the scarcity of trees and stunted tree growth in the area around the smelter.

The expansion of the smelter after the turn of the century was the result of the company's domination of the world's copper industry. By the mid 1880s, the Anaconda had become the most productive copper mine in the U.S., producing over 50 million pounds of copper in 1887 alone. During the 1890s, the owners purchased several other mining properties in Montana and built the Butte, Anaconda & Pacific Railroad, which linked Butte and Anaconda. The company also created the Butte City Water Company; invested in coal mines in Wyoming and in Park, Cascade, and Carbon counties; and purchased the Big Blackfoot Milling Company at Bonner to provide a stable supply of lumber. At the turn of the century, as one historian wrote, the Anaconda Copper Mining Company "loomed over Butte, and over Montana itself, like a monstrous leviathan whose every twist and lurch became a life and death concern."

During the first decade of the 20th century, the copper mines on the "Richest Hill on Earth" reached new production levels after the Amalgamated Copper Company had bought the Anaconda Copper Mining Company and other Butte copper mines. In 1908, the company built a new reduction works at Great Falls. In 1910, the officials and stockholders of the companies that comprised the Amalgamated Copper Company voted to become a single corporation, the Anaconda Copper Mining Company, nearly establishing a monopoly in the copper industry. From 1910 to 1940, Anaconda converted old machinery and installed technologically advanced equipment; by World War II, Butte copper production had soared to record levels.

By the 1950s, the high-grade ore at Butte had been mined and activity began to shift away from the deep mines. The huge headframes you see in Butte today are visible remnants of those mines that were drilled over a mile deep into Butte Hill. Over the years, the company had built over 100 steel headframes, ranging from the 70-foot-high Orphan Girl to the 178-foot-high frame at the Kelley No. 1 mine shaft. Today, 13 headframes dot the Butte landscape. Headframes are derrick-like structures constructed above the main mine shaft to house machinery that lifted miners and ore to the surface. You can still see the Kelley headframe on Copper Street (off Wyoming Street) in Butte.

In the mid 1950s, Anaconda company officials decided to open a new mine on Butte Hill. Instead of a deep mine, Anaconda proposed its first open-pit strip mine on the site of Meaderville, a small community on Butte's east side. Promising decades of continued prosperity and additional mining employment, Anaconda persuaded the residents of Meaderville to move to another part of Butte.

The Berkeley Mine began production in July 1955. Miners stripped the low-grade ore from the surface, using huge power shovels. For every ton of ore, which might contain no more than .8 per cent copper, miners dug three tons of rock, sometimes stripping as much as 50,000 tons a day. You can see the Berkeley Pit—which is 7,000 feet long, 5,500 feet wide, and 1,800 feet deep—and the concentrator complex, built in 1963 on the edge of the mine, by taking the Continental Drive exit off I-90.

During the 1970s, the Anaconda Company experienced some economic set-backs when low zinc and manganese prices forced the company to curtail operations in Great Falls and when the government of Chile nationalized the company's profitable copper mines there in 1972. To raise cash to pay short-term debts, the company sold its Bonner lumber operations to Champion International. In 1977, Atlantic Richfield (ARCO) bought the Anaconda Company; but by the 1980s, copper mining at Butte had come to a standstill. ARCO, claiming that the Butte operations were no longer profitable, permanently closed the Washoe smelter, ceased mining in the Berkeley Pit, and turned off the pumps in the Butte deep mines. The "Richest Hill on Earth" began filling with water. The days were over when the Anaconda Copper Mining Company controlled the destiny of thousands of workers in Montana and in other parts of the world.

Landscape 16: The Deerlodge Valley and the Garnet Mountain Range

Traveling southeast on I-90 from Drummond to Anaconda, you will pass through some of the best agricultural country in the Northwest. The Deerlodge Valley is a wide expanse of rich soil, watered by Warm Springs Creek and the Clark Fork and Little Blackfoot rivers. "Deerlodge" comes from the Shoshoni phrase *it-soc'ke en car'ne*, which means "white-tailed deer's lodge." At one time, thousands of deer populated the valley; and although their numbers have diminished over time, you can still spot deer in the relatively undeveloped areas of the valley. In 1831, fur trader Warren Ferris described the valley's resources:

This is a valley somewhat larger than the Big Hole, and like that surrounded by mountains, generally, however low, barren and naked, except to the south and east where lofty snow-clad peaks appear. All the streams . . . are decorated with groves and thickets of aspen, birch and willow, and occasional clusters of currant and gooseberry bushes. The bottoms are rich and verdant, and are resorted to by great numbers of deer and elk. The several streams unite and form "La Riviere des pierres a fleches" [Arrow Stone River, now known as Flint Creek], thus named for a kind of semi-transparent stone found near it. . . . This river is one of the sources of Clark's River, and flows through the valley to the north[west].

For centuries, this landscape of rich grasses, plentiful water, thick stands of trees, and deposits of precious minerals has attracted and sustained both Indians and white settlers.

Route 49: Ranching in the Deerlodge Valley

Route A: Interstate Highway I-90, from Garrison to Deer Lodge
Route B: Montana Road 141, from Avon to Helmville

Even before prospectors discovered gold at Bannack and Virginia City, there were cattle ranchers in the Deerlodge Valley. Today, at the site of the John Grant ranch near Garrison, the Grant-Kohrs Ranch in Deer Lodge, and the old Fitz-patrick Ranch near Helmville, you can see the topography and natural resources that attracted Montana's ranchers to the Deerlodge country.

Route A: Interstate Highway I-90, from Garrison to Deer Lodge

John Grant, one of the earliest stock-growers in Montana, built two log cabins at the confluence of the Little Blackfoot and Clark Fork rivers in 1859 and became the first permanent settler in the Deerlodge Valley. You can see a monument that marks the site at the westbound I-90 exit for Garrison. Grant raised a small herd of cattle and carried on a brisk trade with Native Americans who traveled through the Deerlodge country. In 1862, he built a new home at Cottonwood (present-day Deer Lodge), 10 miles south of his original cabin. Grant's new two-story home had 28 glass windows and was built from lumber hauled by ox team from the mill at St. Ignatius Mission in the lower Flathead Valley, over 100 miles to the north.

During the early 1860s, when thousands of people were traveling through the valley on their way to the Bannack and Virginia City goldfields, Grant made enormous profits by selling cattle to the miners at very high prices. He made even more money by trading his herd of 2,000 horses at Salt Lake City for flour, which he promptly sold to Montana's hungry miners. By the mid 1860s, Grant was probably one of the territory's richest citizens.

In 1866, Grant sold all of his property, including "farmhouses with household furniture, stables, corrals, ricks of hay, all my farming implements, wagons, yokes and chains. . . . also my cattle, sheep, goats and grain" to Conrad Kohrs, who became one of the fathers of the open-range stock-growing business in Montana. The purchase price was $19,200.

While his half-brother John Bielenberg managed the ranch's daily affairs, Conrad Kohrs became a cattle baron. Kohrs began experimenting in 1871 when he went to Illinois to buy a herd of shorthorn cattle, which he later bred in the Deerlodge Valley. Because of his success as a stockbreeder, his herd was strong enough to survive the terrible winter of 1886-1887. In 1890, Kohrs introduced Hereford cattle to the Montana plains. He also joined with several partners in 1867 to construct the 13-mile-long Rock Creek ditch, which was initially constructed to supply water to the placer mines at Pioneer (near Gold Creek) and later served as an agricultural water supply.

By the 1890s, the Kohrs ranch covered some 25,000 acres and shipped at least 8,000 head of cattle each year, a level of stock production it maintained from 1888 to 1913. In one year alone, Kohrs's cattle filled 365 boxcars. Conrad Kohrs died in 1920, but the ranch stayed in family hands until the early 1970s.

The Grant-Kohrs Ranch is the best place in Montana to see a stock-growing operation. The National Park Service began administering this working ranch in 1972, and it conducts year-round tours of the ranch house and outbuildings.

Route B: Montana Road 141, from Avon to Helmville

North of the Deerlodge Valley and along the drainage of Nevada Creek along Montana Road 141, you can see another area that is important to Montana's

C. V. West, photographer, MHS SHPO

Main Street, Helmville, Powell County. *One long-time resident regretted how times have changed in Helmville: "Why we don't even have the Sunday fights we used to. 15 fights! Best Sunday we had."*

ranching history. At the eastern end of the Nevada Creek Reservoir near mile marker 17, you can see the historic Fitzpatrick Ranch on the south side of the highway. The ranch has an excellent location, tucked between the slopes of Buffalo Gulch, which protects the buildings from harsh winds. The ranch is listed in the National Register of Historic Places and is on private property. Do not trespass.

Jimmy Isbel, a prospector, built the first log cabin here in 1872, and 13 years later he sold his houses to J. F. Fitzpatrick. In the beginning, Fitzpatrick and his family did little ranching, but their place became the community center for an increasing number of Nevada Creek ranchers. The Fitzpatrick home was a stage stop and the local post office, and Fitzpatrick was the postmaster for "Isbel, Montana Territory." In 1899, he would be elected to the state legislature.

In 1890, Fitzpatrick patented his homesteading claim, and within two years he had built a substantial two-story log home. During the 1890s, he built a large wooden-frame barn, a wooden-frame chicken house, and a frame storage shed. He also added siding and two gable-ended frame additions to the 1892 log home, making it into a fashionable "L-shaped" Victorian house for his wife and 14 children.

The Fitzpatricks sold the ranch in 1917 and moved to California. Different families have lived on the property since, but the ranch still retains its turn-of-the-century appearance. Isbel's 1872 log cabin, which Fitzpatrick altered to serve as a dwelling and a post office, still stands, as does a log dairy barn, a smaller storage barn, and all of the buildings from the 1890s except for the wooden-frame barn.

Between the Fitzpatrick Ranch and Helmville on Montana Road 141, you can see several barns that date to the early years of settlement along Nevada Creek. In Helmville, you can see several historic barns. Some have gable roofs with the logs joined by saddle or V-notching, and some have gambrel roofs with square notching—two styles that may derive from the ethnic origins of the early settlers. Germans usually constructed gambrel-roof barns with square notched logs, and the Irish usually built gable-roof barns with saddle or V-notching.

Route 50: Mining in the Deerlodge Country
Route A: Montana Road 141, from Helmville to Avon
Route B: Interstate Highway I-90, at Gold Creek
Route C: Garnet Range Road, from Montana Highway 200 to Garnet

As you return to Avon from Helmville, traveling on Montana 141, you can look to the north and see the Garnet Mountain Range. From the prehistoric period until the 1940s, precious stones and metals were mined in the mountains' high peaks and foothills. For centuries, Native Americans mined valuable rocks along Nevada Creek; during the late 1850s, prospectors discovered the first gold in Montana at Gold Creek; and at the turn of the century, there were thriving boom towns at Coloma and Garnet.

Route A: Montana Road 141, from Helmville to Avon
The first people to mine the precious stones of the Garnet Mountains were the Native Americans who made the Deerlodge country their home hundreds of years ago. In the foothills of the mountains, which rise above Nevada Creek to the south of Montana Road 141, the Indians mined blue-black chert, basalt, and the extremely valuable Avon chert. For thousands of years during the summer and early fall, Indians mined rock outcroppings in the area to make tools and arrowheads. As technology advanced, the prehistoric Indians were able to exploit the outcroppings to a greater degree. The pits they dug left an altered landscape, which archaeologists have identified as one of the most important Native American mining sites in Montana.

Route B: Interstate Highway I-90, at Gold Creek
The first verified gold strike by whites in Montana was in 1858 near Gold Creek, eight miles west of Garrison on I-90. There is some evidence, however, that gold was discovered here as early as 1852 by Francois Finlay, a French-Canadian fur trapper who worked for the Hudson's Bay Company. The company apparently hushed up Finlay's discovery because it feared that a gold rush would ruin the fur trade. If you take the gravel road southwest from the town of Gold Creek, you will see the remains of years of mining in this district, marked by ditches, abandoned equipment, and huge piles of placer tailings on both sides of Gold Creek.

In 1858, James and Granville Stuart and Reece Anderson discovered gold at Gold Creek. They began mining here three years later; and by the early 1860s, hundreds of merchants, miners, and prospectors had come to the district. In 1865-1867, the town of Pioneer was settled along Gold Creek, with a population of from 800 to 1,000 people.

Within 10 years, the Gold Creek claims had yielded over $20 million in gold. Once the richest deposits had been mined, however, most white miners moved on to other gold strikes; and during the early 1880s, Tim Lee, a Chinese miner, bought up most of the Pioneer claims. Throughout the 1880s, Lee employed over 800 Chinese miners to rework the placer claims at Gold Creek. The Chinese produced enough gold to interest a group of English capitalists, who formed the Gold Creek Mining Company Limited and bought Lee's property in 1890.

The new company used heavy machinery and hydraulic nozzles and hoses to mine the district. Most of the mining scars and piles of placer tailings you see today at Pioneer are a result of the hydraulicking. Mining continued at Pioneer throughout the early 20th century, and by as late as 1939 Pioneer mines were producing $1 million in gold.

Route C: Garnet Range Road, from Montana Highway 200 to Garnet

The Garnet/Coloma mining district was the most important mining area in the Deerlodge country. You can reach Garnet, which was one of the last Montana mining boom towns and is one of the best preserved ghost towns, by leaving Montana Highway 200 at the Garnet Range Road, 9.6 miles west of the junction of Montana 83 and 200. About 12 miles up this gravel road is the sign for Garnet. The ghost town is located approximately one mile farther, through the forest on an unimproved road.

The BLM manages the ghost town, providing protection for the town's buildings, and together with the Garnet Preservation Society it hires a year-round caretaker. At about 5 miles and again at 10 miles along the Garnet Range Road, you can look to the left and see the beautiful Blackfoot Valley and the Mission Mountains in the distance.

Mining began in the Garnet Mountains during the fall of 1865, when prospectors uncovered rich gold deposits in Bear Gulch, near present-day Bearmouth on the Clark Fork River. Within weeks, miners had arrived in the area by the thousands, and Beartown was established. To move the huge boulders that covered the rich ground, miners cut down pine trees, shaped them into levers, and rolled the boulders away. The rich placers only lasted for a short time, but prospectors continued to mine the Beartown placers into the 1880s. For the most part, however, those who remained were "family men" who had made their permanent homes in the foothills.

The biggest obstacle to developing the area's mineral deposits was the absence of good roads. The first crude wagon road to the Beartown area was not built until 1878-1879, when the mines were connected to the Mullan Road. During the early 1880s, however, the Northern Pacific Railroad built through the area, solving the region's transportation problems and providing an efficient way to ship the mined ore. The railroad's presence meant that miners could develop quartz lodes that had been discovered at Beartown during the 1860s and 1870s.

Garnet, Granite County. *From its beginnings in 1896, Garnet grew rapidly and had over 1,000 residents by 1898. Today, it is one of Montana's best preserved ghost towns.*

Not until the 1890s, however, did outside capitalists and hard-rock miners turn their attention to the Garnets.

Large-scale quartz mining began in 1894-1895, when the owners of the Mammoth and Comet mines directed the construction of a 10-stamp mill about 10 miles north of Beartown in First Chance Gulch. During the summer of 1895, more gold mines were opened, and Dr. A. H. Mitchell constructed another large stamp mill in the gulch. Near the mill, Mitchell laid out the town of Mitchell, which later became Garnet. Mitchell also built a road connecting the railroad, Garnet, and Coloma, which had been founded in the spring of 1895 about four miles east of Garnet. You can still see Coloma's abandoned log and plank buildings just off the Garnet Range Road.

The Garnet mines were most prosperous at the turn of the century, when nearly 1,000 people lived in Garnet. A major fire destroyed much of the town in 1911, but Garnet briefly came to life again in the 1930s after gold prices doubled. When dynamite prices dramatically increased during World War II, mining low-grade ore became unprofitable and the town was soon abandoned.

The 50 extant buildings at Garnet exhibit a range of construction techniques, materials, and architectural styles. The log buildings usually have log foundations and dirt or wooden-plank floors. The miners used local clay deposits to chink between each log and made the roofs of corrugated metal, wooden shingles, or asphalt-based coverings. A few buildings feature board-and-batten construction, with either no foundation or a foundation made of rubble stone or wood. Garnet miners and storeowners did not build wooden-frame structures until the 20th century, and most of those buildings were constructed with rough-sawn lumber.

High school, Philipsburg, Granite County. *This school, which still serves the people of Granite County, was constructed in 1911 at a cost of $28,000.*

C. V. West, photographer, MHS SHPO

Bi-Metallic Mill, Philipsburg, Granite County, 1888. *The Granite Mountain and Bi-Metallic lode, which fed the Bi-Metallic Mill, was one of the world's most productive silver-mining operations. In 1890, the mines produced over 4 million ounces of silver.*

MHS Photo Archives

The most impressive building in Garnet is the three-story J. K. Wells Hotel, which has a wooden post foundation. The rubble stones that you see on the building's foundation merely closed the crawl space between the ground and the first floor.

When you visit Garnet, stop at the Garnet Preservation Society at Ole's Tavern for more information about the town and its buildings. While at Garnet and Coloma, do not enter any mine adits or closed buildings and do not remove any material from the town or the surrounding mines.

Landscape 17: The Pintler Scenic Route

One of the most popular roads in Montana is the Pintler Scenic Route on U.S. Highway 10A. On this 65-mile-long road, you can see some of the state's most striking scenery, from the beauty of the Flint Creek bottomlands to the spectacular views of the Pintler and Flint Creek ranges and Georgetown and Silver lakes. This road also takes you near an area where miners discovered some of Montana's most valuable gold and silver deposits a century ago: the mining districts at Cable, Georgetown, Philipsburg, and Granite.

Route 51: Mining in the Granite Mountains
U.S. Highway 10A, from Anaconda to Philipsburg

Along the east side of U.S. Highway 10A between Anaconda and Georgetown, you will see many mine dumps, depressions, adits, and abandoned mills, especially in the Silver Lake area. Prospectors struck placer gold at Georgetown in 1865. East of Georgetown, at Cable, the Atlantic Cable Mine was the area's largest strike, and legend has it that pure gold ore was discovered here. Southern Cross, just a mile north of Georgetown in the Deerlodge National Forest, is the site of the last major strike in the area. Between Georgetown and Silver lakes, you can see the Gold Coin mill, a 10-stamp mill that processed low-grade gold ore mined in the mountains to the south.

The center of mining history in the Pintler Mountains is at Philipsburg, the county seat of Granite County, located 14 miles north of Georgetown. North of Philipsburg are several old mining dumps and depressions. High on Granite Mountain, about five miles southeast of Philipsburg, is the Granite State Monument, which commemorates what was once the silver capital of Montana. The dirt road to the monument, which is open only during the summer, is narrow and extremely hazardous.

In 1875, James W. Estill, Eli D. Holland, and Josiah M. Merrell discovered Granite's first quartz lode, but they lacked the money to develop the claim. They sold the mine to Charles D. McClure of the Hope Mining Company; and in 1881, he and Charles Clark, his brother-in-law, and several other St. Louis businessmen formed the Granite Mountain Mining Company.

After a year of drilling, the company struck a lode of silver ore, which they first milled at the Hope mill in Philipsburg and later at the Algonquin mill, which was not far from town. By late 1884, however, the Granite company had opened its own 20-stamp mill. As silver prices rose and the mines increased production, the new mill suddenly had more ore than it could handle, and in 1886 McClure directed the construction of a 40-stamp mill. By 1890, the mills had used up all of the surrounding timber, so McClure approved the construction of a 100-stamp mill at Flint Creek Gulch.

In 1882, McClure had paid $1,800 for the Bi-Metallic Mine, a sister mine to the Granite. Four years later, he and his partners had sold the Bi-Metallic to a new corporation, the Bi-Metallic Mining Company. Even though the two mines were located next to each other and were owned by the same people, the Granite Mountain and Bi-Metallic companies operated the mines separately, each with their own workers, superintendents, and offices.

The Granite and Bi-Metallic companies prospered until the spring of 1891, when silver prices began to fall. Within two years, company stock that once sold for $50 a share interested few buyers at $1 a share. In July 1893, the Granite Mountain Mining Company ceased operations. The Bi-Metallic Mine remained open for several years, but on a limited scale. After the depression of 1893-1896, McClure and his St. Louis partners reopened both mines as the Granite-BiMetallic Consolidated Mining Company, but silver prices were too low to sustain large-scale mining. In 1907, Granite-BiMetallic Consolidated leased its mines, retaining 25 per cent of the output. The Great Depression crushed any hopes that the mines could ever be profitable, and in 1934 Granite-BiMetallic Consolidated ceased operations.

You can see what remains of the Granite company on the outskirts of Philipsburg and at the Granite State Monument. Less than a mile south of town are the remains of the Bi-Metallic mill, the 100-stamp concentrator built in 1890. Six stories high and over 800 feet long, the mill that sat on the side of Granite Mountain produced over $5 million in silver from 1890 to 1893. In 1967, the mill was burned because it had become a fire hazard. The foundations and two large brick smokestacks, which tower over Philipsburg, are all that remain of the mill.

High on Granite Mountain, four miles east of the Bi-Metallic mill, are the ruins of the Miners' Union Hall, once Granite's community center. The hall was a three-story brick and stone building with a facade made of wood, metal, and brick. Constructed in 1890, the Miners' Union Hall had club and pool rooms on the first floor, a combination dance hall and auditorium on the second floor, and a large meeting room on the third floor. The hall is listed in the National Register of Historic Places.

The superintendent's house, located about 100 yards southeast of the Miners' Union Hall, is also listed in the National Register of Historic Places. This building was constructed in the 1880s from granite from a nearby quarry and was the first significant stone structure in Granite. The 32- by 42-foot two-story building, with dormer windows and a gable roof, was the camp's most impressive structure and emphasized the superintendent's importance to the mining operations on Granite Mountain.

In Philipsburg, you can see some excellent examples of the late Victorian architecture that is often found in western mining towns. The Granite County Jail, built in 1896, is listed in the National Register of Historic Places. The Victorian style is also apparent in the Masons' Building and in the facades of the Ross Building and the Sayrs Block.

Landscape 18: The Missouri River Country

You can get an excellent view of the Missouri River country by traveling on I-15 between Great Falls and Wolf Creek and on U.S. Highway 287 between Winston and Toston. Between Great Falls and Wolf Creek, the Missouri River Valley contains good soil for cultivation and rich grasses for grazing. One writer has described this section of the valley as a "sleeping valley with its winding, willow-fringed streams, its yellow fields and meadows, and its nestling cottage homes."

Traveling south through the valley from the Gates of the Mountains to Toston, you see a landscape that has changed dramatically since Native Americans controlled the land. The river's flow has been manipulated by three major dams: the Hauser and Holter dams north of Helena and the Canyon Ferry Dam east of Helena. Upriver from Canyon Ferry Reservoir near Townsend, you can see the river as Lewis and Clark and the Indians saw it nearly 200 years ago.

Route 52: Lewis and Clark on the Missouri River

Route A: U.S. Highway 87, to the Ryan Plant Recreation Area and to River Drive in Great Falls
Route B: Interstate Highway I-15, to the Gates of the Mountains

Meriwether Lewis and William Clark found this section of the Missouri River to be the most difficult part of their journey up the river in their search for the headwaters. The difficulties began at the Great Falls of the Missouri, the major obstacle on this part of the expedition's route.

Route A: U.S. Highway 87, to the Ryan Plant Recreation Area and to River Drive in Great Falls

You can see the Great Falls of the Missouri by leaving U.S. Highway 87 at the turnoff for the Ryan Plant Recreation Area, about 3.5 miles north of the 15th Street Bridge in Great Falls. The Montana Power Company now maintains a park at the falls, and there are several monuments about the expedition's activities.

For five days in June 1805, Capt. William Clark and five members of the expedition explored the area around the Great Falls, mapping a portage route of about 18 miles. The weather was hot, and the men complained as they carried supplies from one camp to the other, slapping at mosquitoes and worrying about the possibility of grizzly bears in the area. Even though expedition members built primitive wagons to make the portage easier, it was still a harrowing experience. It took several weeks for the expedition party to complete the portage, and its route has been designated a National Historic Landmark.

MHS Photo Archives

Gates of the Mountains, Missouri River, Lewis and Clark County. *The Missouri River has cut a narrow defile through precipitous limestone cliffs, forming what Meriwether Lewis named "gates of the Rocky Mountains."*

In his journal of June 18, 1805, William Clark recorded a remarkable discovery: "We proceeded on up the river [from the Great Falls] a little more than a mile to the largest fountain or spring I ever saw, and doubt if it is not the largest in America known. . . ." What they had found was Giant Springs. This huge cold water spring pours 388 million gallons of water into the Missouri every day. As Clark described it: "This water boils up from under the rocks near the edge of the river and falls imediately into the river 8 feet, and keeps its colour for ½ a mile which is emencely clear and of a bluish cast." To reach the Giant Springs, leave U.S. 87 at River Drive and follow this city street for about a mile to its junction with Montana 557. Then follow the signs to the Giant Springs State Park. Historical markers at the park describe the portage route and explain the importance of the springs to the expedition.

Route B: Interstate Highway I-15, to the Gates of the Mountains

Once Lewis and Clark and their men had passed the Great Falls, the expedition traveled upriver through the Missouri River Canyon. You can get a good idea of what the route was like by stopping at a scenic overlook off the southbound lanes of I-15, about 38 miles south of Great Falls.

After leaving this canyon, the expedition proceeded upriver for about 30 more miles, where it entered the most spectacular canyon on the Missouri River above Great Falls. On July 19, 1805, Lewis described the Gates of the Mountains, which is located 72 miles south of present-day Great Falls:

[The] river appears to have woarn a passage just the width of its channel over 150 yds. It is deep from side to side nor is there in the 1st 3 Miles of this distance a spot except one of a few yards in extent on which a man could rest the soal of his foot. . . . This rock is a black grannite below and appears to be of a much lighter color above and from the fragments I take it to be flint of a yellowish brown and light creem-coloured yellow. From the singular appearance of this place I called it *gates of the Rocky Mountains.*

Many people consider the Gates to be one of the state's most scenic places, but the area looks much different today than it did when the expedition passed through in 1805. When the Hauser Dam was constructed in 1907, the water level of the Missouri was raised, giving the river a much different appearance. (The dam was destroyed by a flood and rebuilt in 1911.) You can still gain an appreciation for the spectacular natural gateway, however, by taking a boat tour of the river.

Route 53: Charlie Russell's Missouri River Country
Frontage Road (old U.S. 91), from Great Falls to Cascade

Born in St. Louis in 1864, Charlie Russell was 16 when he came to Montana, where he worked as a cowboy in the Judith Basin and around Cascade. In 1892, Russell moved to Great Falls, where he set up a studio and began to paint for a living. Russell produced thousands of works of art, most of them depicting the romantic, open-range stock-growing era in Montana's history. The cowboy artist made the area south and west of Great Falls famous in his paintings. The landscape surrounding Square Butte, the Missouri River, and the town of Cascade appears in paintings such as *When the Land Belonged to God* and *Charlie Russell and His Friends,* which you can see in the Mackay Gallery of Charles M. Russell Art at the Montana Historical Society in Helena. Other important collections of Russell's works are on exhibit at the C. M. Russell Museum in Great Falls and at the Amon Carter Museum in Fort Worth, Texas. Next to the museum in Great Falls, at 1201 4th Avenue North, you can visit Russell's log cabin studio and his wooden-frame house, a site that is a National Historic Landmark.

Route 54: The Sun River Valley
Montana Highway 200, from Vaughn to Fort Shaw

When you leave I-15 at Vaughn, 10 miles north of Great Falls, you will see the Sun River, a major tributary of the Missouri. The Sun River Valley is where the region's first white residents settled. For 12 miles along Montana 200, between Vaughn and Fort Shaw, you will follow the route of the Mullan Road, the first military road in Montana. The place where this road crossed the Sun River—the Sun River Crossing—became a strategic location. During the mid 1860s, the U.S. Army built Fort Shaw near here and whites came to settle the area.

Seven miles west of Vaughn, near the junction of Montana 200 and U.S. 89, is the J. C. Adams Stone Barn, a reminder of the diversified enterprises of the early settlers. Between 1882 and 1885, stock-grower and freighter J. C. Adams built this 120- by 40-foot unique stone barn to serve as the center for his freighting operations. Adams also sold supplies and livestock to stage companies and freighters who used the Mullan Road. The barn's second story has hardwood floors, and the community often held dances and other social events in this loft. Two Swedish stonecutters carved the building's distinctive architectural details, taking the sandstone blocks from a quarry a few miles away. The J. C. Adams Stone Barn is listed in the National Register of Historic Places. It is private property; do not enter without permission.

Fort Shaw, which is also listed in the National Register of Historic Places, is located five miles west of the J. C. Adams Stone Barn on Montana Highway 200. If you look north from the highway historical marker in the town of Fort Shaw, you can see the buildings that remain at this army post.

Built in 1867 in what was then the heart of the country dominated by the Blackfoot Confederacy, Fort Shaw stood just a few miles west of where the Mullan Road crossed the Sun River. Colonel I. V. D. Reeves designed the fort, which was built with timber from the nearby hills and sandstone and fieldstone found nearby. The soldiers also made adobe bricks that were used to construct the walls of many buildings at the fort. You can still see several of the original buildings, including two sandstone washhouses for the officers, the officers' living quarters, and the commanding officer's house. For much of this century, the old post hospital has been used as part of the Fort Shaw public school.

Fort Shaw was built mainly to protect the Mullan Road and the large mining camps to the south from the possibility of Indian attack, but the fort was also a focal point for white settlers who had come to the Sun River Valley. By the 1870s, several hundred people lived in the valley, enjoying prosperity as traders and stock-growers. The army maintained the post until 1891.

Route 55: Mining in the Missouri River Country
Route A: Montana Road 284, from Townsend to Canyon Ferry
Route B: Montana Road 360, from White Sulphur Springs to Fort Logan

Although Broadwater County is best known for its agricultural productivity, it also has an important mining past. At Diamond City in Confederate Gulch on the east side of the Missouri River, rich placer gold discoveries attracted thousands of miners. North and east of Confederate Gulch in Meagher County's Smith River Valley, the U.S. Army built Fort Logan to protect the mining camps and other settlements in the area.

Route A: Montana Road 284, from Townsend to Canyon Ferry

Miners first struck gold in what would become Broadwater County in the gulches of the Missouri River. You can see these old mining districts by leaving U.S. Highway 12 one mile east of Townsend and taking Montana Road 384 north for 19 miles to the Confederate Gulch Road. About five miles east on this dirt road, three veterans of the Confederate army found gold during the summer of 1864. Washington Baker, Fountain M. Dennis, and John Wells discovered gold flakes in this tiny tributary of the Missouri River; and as the fame of the Confederate Gulch placer deposits spread, thousands of miners arrived to work the stream. In 1866, at Montana Bar, a sandbar located a few miles away on the Missouri, 20 men discovered 700 pounds of gold on one claim in one day; and later that fall another group of miners sent four and a half tons of gold from Montana Bar to New York City banks.

Other entrepreneurs made their fortunes by providing important services to the miners. About 14 miles north of the Confederate Gulch Road, at present-day Canyon Ferry Dam, a ferry carried the miners and their gold across the Missouri River. The ferry was also a primary transportation link between Helena and Diamond City, the major town in Confederate Gulch.

Diamond City began as a camp of tents and crude log buildings, but in less than a year the town was one of the largest in the territory. By 1867, Diamond City had 2,000 residents, had become the county seat of Meagher County, and had general stores, hotels, dwellings, several houses of prostitution, and many saloons. During 1868-1869, placer mining became less profitable, and most of the miners left. Diamond City remained the county seat until 1879, but the population was small—only 460 people lived here in 1870 and only 64 by 1880.

There is not much left at Diamond City to remind us of the thousands of people who once sought their fortunes here. During later decades, miners using hydraulic mining techniques eroded away the gulch, which finally led to the town's destruction. Tailings from the hydraulicking operations are the only remains you can see today.

Route B: Montana Road 360, from White Sulphur Springs to Fort Logan

East of Confederate Gulch on the other side of the Big Belt Mountains, are the remains of Fort Logan, an army post built to protect the mining camps in the area. You can reach Fort Logan, which is listed in the National Register of Historic Places, by continuing east past Diamond City on the Confederate Gulch Road for about 25 miles, but this road is unimproved and travel on it is not advisable. A better way to reach Fort Logan is to take Montana Road 360 out of White Sulphur Springs and follow this paved road northwest for about 18 miles.

In 1869, the U.S. Army constructed Camp Baker on the Smith River. It was a simple post, with 10 dirt-roofed buildings made from pine logs. Fort Logan was built during the next year as a more permanent fort not far from Camp Baker. Using pine logs found in the Big Belt Mountains, the soldiers built company quarters, officers' residences, a blacksmith shop, stables, a granary, a chapel, a hospital, several storehouses, and a blockhouse. The soldiers had tried using adobe bricks, but they soon found that the soil in the area did not make good bricks. They later covered the adobe buildings with weatherboard, a beveled or clapboard siding.

Fort Logan was constructed to protect the Helena-Fort Benton stage route and the settlements in Meagher County, and it fulfilled that charge until 1880, when the army transferred the garrison and much of its equipment to Fort Maginnis, a new post in the Judith Mountains. You can still see the original blockhouse, an officer's quarters, and other log buildings at the fort. The blockhouse has been moved from its original location to what would have been the center of the fort's parade grounds. The fort is now part of a working ranch. Do not trespass.

In White Sulphur Springs, the county seat of Meagher County, you can see the "Castle," which is located at 310 2nd Avenue N.E. Built in 1892 by rancher and businessman Byron Roger Sherman, the Castle overlooks the town and the surrounding countryside, dominating the local built environment. The Castle, which serves as the Meagher County Museum, is open for public tours.

Route 56: The Tipi Rings in the Broadwater Valley
U.S. Highway 287, from Townsend to Toston

As you travel on U.S. Highway 287 south of Townsend, you will see many wheat farms nestled in the lower Broadwater Valley along the Missouri River. Earlier residents of the valley, however, did not settle near the river. The Native Americans who lived in this area preferred the foothills of the Elkhorn Mountains to the west and the Big Belt Mountains to the east.

In the foothills south of Townsend are hundreds of tipi rings, circles of rocks that Native Americans used to anchor their tipis to the ground. More than curiosities on the landscape, tipi rings can tell us much about how people lived thousands of years ago.

Three thousand years ago, prehistoric Indians camped each spring and summer in the foothills of the Elkhorn Mountains overlooking the Missouri River Valley between present-day Townsend and Toston. The women gathered the abundant bitterroot and wild parsley plants, while small groups of men hunted in the valley. The Native Americans preferred the foothills to the valley because there was a stable supply of plants and water and they could find shelter quickly.

Evidence from the tipi rings at the Pilgrim archaeological site south of Townsend, indicates that the area was often a base camp for the summer hunt. Before the Indians acquired horses, they hunted in the valley and brought their kill back to the base camp. The Pilgrim site was a seasonal settlement that prehistoric Indians used repeatedly for over 3,000 years.

J. C. Adams Stone Barn, Sun River, Cascade County. *The Adams Stone Barn "looks as if it would stand the storms and decay of a century at least."*—Sun River Press, *September 10, 1885*

The Great Falls of the Missouri, Cascade County. *After describing the Great Falls, the largest cataract on the Missouri River, Meriwether Lewis wrote: "the river was one continued sene of rappids and cascades . . . the river appears here to have woarn a channel in the process of time through a solid rock."*

Beaverhead Rock, Montana Highway 41, Beaverhead County

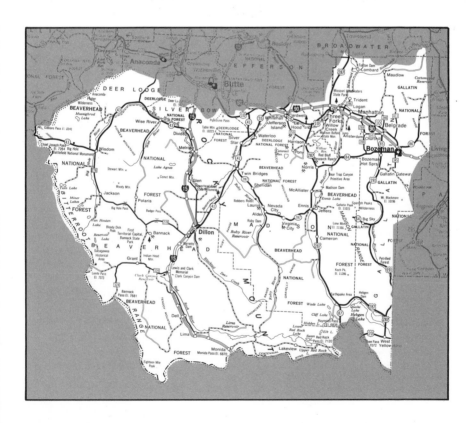

Chapter 7

The Upper Missouri Country

For thousands of years, Montanans have used the natural resources found in southwestern Montana's grassy hills, pine-covered mountains, and Big Hole, Beaverhead, Ruby, Red Rock, Madison, Jefferson, and Gallatin river valleys. Centuries ago, small groups of Native Americans hunted the region's animals. Some prepared buffalo jumps on the bluffs and steep cliffs; and others, like the Tukudika Shoshoni, built traps deep within the pine-covered mountains to snare deer and mountain sheep.

The Tukudika Shoshoni, who lived in the region during the late 18th and 19th centuries, had few horses when compared to other Montana Indians, but they nevertheless thrived in the mountainous environment of the present-day Beaverhead National Forest. When the Lewis and Clark expedition was traveling through this area in 1805, the Shoshoni considered the southwestern corner of present-day Montana to be their land. And it was Sacagawea, the Shoshoni woman who traveled with Lewis and Clark, who spotted Beaverhead Rock on the Beaverhead River and told the Americans that they had reached the country of the Shoshoni, where they could trade for needed horses.

Fur trappers came to southwestern Montana soon after Lewis and Clark, but hostility from Indians who lived in the area prevented them from doing much more than building a temporary fort at the headwaters of the Missouri in 1810.

During the early 1860s, gold drew thousands of whites to the area. Beginning at Bannack, which became Montana's first territorial capital in 1864, and then at Virginia City and Nevada City, the miners built camps that would grow to become the leading towns of the new territory. Quartz gold discoveries at Glendale, Melrose, and Pony attracted more miners. The landscape changed dramatically as entrepreneurs built smelters to process the ore and constructed large charcoal kilns to supply the smelters with fuel and as miners stripped the surrounding hills of timber.

In the 1880s, the Utah and Northern Railroad built through the Beaverhead and Big Hole valleys, bringing farmers and ranchers who would also transform the landscape. The Utah and Northern, the first railroad in Montana, entered the territory at Monida Pass, followed the Red Rock and Beaverhead rivers to Dillon, and continued north to Butte. The Utah and Northern gave southwestern Montana a direct connection to the Union Pacific transcontinental railroad in Utah, ending Montana's transportation isolation.

As Montana's economy expanded during the 1880s and 1890s, there were other alterations to southwestern Montana's landscape. One of the most eye-catching additions to the landscape is the Big Hole River Pumpstation near the town of Divide, which supplies water to Butte's mines and residents by lifting 15 million gallons of water per day over the Continental Divide.

East of the Beaverhead and Big Hole valleys is the Gallatin Valley, the agricultural center of southwestern Montana. Farmers first came to the Gallatin Valley during the 1860s, and they grew grain, raised livestock, and processed flour to sell to Bannack and Virginia City miners. More farmers came in the 1870s and 1880s; thousands of homesteaders arrived during the early years of the twentieth century. By 1915, one-room schoolhouses dotted the countryside, evidence of thriving communities and the homesteaders' commitment to education. Although many homesteaders failed and the small communities faded, those who remained continued to use some of these buildings. Most, however, remained empty until other Gallatin County residents converted them into homes and community centers.

The mines of southwestern Montana have been quiet for decades. Now, as you travel from the haystacks of the Big Hole Valley to the grainfields of the Gallatin Valley, you can see that the region's true riches lay in cultivating the land.

Landscape 19: The Madison River Country

The headwaters of the Madison River, one of the three forks of the Missouri, lie deep in Yellowstone National Park. The Madison flows northwest out of the park into Hebgen Lake, which was created by the Montana Power Company's Hebgen Dam in 1915. The river then flows into Quake Lake, which was formed in 1959 by one of nature's most powerful forces—an earthquake. After passing through a narrow canyon, the river flows into the magnificent Madison Valley, flanked by the Gravelly Range on the west and the towering Madison Range on the east. This is some of the best grazing land in southwestern Montana.

It was along the gulches and uplands just off the Madison River in the Ruby Valley that prospectors found some of Montana's great placer gold deposits. The Madison country's first mining camp developed in the foothills of the Tobacco Root Mountains, where Daylight Gulch meets Alder Gulch. Mary C. Ronan remembered it as an odd-looking place:

> Hundreds of tents, brush wikiups, log cabins, and even houses of stone quarried from the hills were springing up daily in the windings of Alder Gulch and Daylight Gulch, in the hollows of the hills, and along the ramblings of Alder Creek and The Stinking Water [Ruby River] as they flowed through the valley. Soon over a stretch of fifteen miles a cluster of towns had assumed the importance of names,—Junction, Adobetown, Nevada, Virginia City, Pine Grove, Highland, and Summit. . . . Every foot of earth in the gulches was being literally turned up side down. Rough-clad men with long hair and flowing beards swarmed everywhere. Some were digging for bed rock, others were bent over barrow loads of the pay dirt which they were wheeling to the sluice boxes, into these boxes yet others were shoveling the dirt.

North of the gold mining area, the land takes on a different look. Near where the Madison joins the Jefferson and Gallatin rivers to form the "Great Muddy,"

Hydraulic mining, Alder Gulch, Madison County, 1871. By 1871, *miners had begun to use hydraulic techniques to wash gold from the Alder Gulch gravels, dramatically changing the mining landscape.*

the topography makes this region ideal for Indian bison hunts. For hundreds of years, Indians drove bison over the Madison country's steep cliffs and high plateaus. Along the Madison River, you can also see the resources that later attracted white settlers to the region: the rich bottomland, the stands of timber in the mountains, and the high plateaus and bluffs. Much of the history of the Madison River country tells us how Indians and whites have used the region's natural resources.

Route 57: The Alder Gulch Gold Rush
Route A: Montana Highway 287, from Virginia City to Sheridan
Route B: U.S. Highway 287, at Pony Road exit in Harrison
Route C: Montana Highway 84, at Red Bluff

In 1863, the first miners at Alder Gulch (present-day Virginia City) used a simple, inexpensive pan to wash away the gravel from the heavier gold flakes and nuggets. Within a short time, however, placer mining techniques became more sophisticated; miners used a sluice box and a rocker, which was "somewhat like a child's old fashioned cradle, having at one end a perforated sheet of iron." Two miners worked the rocker, which they placed by the side of a stream: "one man rocked and poured water, while another dug and carried dirt." The sluice allowed the miners to wash gravel faster and more efficiently. William A. Goulder, a miner in the Bitterroot Mountains, described sluice mining in his memoirs:

First, the tough, grassy sod and the . . . loam, as the miners called it, is removed from a space measuring some forty feet in length and twelve feet in width and carried to a distance from the spot. . . . This operation exposes the gravel. Next the creek is dammed . . . and the water thus raised above the surface is brought in boxes to the place where it is to be used. Before

Edgar H. Train, photographer. MHS Photo Archives

Wallace Street, Virginia City, Madison County, ca. 1878. *For years after the mining rush of the 1860s, Virginia City was an important Montana town and was territorial capital from 1865 to 1875.*

proceeding further, the gravel must be removed from the pit, or enough of it to allow the sluice boxes to be placed at the angle . . . necessary to produce the required current. Then, at the lower end of the sluice, a strong dam must be built to prevent the water from washing back into the pit. . . . Now the water is rushing through the sluices at the required velocity, and the gold-bearing gravel is all exposed and ready to be thrown into the boxes.

To mine the placer deposits efficiently, miners also constructed a "bed-rock drain," a ditch about half a mile long that supplied "a channel through which the seepage water is to flow from the claim to the bed of the creek below."

During the late 1870s, miners began using a mining technique that shaped the landscape in an even more dramatic way than had placer mining. Hydraulic mining allowed miners to use iron pipes and special nozzles to create a high-pressure stream of water that could be directed at hillsides. In this way, they could wash huge amounts of gold-bearing gravel into sluices, where the ore could be separated.

You can see the tailings produced by sluice-box and hydraulic mining throughout the Virginia City region. These piles of gravel and dirt mark an area where thousands of miners once toiled and where later gold-seekers used dredges to look for gold that the early placer miners could have missed.

Route A: Montana Highway 287, from Virginia City to Sheridan

Virginia City lies at the heart of Montana's richest placer mining district, which has produced over $100 million in gold. In the late spring of 1863, Henry Edgar and Bill Fairweather returned to their camp at Bannack with news that they had discovered gold in Alder Gulch, about 75 miles to the west. The announcement sparked a rush that brought thousands to the gulch. In 1864-1865, when activity in the district peaked, some 10,000 people arrived in Alder Gulch, most of them to work in the mines.

Virginia City was a mining town whose purpose was to provide miners with shelter, food, equipment, clothing, and entertainment. In 1864, Albert Dickson wrote that he was surprised by the town's appearance. According to Dickson, Virginia City was "an orderly village of neat log and frame buildings nestled in a sheltered basin where a tiny stream, fed by a series of springs, reached Alder creek from the north through a tangle of alder and willow." Dickson also observed that Virginia City "was no 'Main Street town' like those to which we were accustomed . . . but a community where life was lived to the full."

The variety of building materials used and the range of architectural styles in its buildings made Virginia City one of the most striking examples of a typical western mining town. These are the qualities that earned the town its designation as a National Historic Landmark. Some of the buildings in Virginia City are of log construction with metal or sawn-timber sheathing, and others are built of brick or locally quarried rock. Most of the buildings are wooden-frame structures, made from hewn logs covered with pine siding. These buildings reflect many architectural styles, including Classical Revival, Gothic Revival, and Italianate. Many of the buildings have been restored as period pieces of the 1860s and 1870s.

You can see several important structures along Montana Highway 287, which passes through the center of town. The Madison County Courthouse (1875) dominates the east end of Virginia City. This two-story brick building, featuring a cupola and columned front porch, is still used as the seat of county government. Content Corner (1864), which now houses a restaurant and general store, is an early two-story stone building with gothic-style windows. The Montana Post Building (1864) is a stone structure that features gothic arched windows and a decorative board-and-batten storefront section. Partially destroyed by fire in 1937, this building has been restored, and it now appears as it did during the 1870s.

The Masonic Hall (1867) and Rank's Drugstore (1864) are two-story, stone buildings. The building that currently houses the town's carriage collection, a two-story log and stone livery stable, was once the headquarters for a group of vigilantes. The harness shop and mechanical bakery also date to the 1860s. Each building is of log construction with weather-board siding and a false front.

About one mile west of Virginia City is Nevada City, another Alder Gulch mining camp. No more than a dozen original buildings remain at the town; and Bovey Restorations, which is responsible for restoring Virginia City, has moved several buildings to Nevada City from different parts of Montana.

Several stage roads connected the early mining camps in southwestern Montana. Three distinctive sidehill road cuts are located west of Montana Highway 287 and north of the Norris Hill near Virginia City. The middle cut is a remnant of the Bozeman Road, which John Bozeman established in 1863. The road was popular with miners traveling to Alder Gulch; and in time the emigrant trail became an all-season road used by freighters, Wells, Fargo & Co., and the Overland Mail and Express Co.

Robbers' Roost, an important stage stop near Virginia City, is located about 15 miles west on Montana Highway 287. Peter Daly built this two-story roadhouse and stage stop in the 1860s, and the building's fame rests on its connection with outlaw Henry Plummer and his highwaymen who supposedly plotted their robberies there. Some experts dispute that claim, however, maintaining that the building dates to 1866-1867, about three years after the vigilantes had hanged Plummer and his men. Robbers' Roost's square-hewn log construction is a rare surviving example of early Montana architecture. It is listed in the National Register of Historic Places and is open to the public.

Route B: U.S. Highway 287, at Pony Road exit in Harrison

Pony, another Madison River country mining camp, is located about 40 miles northeast of Virginia City. You can reach this old town by turning west of Harrison off U.S. Highway 287 and following the paved Pony Road for about six miles.

Tecumseh "Pony" Smith made the first placer claims in Pony in 1868, and miners worked the placers for the next seven years. In 1875, George Moreland opened the Strawberry Mine, which had rich quartz gold deposits. Mallory, Barnes, and Meader operated one of the stamp mills that processed the ore. The Morain 15-stamp steam mill, the Getchell 10-stamp water mill, the W. W. Morris 20-stamp water mill, and several arastras (a type of crude ore mill first developed by the Spanish during the 16th century) also pounded away at Pony's ore deposits.

The Boss Tweed-Clipper partnership, headed by W. W. Morris and Henry Elling, produced the most gold in the district. At the turn of the century, the owners sold the mines to A. C. Burrage and a group of Boston capitalists, who built a huge, 100-stamp mill—at the time the largest gold-processing center in Montana. The Strawberry-Keystone property, the second most productive mine at Pony, was purchased in 1889 by A. M. Holter and other Helena businessmen. At Holter's urging, the Northern Pacific built a branch line to Pony, increasing the value of the local mines and spurring the town's commercial development.

Pony's abandoned buildings, old commercial structures, and late Victorian cottages, which are still used as residences, are reminders of the town's halcyon days when it was a leading mining district in Madison County. You can still see the two-story brick Morris State Bank Block looming over what remains of the town's commercial district and the closed Swanson Hardware shop and the abandoned concrete-block town church standing along Pony's main street. The town's 20th century two-story brick schoolhouse and gymnasium are Pony's most visually imposing buildings, serving as monuments to past community pride.

Route C: Montana Highway 84, at Red Bluff

About 19 miles southeast of Pony, you can leave U.S. Highway 287 at Norris and take Montana Highway 84 to Red Bluff, where only two stone buildings remain to mark the town's location. The large two-story stone building that still stands probably dates to the mid 1860s when prospectors discovered placer gold in the area. During the 1870s, an Anglo-American mining company invested in the mines, but the mines produced less and less over the next two decades.

Red Bluff, Madison County, ca. 1895. *Only the two-story stone building, located in the center of the photograph, remains at the site of Red Bluff today.*

During the 1880s and 1890s, Red Bluff became an important stage stop on the road connecting Bozeman and Virginia City; and by 1900, A. W. Tanner and his wife had transformed the two-story stone office building into a combination store, hotel, and stage stop. About 15 years later, George B. Rowe claimed the buildings in Red Bluff under the homesteading act and used the stone structure for his residence. The Montana Agricultural Experiment Station acquired the property in 1956 to use as a range management station.

Route 58: Buffalo Hunting on the Plateaus of the Madison

Interstate Highway I-90, from Logan to Madison Buffalo Jump

The Madison Buffalo Jump State Monument, which is listed in the National Register of Historic Places, is the only bison kill site in southern Montana that is open to the public. Located on a steep limestone bluff on the eastern wall of the Madison River Valley, the jump is a 30-foot-high cliff that drops into a 150-foot-high steep slope. At the bottom of the slope is a small creek, where Indians made their camps and processed the kill. You can see many different facets of this typical bison kill site by taking the trails to the cliff, to the tipi rings marking the campsite, and to the processing center near the creek.

It is certain that various Native American tribes used the Madison Buffalo Jump for over 4,000 years, but it is impossible to attribute this use to any particular tribe. Evidence suggests, however, that Shoshonean groups might have used this cliff at least 800 years ago to trap and maim and then kill bison.

Albert Schlecten, photographer. MHS Photo Archives

Wheat field, west of Bozeman, Gallatin County, ca. 1910. *Gallatin Valley, the site of the earliest homesteads in Montana, was a productive wheat-producing area at the turn of the century.*

Landscape 20: The Gallatin Valley

"In beauty and fertility the valley of the Gallatin surpasses all others in Montana which have come within the limit of our explorations," wrote geologist F. V. Hayden in 1872. "This valley is about forty miles in length from north to south, and five to fifteen miles in width. . . . [It is] occupied to a greater or less extent by thriving farmers, with here and there prosperous villages."

At the time when Hayden described the Gallatin Valley, the area had already been settled for nearly a decade. During the 1860s, the first settlers arrived here, where they found rich soil and ample supplies of water. The land, wrote Isabel Randall in 1886, is "covered with flowers; pink and white ox-eyed daisies in tiny round bunches, growing quite close to the ground . . . yellow flowers (called prickly pear, really a sort of cactus), small pansies, lenten lilies, and many others. The air is literally scented with them all."

The Gallatin Valley, as Hayden remarked over a century ago, "surpasses all others in Montana." With many multi-generational farms and ranches, this valley is an agricultural paradise for horticulturalists and stock-growers.

Route 59: Homesteading in the Gallatin Valley

Route A: Interstate Highway I-90, from Bozeman to Three Forks
Route B: Montana Road 288, from Manhattan to Churchill
Route C: U.S. Highway 191, at Big Sky Resort

The best way to see how agriculture has affected the Gallatin Valley is to drive the 30 miles from Three Forks to Bozeman on I-90. A less direct and slower route, but one that is still visually informative, is to take old U.S. Highway 10 from Three Forks to Bozeman, a road that parallels the tracks of the Burlington Northern Railroad (the former Northern Pacific route). Whichever road you take and whether you are near Belgrade, Manhattan, or Bozeman, you will see many similarities in the built environment.

Route A: Interstate Highway I-90, from Bozeman to Three Forks

The first farmers arrived in the Gallatin Valley in 1863 and 1864. They realized that the booming mining camps to the southwest needed fresh food and that the valley could become a productive agricultural area. They homesteaded, choosing land claimed either under the Homestead Act of 1862 or under squatter's rights. The homesteaders chose their land carefully, ensuring that they had easy access to their farms and a constant supply of water. Many farmers first settled on river bottomland, and the remains of homesteads you see along or near a creek or river probably date to the earliest years of settlement.

Homesteaders also understood that they needed to irrigate the land. As early as 1864, they constructed irrigation ditches from the East Gallatin River; the following year, they diverted water from the West Gallatin River and Middle Creek. The ditches were easy to operate and were designed to irrigate four or five farms. As one resident remembered, "It seems very interesting work; they fill the different ditches with water, then dam them up at the highest point, cut a hole in one of the banks, and let the water run out on to the land on both sides of the ditch."

Some 20 years later, after the Northern Pacific Railroad had built through the Gallatin Valley, major irrigation systems were constructed to bring water to those parts of the valley not crossed by natural streams. These "big ditches" opened more of the valley to homesteaders, who usually located their farms near irrigation ditches. In 1888-1889, an irrigation company headed by Albert Kleinschmidt of Helena built a large ditch to irrigate land east of the West Gallatin River. Two years later, homesteaders constructed a ditch to irrigate the same area and the Manhattan Malting Company built the High Line Canal to irrigate the land west of the West Gallatin. The valley's productivity increased significantly. In 1865, farmers harvested 20,000 bushels of wheat; two years later, they harvested 300,000 bushels.

Bozeman, the commercial center for homesteaders in the valley and the seat of government for Gallatin County, grew rapidly. Large grain harvests during the 1860s and 1870s, for example, prompted the construction of several flour mills. P. W. McAdow and Thomas Cover built the first mill in 1865, and the Penwell brothers at Springhill and John J. Tomlinson at Salesville (present-day Gallatin Gateway) built additional mills during the next eight years. In 1879, George D. Thomas constructed a modern mill at Springhill, and three years later Nelson Story built a flour mill at the mouth of Bridger Canyon. You can see the Story Mill from Montana Highway 86 on Bozeman's northeastern outskirts.

During the first 25 years of settlement in the Gallatin Valley, homesteaders took up claims in the rich bottomland and avoided the higher and drier uplands.

C. V. West, photographer. MHS SHPO

Abandoned farm, Gallatin Valley, Gallatin County. Many 20th century homesteaders whose crops failed found the Gallatin Valley's boast that "no place in the northwest . . . offers the same opportunity for profitable investment" to be a hollow claim.

A few homesteaders settled the uplands of northern Gallatin County during the 1890s, but not until dry farming techniques became popular during the 1910s did large numbers of homesteaders move into the northwestern part of the county, north of the Gallatin River and Bozeman and east of the Missouri.

Homesteaders moved to the dry uplands in response to the construction of the Milwaukee Road, promotional literature that lauded the technology of dry farming, and the new laws that allowed homesteaders to claim more acres. This second rush of homesteaders took up some of the less desirable land in the valley and established towns like Maudlow and Three Forks.

The location of the homesteads in the Gallatin can tell you their approximate age and what type of crops they produced, and the types of buildings can tell you how successful the homesteaders were.

Homesteaders usually came to the Gallatin Valley in the spring and summer and often lived in tents or converted covered wagons until they could build a one-room log cabin. Some had time to construct outbuildings, such as the all-important granary, which the farmers had to have before the first harvest. Most homesteaders built their granaries with commercial lumber or they waited until their own hand-hewn lumber had cured.

Successful homesteaders constructed other buildings and often replaced their log cabins with more substantial framed, multi-story homes. In the townships of Springhill and Willow Creek, prosperous homesteaders hired carpenters to build their second homes. Many of these pattern-book dwellings exhibit superb local craftsmanship and are excellent examples of popular architecture.

Larger homes also meant that the division of labor changed in many homestead families. In their diaries and memoirs, women described how rugged their lives were during the early years in the valley. They told how they began with little experience in dry farming and how, in addition to tending to the housework of a one- or two-room shack, they worked in the fields, helped with the livestock, and managed the farm's daily affairs. Because cleaning and other domestic chores took relatively little time, the women had more time to work outdoors. Once the family built a larger home—perhaps one with two stories—many women found that their domestic duties were more time-consuming and that they had less time to help with other farm operations.

The location of the permanent farmhouses on homestead claims can tell us a lot about each homesteader's concerns. Some families placed their houses near a road; others built near a reliable supply of water; some located homes on the worst farmland on the claim; and still others built their homes where they would be protected from the winter weather.

The final pattern on the landscape in Gallatin County that relates to the homestead era is the many dirt and gravel roads that run in straight lines. These roads usually follow the survey lines between homesteads; the township plat, not topography, determined where the first local roads were built.

Route B: Montana Road 288, from Manhattan to Churchill

Homesteaders in the Gallatin Valley created communities, which were nearly as important to the settlers as plentiful water and good land. Amsterdam and Churchill on Montana Roads 288 and 347 are excellent examples of community building in the Gallatin Valley. The miniature windmills that you can see from Montana Road 288 demonstrate the residents' pride in their Dutch ancestry, which in turn reinforces their sense of community.

During the 1890s, about 30 years after farmers had settled here, the Manhattan Malting Company proposed using dry farming technology to raise barley in western Gallatin County. To encourage his fellow countrymen to emigrate to the area, company president Henry Altenbrand sent Reverend A. J. Wormset to the Netherlands to persuade farmers to move to the Gallatin Valley to grow barley.

Homesteaders found another important center of community in their local schools, where people from miles around gathered to participate in political meetings, socials, and other community events. The Dry Creek School, east of Manhattan at the junction of Dry Creek Road and Montana 346, is a good example of a schoolhouse built during the homesteading era. This balloon-frame wooden-plank school, which dates to 1902, features an open cupola and a recessed front door, which provided additional protection to students during cold and windy weather. Another outstanding schoolhouse is at Maudlow, about 20 miles north of the Dry Creek School at the end of Dry Creek Road. Both of these schools, along with 16 others in Gallatin County, are listed in the National Register of Historic Places.

Route C: U.S. Highway 191, at Big Sky Resort

The Crail Ranch, now surrounded by condominium buildings off U.S. Highway 191 on Montana Road 64 at the Big Sky Resort, is a superb example of

Gallatin River Canyon, Gallatin County, ca. 1910. *It would not be until 1930 that tourists traveling to Yellowstone National Park could drive on a modern road (U.S. Highway 191) up the Gallatin Canyon; but as early as the 1890s, the canyon's scenic wonders had drawn, first, tourists in wagons and, then, automobile traffic.*

Karst's Kamp, Gallatin River Canyon, Gallatin County, ca. 1925. *Peter Karst began the dude ranching and tourist business in the Gallatin River Canyon in the early 1900s. Karst's Kamp, which was destroyed by fire and has since been rebuilt, still operates in the canyon.*

homestead architecture. A. F. Crail and his family built the house in 1905, and it was the headquarters for their sheep and cattle ranching operation for almost 50 years.

The Crails built their one- and one-half-story house out of hand-hewn logs and rough-sawn lumber from their own sawmill. They used a sophisticated notching technique that was common in Gallatin County: the sides of the logs were flattened with an axe and then dove-tail notches were cut to connect the logs at the corners.

Near the ranch house is the Crails' first home, a simple one-story building, measuring 12 by 16 feet, of round log construction with V-notching. The family lived in this small log cabin for several years while they painstakingly prepared the logs for the larger ranch house. At several places in Gallatin County, you can see this pattern of homestead development, where families built a second home near a simple log or plank structure. As you travel through the valley, look for small log buildings near larger, permanent farmhouses. The families' first homes might now be used as sheds for animals or equipment.

Route 60: Tourism in Gallatin County
U.S. Highway 191, from Bozeman to West Yellowstone

U.S. Highway 191 from Bozeman to West Yellowstone runs through the Gallatin River Canyon, one of the most scenic river routes in Montana. During the last half century, the traditional occupations in the canyon of ranching and lumbering have been superceded by tourism. Dude ranches, backcountry outfitters, and luxury resorts now cater to the tourists who come to the Gallatin River Canyon during all seasons. This new industry has been changing the Gallatin Canyon landscape for over 50 years.

About 14 miles southwest of Bozeman on U.S. Highway 191 is the Gallatin Gateway Inn, one of the earliest structures to take advantage of the tourist traffic to Yellowstone National Park. The Milwaukee Road built the inn in 1927, locating it at the terminus of its branch line from Three Forks. Promoters believed that the inn would be the perfect place to entertain Milwaukee Road passengers before taking them on to the park by bus.

Located at Salesville (which soon changed its name to Gallatin Gateway), the inn differed from most resorts of the era. There was a large lounge and ballroom and a dining area for several hundred people, but the inn had only 35 guest rooms. The Milwaukee expected most tourists to sleep in Pullman cars and to go on to Yellowstone the next day. But the Milwaukee Road's timing was off: within ten years, tourists were using automobiles, not trains, to travel to Yellowstone National Park. The resort never made much money, and the railroad sold it in the early 1950s.

The Gallatin Gateway Inn was designed by Schack, Young and Myers of Seattle and is an excellent example of Spanish Colonial Revival architecture. The inn, which is 250 feet long and 40 feet wide, features a buff-colored stucco exterior and a red tile roof. When the inn opened in the late 1920s, the building was surrounded by 12 acres of gardens, what the Milwaukee called the "Flower Garden

MHS Photo Archives

Gallatin Gateway Inn, U.S. Highway 191, Gallatin County, ca. 1920. *The opening of the inn began with a parade in Bozeman, a picnic at Specimen Creek, a speech by Governor John Erickson, and a dance that attracted some 2,000 people.*

of the West." Today, only traces of the original gardens remain. Because of its connection to railroad promotion and its striking architecture, the Gallatin Gateway Inn is listed in the National Register of Historic Places.

Thirty-one miles south of the Gallatin Gateway Inn, off U.S. Highway 191 on Montana Road 64, is the Big Sky Resort, the newest resort in the Gallatin River Canyon. Unlike the Gallatin Gateway Inn and the area's dude ranches, the Big Sky Resort was more than just a place to spend the night before venturing into the rugged wilderness of Yellowstone National Park. The developers of Big Sky shaped the landscape into patterns that are ideal for skiing, golfing, and horseback riding; and they built luxurious tourist accommodations that contrast with the ruggedness of the Gallatin Canyon environment.

Near the Montana-Wyoming state line, 47 miles south of Big Sky on U.S. Highway 191, is West Yellowstone and the West Entrance to Yellowstone National Park. West Yellowstone is Montana's best example of a town dominated by tourism.

Tourists had used the Madison River area as an entrance to Yellowstone for many years, but it was not until the Union Pacific Railroad constructed a spur line from Ashton, Idaho, to the park's West Entrance in 1905-1908 that West Yellowstone became a popular entryway. During the next 20 years, the Union Pacific constructed a depot, a dining hall, dormitories, and a baggage storage building, which encouraged other businesses to build near the depot.

The Union Pacific depot, designed by Gilbert Underwood, is listed in the National Register of Historic Places. It is an excellent example of rustic architecture, which uses native materials to match the natural landscape. The depot, which is a log building similar in style and appearance to National Park Service buildings in

MHS SHPO

Union Pacific Railroad Depot, West Yellowstone, Gallatin County. *After over a decade of promotion by Bozeman-area merchants, the Union Pacific built a spur line to West Yellowstone in 1907. A year later the town of West Yellowstone developed.*

the Park, established an architectural style that others quickly copied in commercial buildings and private residences throughout the West Yellowstone area. Located at the intersection of Yellowstone and Canyon avenues, the town's focal point, the depot now houses the Museum of the Yellowstone, which is open to the public.

West Yellowstone was originally a strip town, with the leading businesses lining Yellowstone Avenue, directly across from the railroad depot. Two of these early businesses, the Madison Hotel and Cafe at 137 Yellowstone Avenue and the Kennedy Building at 127 Yellowstone Avenue, are listed in the National Register of Historic Places. As automobiles grew in popularity, however, the business district shifted to Canyon Avenue, the route of U.S. Highway 191. Today, West Yellowstone resembles a "T"-style railroad town.

Route 61: The Headwaters of the Missouri River
Interstate Highway I-90, at Three Forks

You can reach the Missouri River Headwaters State Park by leaving I-90 and taking the Frontage Road (old U.S. Highway 10) east for three miles to the park's entrance.

The Three Forks of the Missouri River, which has been designated a National Historic Landmark, has great historical significance. During the 18th and into the 19th centuries, the Three Forks was a rendezvous point and a shared hunting ground for several Montana tribes, including the Blackfoot Confederacy, Atsina, Shoshoni, and Flathead. By the early 1800s, however, the Blackfoot Confederacy controlled the resources found in the Three Forks area, even though their homeland was hundreds of miles to the north.

Three Forks of the Missouri, Gallatin County, 1883. *When Lewis and Clark reached the headwaters of the Missouri in July 1805, they named the principal tributaries after the three men who had made the expedition possible: President Thomas Jefferson, Secretary of State James Madison, and Secretary of the Treasury Albert Gallatin.*

Members of the Lewis and Clark expedition were the first white Americans to reach the Missouri headwaters. On July 25, 1805, William Clark recorded that the three forks are nearly of a Size, the North fork [Jefferson] appears to have the most water and must be Considered as the one best calculated for us to assend Middle fork [Madison] is quit[e] as large about 90 yds. wide. The South Fork [Gallatin] is about 70 yds wide & falls in about 400 yards below the midle fork those forks appear to be verry rapid & contain some timber in their bottoms which is very extencive.

Fur trappers and traders in search of beaver skins made up the next group of Americans who came to the Missouri headwaters. In 1808, Manuel Lisa sent John Colter and John Potts, both former members of the Lewis and Clark expedition, to the Three Forks area. Their task was to persuade the Indians to visit and trade at Fort Remon on the Yellowstone River. But instead of willing traders, Colter and Potts found a group of Piegan warriors, who killed Potts and gave Colter little chance of saving his life. The barefooted Colter ran across the cactus and rock-strewn landscape pursued by several young Piegan warriors. Colter outran the Piegan, hid in the brush along the banks of the Madison River, and eventually made his way back to Fort Remon.

Two years later, 32 American and French-Canadian trappers used the cotton-wood trees in the bottomland to build a post at Three Forks. But constant harass-ment from the Blackfoot Confederacy scuttled their hopes of trading and forced them to abandon the post.

At the Missouri Headwaters State Park, off Frontage Road (U.S. Highway 10) some five miles east of the town of Three Forks, you can read about the geological history, the Lewis and Clark expedition's discoveries, and the location of the 1810 trading post. Interpretative markers are posted along several easy trails to interesting sites.

Landscape 21: The Big Hole River Country

Flowing out of the Bitterroot Mountains, the Big Hole River heads north through the wide Big Hole Basin. It then turns east through a narrowing valley and canyon on its way to joining the Beaverhead River and creating the Jefferson River. The Big Hole Basin is rich farming country. As one promoter claimed, the basin is the "Valley of 10,000 Haystacks,"

a fertile bowl set down among the mountains of the Continental Divide, a broad expanse of rich soil blanketed in winter by the heavy snows of high altitudes and in the summer by acre after acre of luxuriant and nutritious grasses, a cattle kingdom isolated from railroads yet supporting two progressive towns and scores of prosperous ranches, the home of the happiest people, the richest hay and the fattest beef steers in the world.

East of the basin, the valley narrows and you can see the mountains of the Beaverhead National Forest, which hold valuable natural resources. During the 1870s and 1880s, prospectors and miners found riches in the mountains that tower above the Big Hole River. This area became one of Montana's mining centers, and it is one of the best preserved mining landscapes in Montana.

Route 62: Mining Along the Big Hole River
Interstate Highway I-15, from Melrose to Divide

The first significant mining claim in the Big Hole River country was made in 1868, and for the rest of the century the region's miners produced a considerable amount of the profitable precious metals. You can see remnants of those mining operations at several sites near Melrose, 30 miles north of Dillon on I-15.

The major quartz strikes in the Big Hole River country occurred at Glendale, west of Melrose in the Pioneer Mountains. To reach Glendale, take the Glendale Road bridge over the Big Hole River and travel for about 15 to 20 minutes. The road can be hazardous during the winter and spring, so check road conditions before visiting the area. You can still see a smelter stack and other mining structures at Glendale, and there are several charcoal kilns at Canyon Creek about two miles west of the old town.

Miners made the first placer strikes near Glendale along Trapper Creek in 1873, and the discovery of more valuable silver lodes set off a rush to the area. Soon, the miners had established Trapper City and Lion City near the mines. Trapper City boasted several log dwellings and many saloons, but it lasted for only a few years. Lion City enjoyed more success, with several hundred residents, two general stores, three saloons, and two hotels. The Hecla Mining Company also operated a few boarding houses in Lion City for its employees.

Hecla Mining Company smelter, Glendale, Beaverhead County. In 1882, *when the Utah and Northern built a spur to Glendale, the mining town had nearly 3,000 people and over 30 businesses. This smelter stack is one of the few remnants of the extensive works, which included a half-mile-long flume to bring water from Trapper Creek.*

Big Hole Pumpstation, Divide, Montana Highway 43, Silver Bow County. *An unusual feature of the historical landscape near the Big Hole River is this pumpstation, which pumps 5 million gallons of water over the Divide to Butte every day.*

In 1875, Charles Dahler and Noah Armstrong constructed a small smelter where the road from Melrose to the mines crossed Trapper Creek. The town of Glendale was established near the smelter. Fire destroyed the smelter in 1879, and the Hecla Mining Company built a new, larger, and more productive one on the site. The new smelter and the arrival of the Utah and Northern Railroad at Melrose in 1881 made the Glendale operations the most important in the Big Hole River country.

In 1881, Glendale had a population of over 1,500 people, a Methodist church, a school for 200 pupils, a water works system, and many commercial stores. The Hecla Mining Company, the town's leading employer, operated the smelter, a roaster, two crushers, an assay office, a sawmill, a tramway, and three blast furnaces. Between 1881 and 1900, the company mined ore that was valued at $22 million.

The Hecla company also constructed 28 charcoal kilns, which produced about 100,000 bushels of charcoal a month to fuel the smelter. In 1882, Hecla constructed what some historians believe was the first concentrator in the territory. The concentrator was located at the base of Lion Mountain, about seven miles west of Glendale.

After the Hecla Mining Company ceased operations in 1904, Glendale's residents quickly deserted the town. Since then, most of the town's buildings have been removed, and only a few stone foundations and buildings remain of this once vibrant mining camp.

Near Divide, about nine miles north of Melrose on I-15, is the Big Hole Pumpstation, another structure important to the mining history of western Montana. Each day, the pumpstation sends 5 million gallons of water from the Big Hole River over the Continental Divide and on to the city of Butte, 22 miles to the north. The pumpstation is located just west of Divide on the north side of Montana Highway 43 near a bridge over the Big Hole River.

Designed in 1893 by Eugene Carroll and built in 1898, the pumpstation required five different distribution systems and was quite an engineering accomplishment. Now powered by electricity, the pumps were originally driven by steam engines, and the station's 150-foot-high steel smokestack was a landmark along the Big Hole River. The building is owned by the Butte Water Company and is listed in the National Register of Historic Places. Several houses, which the company built for its employees, can be seen near the pumpstation.

Route 63: The Valley of 10,000 Haystacks

Route A: Montana Highway 43, at the Big Hole Battlefield National Monument
Route B: Montana Road 278, from Wisdom to Jackson

Some of southwestern Montana's most prosperous stock-growing ranches are in the Big Hole Basin, an area that locals call "the land of 10,000 haystacks." As you travel along Montana Highway 43 or Montana Road 278, you can see evidence that the bottomland's rich soil is ideal for producing hay.

C. V. West, photographer, MHS SHPO

Slide haystacker, Sula, Ravalli County. *One of the inventors of the Sunny Slope—or beaver—slide haystacker, H. S. Armitage, bragged that "there is no country in the world where there is so much hay stacked in three weeks as in the Big Hole."*

Route A: Montana Highway 43, at the Big Hole Battlefield National Monument

Ranchers did not come to the Big Hole until well after the fur trappers, the traders, and the miners had entered the basin and after a pivotal battle in the Nez Perce War of 1877 took place on the basin's western edge. The Big Hole Battlefield National Monument, located on Montana Highway 43 about 12 miles west of Wisdom, marks the site of the battle, where the U.S. Army surprised the Nez Perce Indians, who were fleeing from Idaho Territory. On August 9, 1877, 89 Nez Perce lost their lives here in the bloodiest battle of the Nez Perce war. Despite the loss, the Nez Perce successfully repulsed the army's attack and escaped to the east to continue their ill-fated journey, which ended in surrender two months later near present-day Havre, Montana. There are several fascinating exhibits on the battle at the monument, and you can follow marked trails to explore the Nez Perce camp and the battlefield.

Route B: Montana Road 278, from Wisdom to Jackson

In 1882, five years after the Battle of the Big Hole, the first white settlers arrived in the valley. You can see how farmers and ranchers have changed the look of the land by traveling on Montana Road 278 from Wisdom to Jackson, a 19-mile route that will let you see most of the Big Hole Valley.

Among the early residents of the basin were Alvin and Hattie Noyes, who settled at the Crossings (present-day Wisdom) in 1882. The following winter, Nick Bielenberg brought 100 head of cattle into the Big Hole, the first participant in what would become a healthy stock-growing industry in the valley. In 1884, B. O. Fournier settled at the basin's hot springs, and the town of Jackson developed around his ranch.

There are two prominent elements in the landscape that link modern ranchers to their past: the beaver-slide haystacker and the buck-and-rail fence. In 1910, D. J. Stephens and H. S. Armitage patented the "Sunny Slope Slide Hay Stacker," better known as a beaver-slide haystacker. These distinctive contraptions allowed ranchers to stack more hay than ever before. Horse teams powered the belts that carried the hay to the top of the stacker's inclined slide, where the hay dropped on to the haystack. Farmers now use machines to power the haystackers, but the contraption has changed little over the years. You will also see buck-and-rail fences surrounding many of the basin's ranches. Some ranchers have added wire to this wooden fence. In the Big Hole Basin, you can see evidence of the revolution that has occurred in agricultural technology during the 20th century, but you can also see how Big Hole ranchers have maintained some of the traditions of their parents.

Landscape 22: The Beaverhead River Country

In 1805, Meriwether Lewis recorded in his journal that the Beaverhead River "is from 35 to 45 yards wide very crooked many short bends constituteing large and general bends; insomuch that altho' we travel briskly and a considerable distance yet it takes us only a few miles on our general course or rout." Lewis also described the area's flora:

there is but little timber on this fork principally the under brush frequently mentioned. I observe a considerable quantity of the buffaloe clover in the bottoms. the sunflower, flax, green swoard, thistle and several species of the rye grass some of which rise to the hight of 3 or 4 feet. there is a grass also with a soft smooth leaf that bears it's seeds very much like the timothy. . . . it rises about 3 feet high.

William Clark wrote that the Beaverhead country was a

Vallie of 5 or 6 miles wide Inclosed between two high Mountains, the bottom rich Some small timber on the Islands & bushes on the edges of the river Some Bogs & verry good turfs in different places in the vallie, Some scattering Pine & cedar on the mountains in places, other Parts nacked except grass and stone.

Together with the Big Hole and the Ruby rivers, the Beaverhead cuts the headwaters of the Jefferson River, which forms a natural highway through the mountains of southwestern Montana. This route, which Montana Highway 41 from Twin Bridges to Dillon and I-15 from Dillon to the Clark Canyon Dam follow, was first blazed by Indians and later used by whites.

The most noticeable landmark, Beaverhead Rock on Montana Highway 41 about 15 miles north of Dillon, was named by the Shoshoni when they claimed this territory. Sacagawea, the Shoshoni woman who traveled with her husband, Charbonneau, on the Lewis and Clark expedition, recognized this landmark and

Main street, Bannack, Beaverhead County. *"I think the town is very quiet and orderly for such a mining town,"* Mary Edgerton *commented about Bannack in 1863, "much more so than I expected to find it."*

told the Americans that they would soon find her people. Lewis recorded in his journal on August 8, 1805:

> On our right is the point of a high plain, which our Indian woman recognizes as the place called the Beaver's Head, from a supposed resemblance to that object. This, she says, is not far from the summer retreat of her countrymen, which is on a river beyond the mountains running to the west. She is therefore certain that we shall meet them either on this river, or on that immediately west of its source, which, judging from its present size, cannot be far distant.

Route 64: Exploring the Beaverhead River Country
Interstate Highway I-15, at the Clark Canyon Dam
(Montana Road 324)

One of the most exciting periods of the Lewis and Clark expedition was when the Americans were searching for the source of the Missouri River in the summer of 1805. Their quest took them to southwestern Montana, where the expedition traveled up the Jefferson River to its junction with the Beaverhead, near present-day Twin Bridges, and then followed the Beaverhead southward toward Clark Canyon.

The expedition established Camp Fortunate, located near the river at a site that is now covered by the Clark Canyon Reservoir. Here, they bargained with the Shoshoni for the horses they desperately needed to travel over the Continental Divide on the treacherous overland route between the Missouri and Columbia rivers. The expedition cached its canoes and part of its equipment here before heading west toward the Bitterroot Mountain Range. You can see the approximate location of Camp Fortunate at the Clark Canyon Dam exit off I-15 about 20 miles south of Dillon.

In September, the expedition crossed the Continental Divide and left present-day Montana at Lemhi Pass, crossing from the territory of the Louisiana Purchase into Spanish-claimed land. Near the top of the pass, the Americans found what they believed to be the origins of the Missouri, and Lewis wrote: "I had accomplished one of those great objectives on which my mind had been unalterably fixed for many years." To reach Lemhi Pass, where the forest service maintains the Sacajawea Historical Area, take the Clark Canyon Dam exit off I-15 and continue on Montana Road 324 until you see the Lemhi Pass turnoff, a one-lane road that is passable only during the summer.

After Lewis and Clark, the first whites to travel over the Lemhi Pass were the Canadian fur traders of the North West Company and the Hudson's Bay Company, whose brigades often used the pass to reach the Snake River. The Lemhi Shoshoni and members of the Blackfoot Confederacy also regularly used the pass.

Route 65: Mining in the Beaverhead Country
Montana Road 278, from Bannack to Argenta

The first settlers in the Beaverhead River country did not make their homes on the river bottomland but in the foothills where they had discovered gold and silver. The first discovery was the cause of Montana's first large-scale gold rush, which occurred at Bannack, about 22 miles west of Dillon. You can reach Bannack by leaving I-15 about three miles south of Dillon and taking Montana Road 278 west and then south for about 20 miles. The Bannack Road is located a few miles west of Badger Pass.

About half of the buildings at Bannack date to Montana's territorial years. A few of the buildings were constructed during the early 1860s, when Bannack's gold rush was on, but most of the buildings date to the turn of the century, when miners used mechanical dredging to reopen the placer mines.

Bannack was the first territorial capital in 1864 and was later the county seat of Madison County. The town's most distinctive building, the large two-story brick courthouse, was built in 1875. Here you can begin a walking tour of the old town that will explain Bannack's history. Bannack has been designated a National Historic Landmark and is a Montana State Park administered by the state's Department of Fish, Wildlife, and Parks.

About 17 miles northeast of Bannack, on Montana Road 278, you can stop at Argenta, an early silver camp that lies along Rattlesnake Creek. From Dillon, you can reach Argenta by taking Montana 278 for about five miles to the marked turnoff for the Argenta Road.

Argenta began as a placer mining camp, but in the summer of 1864, three miners staked claims on six lodes of silver and other claims soon followed. "The wealth of the Rothchilds is as nothing compared to the riches which lie concealed in the bowels of the Rattlesnake hills," concluded Granville Stuart, "awaiting the coming of the enchanters with their wands (in the shape of greenbacks), to bring forth these treasures."

Stuart had put his finger on why Argenta developed slowly. Silver mining was not easy: processing the ore took machines and money that were beyond the average prospector's means. In 1866, the St. Louis and Montana Mining Company provided the money for the Argenta Smelter, the first smelter in Montana Territory. Samuel T. Hauser and James Stuart directed its construction. The next year, A. M. Esler constructed a second smelter; and in 1868, Tootle, Leach and Company of St. Louis added a third. The only remnants of Argenta are slag dumps, mine shafts, some abandoned mine structures, and several houses that are now private residences.

Route 66: Settling the Beaverhead Country
Route A: Interstate Highway I-15, from Monida to Dillon
Route B: Montana Highway 41, from Dillon to Twin Bridges
When you enter Montana from Idaho on I-15 at Monida, you follow the path of the Utah and Northern Railroad. This is an important historical landscape, combining the highway, railroad tracks, the Red Rock River, and several small towns into a route that can tell you a great deal about how the Beaverhead country was settled.

Route A: Interstate Highway I-15, from Monida to Dillon
Despite the mining activity at Bannack and Argenta during the 1870s, few people settled in the country between Bannack and Virginia City. Once the Utah and Northern Railroad built into Montana in 1880, however, settlements developed along the Beaverhead River. In 1878, Jay Gould and a group of eastern capitalists purchased the Union Pacific Railroad's narrow-gage branch line that reached from Odgen, Utah Territory, to Franklin, Idaho Territory. Gould renamed the line the Utah and Northern Railroad; and in March 1880, he began to extend the line into Montana by building over Monida Pass. The following month, the Utah and Northern moved its construction base from Idaho to Red Rock, Montana, which quickly became a thriving terminus town. Red Rock was a short-lived, temporary town built for freighters and railroad workers who depended on the Utah and Northern for their employment.

At Red Rock, tents and balloon-frame buildings housed hotels, restaurants, saloons, blacksmith shops, and general stores. Because of the constantly changing population, nothing was considered permanent; and carpenters added and removed new buildings, depending on the circumstances. Sometimes, the demand for buildings outstripped the supply of lumber. One lumberman, James Oliverson, sadly noted: "this place [Red Rock] is building up fast. Great call for lumber and I haven't got any."

During the fall of 1880, railroad officials moved the terminus to a pre-selected site near the junction of the Beaverhead River and Blacktail Deer Creek. That October, on land that Richard Deacon once used to raise cattle, the terminus town of Dillon was founded. But Dillon was exceptional: it did not suffer a sudden, inglorious death. Through the foresight and good business sense of several entrepreneurs, Dillon became a permanent settlement and eventually the leading town in southwestern Montana.

C. V. West, photographer, MHS SHPO

Hotel Metlen, Dillon, Beaverhead County. *Dillon's reliance on the Union Pacific Railroad for transportation and the encouragement of commerce is perhaps best documented in the impressive Hotel Metlen, which was built in 1897.*

Several buildings in Dillon remain from the late 19th century. Some old commercial buildings stand near the attractive brick Union Pacific depot in downtown Dillon at 125 S. Montana. The Dingley Block, constructed in 1888, features a facade with pressed-metal decorative ornamentation. Across the tracks and facing the depot is the Hotel Metlen, one of the outstanding railroad hotels in Montana. Built in 1897, this three-story brick hotel with dormer windows on the third floor is listed in the National Register of Historic Places. It stands on the site of Dillon's first hotel, the Corinne. At the turn of the century, showplaces such as the Hotel Metlen played a vital role in the development of towns in Montana. As symbols of the towns' stability and economic opportunities, these buildings helped to attract new businesses and settlers.

On the south end of Dillon is an imposing Victorian building, Old Main at Western Montana College. The college has helped the town achieve economic stability, and this building reflects the important role that the college has played in Dillon's development. This beautiful multi-story red brick building, which was constructed in 1896, is listed in the National Register of Historic Places.

Route B: Montana Highway 41, from Dillon to Twin Bridges

The Beaverhead country is a prime stock-growing area, and many settlers came here to establish ranches. South of Dillon and along Montana Highway 41, you can see a variety of ranch buildings that document the area's stock-growing industry.

The Tash Ranch, three miles south of Dillon at the I-15 exit for Montana 278, features a 30- by 35-foot square-beam log barn with a foundation made of fieldstone. This French-Canadian style of *piece sur piece* sidewall junctions is rarely seen in Montana, and the barn generally matches the appearance of many Canadian barns built during the 19th century. This architectural style suggests that the first owners of the land, Amede Bessette and Xavier Renois, may have built the barn in 1864-1865, before they sold their property to Issac Van Camp. This would make the Tash Ranch barn one of the oldest remaining structures along the Beaverhead River.

On the 28-mile stretch of Montana Highway 41 between Dillon and Twin Bridges, you can see barns with varying architectural styles, some with gambrel and gable roofs and many with architectural ornamentation, such as cupolas. Two miles north of Twin Bridges on the east side of Montana 41 is a unique circular barn. Of board-and-batten construction and with a conical shingled roof, this red painted barn was built by Noah Armstrong, who made his fortune in the Glendale mines. Armstrong bred and trained rare horses on his ranch, and the barn had an indoor track where the horses could exercise in the winter. The racehorse "Spokane," the only Montana horse to win the Kentucky Derby, was foaled at the barn in 1887.

All of these properties, including the Tash Ranch, are still in use and are private property. Do not trespass.

One-room schoolhouse, Maudlow, Gallatin County. *One of 18 schoolhouses listed in the National Register of Historic Places, this frame building was constructed in 1909 to replace an original log structure built in 1901. The Maudlow School was used until 1978.*

Montana Avenue, Dillon, Beaverhead County, 1892. *By the time this photo of Bill Lenkersdorfer and his freight outfit was taken, Dillon was a decade old and had become the leading town in southwestern Montana.*

Montana Properties Listed in the National Register of Historic Places as of November 11, 1985

The listing of a property in the National Register of Historic Places in no way requires the owner to make that property available to the public. We encourage visitors to view Register properties from public roadways and to visit those that are open to the public. We strongly urge visitors to respect the privacy of those who own and use Register properties.

AR: Access restricted, permission required
NO: No access
AC: Active commercial use
OP: Open to the public, set hours
AU: Access unrestricted

Beaverhead County
Bannack Historic District: National Historic Landmark, Montana State Park, 22 miles west of Dillon off Montana Road 278 |OP|

Big Hole National Battlefield: State Highway 48, near Wisdom |OP|

Birch Creek CCC Camp F-60: Birch Creek Road, USFS Road 98 near Dillon |AR|

The LaMarche Game Trap |AR|

Lemhi Pass: National Historic Landmark, Salmon & Beaverhead National Forests, 12 miles west of Tendoy, Idaho |AU|

Sheep Creek Wickiup Cave |AR|

Barrett Hospital: Chapman & S. Atlantic, Dillon |AR|

Dillon City Library: 121 S. Idaho, Dillon |OP|

Hotel Metlen: 5 S. Railroad Ave., Dillon |AC|

Montana State Normal School (Old Main, Western Montana College): 710 S. Atlantic, Dillon |OP|

Big Horn County
Battle of the Rosebud Site: 10 miles south of Kirby |NO|

Big Horn Head Gate: South side of Bighorn River at mouth of Bighorn Canyon |AR|

Chief Plenty Coups Memorial State Monument: 1 mile west of Pryor off Montana Highway 416 |OP|

Custer Battlefield National Monument: I-90 15 miles southeast of Hardin |OP|

Fort C. F. Smith Site: 1 mile east of Fort Smith |AR|

Hardin Commercial District: Roughly bounded by 4th, Crook, BN right-of-way, & Crow, Hardin |AC|

Hardin Residential District: Roughly bounded by 5th, 4th, Crow, & Cody, Hardin |NO|

Lee Homestead (Caretaker's House, Tongue River Dam): Near Decker |NO|

Blaine County
Chief Joseph Battleground of the Bear's Paw: Montana State Monument, 15 miles south of Chinook on Montana Highway 240 |OP|

Lohman Block: 225-239 Indiana, Chinook |AC|

Broadwater County
McCormick's Livery & Feed Stable Sign: Indian Creek Road near Townsend |AU|

Wellington D. Rankin Ranch: National Historic Landmark, 30 miles east of Helena, 2 miles northeast of the Helena-Diamond City Road |NO|

Carbon County
Bad Pass Trail (Sioux Trail): Near Barry's Landing in the Bighorn Canyon National Recreation Area near Lovell, Wyoming |AR|

Cedarvale (Hillsboro): Near Barry's Landing in the Bighorn Canyon National Recreation Area near Lovell, Wyoming |AR|

Ewing-Snell Ranch: South of Barry's Landing in the Bighorn Canyon National Recreation Area near Lovell, Wyoming |AR|

Demijohn Flat Archaeological District |AR|

Petroglyph Canyon |AR|

Pretty Creek Archaeological Site |AR|

Red Lodge Commercial Historic District: Broadway between 8th & 12th, Red Lodge |AC|

Warila Boarding House &
Sauna: 20 N. Haggin, Red
Lodge |AC|

Cascade County
J. C. Adams Stone Barn: 1
mile west of Sun River on
U.S. Highway 81 |AR|

Great Falls Portage: National
Historic Landmark near
Great Falls |AR|

Mullan Road (Benton Lake
Segment): Near Great Falls
|AR|

Belt Jail: Castner St., Belt |AR|

Cascade County Courthouse:
415 2nd Ave. N., Great Falls
|OP|

Timothy Edwards Collins
Mansion: 1003-1017 2nd
Ave. N.W., Great Falls |NO|

Great Falls Central High
School (Paris Gibson
Square): 1400 1st Ave. N.,
Great Falls |OP|

Margaret Block: 413-415 Cen-
tral Ave., Great Falls |AC|

Roberts Building (Elmore
Hotel): 520-526 Central
Ave., Great Falls |AC|

Charles M. Russell House &
Studio: National Historic
Landmark, 1217-1219 4th
Ave. N., Great Falls |OP|

Fort Shaw Historic District &
Cemetery: 1 mile northwest
of Fort Shaw |AR|

St. Peter's Mission Church &
Cemetery: 10 miles west of
Cascade |AR|

Ulm Pishkun State Monument
(Ulm Buffalo Jump, Taft Hill
Buffalo Jump): Near Ulm
|OP|

Robert Vaughn Homestead-
Captain Couch Ranch:
Vaughn Cemetery Road near
Vaughn |NO|

YMCA Building:
101 1st Ave. N.,
Great Falls |AR|

Chouteau County
Fort Benton Historic District:
National Historic Landmark
|AC|

Fort Benton Bridge: Front &
15th, Fort Benton |OP|

Fort Benton Levee |OP|

Chouteau County Courthouse:
1308 Franklin, Fort Benton
|OP|

Chouteau County Jail:
Washington & 14th, Fort
Benton |AR|

Grand Union Hotel: 14th &
Front, Fort Benton |AC|

Masonic Building/Sharps Store
(Benton Pharmacy): 1418
Front, Fort Benton |AC|

St. Paul's Episcopal Church:
14th & Chouteau, Fort Ben-
ton |AR|

Citadel Rock State Monument
(Cathedral Rock): 28 miles
east of Fort Benton |AU|

Judith Landing Historic
District: Secondary Route
236 near Winifred |NO|

Lewis & Clark Camp at
Slaughter River: 40 miles
south of Big Sandy |AR|

Lonetree: Near Geraldine |NO|

Custer County
Fort Keogh (U.S. Range
Livestock Experiment Sta-
tion): 2.5 miles southwest of
Miles City |AR|

Miles City Waterworks &
Pumping Plant: Pumping
Plant Road, Miles City |OP|

Miles City Steam Laundry
(Miles City Laundry & Dry
Cleaners): 800 Bridge, Miles
City |AC|

George M. Miles House: 28 S.
Lake, Miles City |NO|

Dawson County
Hagan Site: National Historic
Landmark |AR|

Charles Krug House: 103 N.
Douglas, Glendive |NO|

Deer Lodge County
Anaconda City Hall: 401 E.
Commercial, Anaconda |OP|

Ancient Order of Hibernians
Hall: 321-323 E. Commercial,
Anaconda |AR|

Barich Block: 416-420 E. Park,
Anaconda |AC|

Davidson Block: 301-303 E.
Park, Anaconda |AC|

Deer Lodge County Court-
house: S. Main Street,
Anaconda |OP|

Durston Block Annex: S. Main
& Park, Anaconda |AR|

Hearst Free Library: Main &
4th, Anaconda |OP|

St. Mark's Episcopal Church:
601 Main, Anaconda |AR|

Washoe Theater: 305 Main,
Anaconda |AC|

Fergus County
Culver Studio: 212 5th Ave.
N., Lewistown |NO|

Fergus County High School:
412 6th Ave. S., Lewistown
|AR|

Fergus County Improvement
Corp. Dormitory (Calvert
Hotel): 216 7th Ave. S.,
Lewistown |AC|

Huntoon Residence: 722 W.
Water, Lewistown |NO|

Lewistown Carnegie Library:
701 W. Main, Lewistown
|OP|

Lewistown Central Business
Historic District: Roughly
bounded by Washington, 1st
Ave., Janeaux, & 8th Ave.,
Lewistown |AC|

Lewistown Courthouse
Historic District: Roughly
bounded by Washington,
6th Ave., Main, & Broadway,
Lewistown |AR|

Lewistown Silk Stocking
District: Roughly bounded
by 2nd Ave., Boulevard &
Washington, & 3rd Ave.,
Lewistown |NO|

Masonic Temple: 322 W.
Broadway, Lewistown |AR|

St. James Episcopal Church &
Parish House: 502 W. Mon-
tana, Lewistown |AR|

St. Joseph's Hospital: High
Street, Lewistown |AR|

St. Leo's Catholic Church: 124 W. Broadway, Lewistown |AR|

Rocky Point: Off U.S. 191, Charles M. Russell National Wildlife Range |AR|

Flathead County
Belton Chalets: West Glacier |AC|

Bull Head Lodge & Studio (Charles M. Russell's summer house): Apgar Cottage Sites, Apgar |NO|

Charles E. Conrad Mansion: 313 6th Ave. E., Kalispell |OP|

A. J. Dean House (C. E. Conrad's private barn): 244 Woodland Ave., Kalispell |NO|

Granite Park Chalet Historic District: Near Going-to-the-Sun Road Loop area, Glacier National Park |AC|

Lewis Glacier Hotel Historic District (Lake McDonald Lodge): Going-to-the-Sun Road, Glacier National Park |AC|

Sperry Chalet Historic District: Near Lake McDonald, Glacier National Park |AC|

Hornet Lookout: Hornet Mountain, Flathead National Forest |AR|

Izaak Walton Inn: Essex |AC|

St. Richard's Church: 505 4th Ave. W., Columbia Falls |AC|

Stillwater Ranger Station Historic District: U.S. Highway 93 near Olney |AR|

Gallatin County
Belgrade City Hall & Jail: Broadway at Northern Pacific Blvd., Belgrade |OP|

R. T. Barnett & Company Building: 13 E. Main, Bozeman |AC|

Blackmore Apartments: 120 S. Black, Bozeman |AR|

Hotel Baxter: 105 W. Main, Bozeman |AC|

Bozeman Carnegie Library: 35 N. Bozeman Ave., Bozeman |OP|

Bozeman National Fish Hatchery (Bozeman Fish Cultural Development Center): 4050 Bridger Canyon Rd., Bozeman |AR|

Burr Fisher House: 712 S. Willson, Bozeman |NO|

Gallatin County Jail (Gallatin County Historical Society Museum): 317 West Main, Bozeman |OP|

Emil Ketter Residence: 35 N. Grand Ave., Bozeman |NO|

South Willson Historic District: Roughly S. Willson between Curtiss & Cleveland, Bozeman |NO|

Spieth & Krug Brewery (Maxey Block, Union Hall): 238-246 E. Main, Bozeman |AC|

Gallatin Gateway Inn: U.S. Highway 191, south of Bozeman |AC|

Crail Ranch: Meadow Village, Big Sky |AR|

Madison Buffalo Jump State Monument: 7 miles south of Logan |OP|

Ruby Theatre: 212 Main, Three Forks |AR|

Sacajawea Hotel: 5 Main Street, Three Forks |AC|

Three Forks of the Missouri (Missouri River Headwaters State Monument): National Historic Landmark, Trident Road near Three Forks |OP|

West Yellowstone Oregon Shortline Historic District (Union Pacific Depot, Museum of the Yellowstone): Yellowstone Ave., West Yellowstone |OP|

Madison Hotel & Cafe: 137 Yellowstone Ave., West Yellowstone |AC|

Kennedy Building: 127 Yellowstone Ave., West Yellowstone |AC|

One-Room Schoolhouses |AR|
Spanish Creek School, Gallatin Gateway
Sedan School, Sedan

Springhill School, Belgrade
Dry Creek School, Manhattan
Reese Creek School, Belgrade
Lower Bridger School, Bozeman
Pine Butte School, Bozeman
Pass Creek School, Belgrade
Anderson School, Gallatin Gateway
Malmborg School, Bozeman
Trident School, Trident
Cottonwood School, Gallatin Gateway
Rea School, Bozeman

One-Room Schoolhouses |NO|
Horseshoe Basin School, Belgrade
Little Bear School, Bozeman
Upper Madison School, Bozeman
Middle Creek School, Bozeman
Maudlow School, Belgrade

Glacier County
Camp Disappointment: National Historic Landmark, 2 miles west of Montana Highway 444, 3.5 miles north of Route 2, Blackfeet Indian Reservation |AR|

Going-to-the-Sun Road: Between West Glacier & St. Mary, Glacier National Park |OP|

Many Glacier Hotel Historic District: 12.8 miles west of Babb, Glacier National Park |AC|

Holy Family Mission: 15 miles southeast of Browning |AR|

Golden Valley County
Grace Lutheran Church of Barber: Near Ryegate |AR|

Sims-Garfield Ranch: North of U.S. Highway 12, about 1.2 miles east of Ryegate |NO|

Granite County
Miners Union Hall: Upper Main Street, Granite, near Philipsburg, Granite |AR|

Superintendent's House (Thomas A. Weir House): Magnolia Ave. (Silk Stocking Row), Granite, near Philipsburg |AR|

Granite County Jail: Kearney Street, Philipsburg |OP|

Hill County
Young-Almas House: 119 4th Ave., Havre |NO|

H. Earl Clack House: 532 2nd Ave., Havre |NO|

Too Close for Comfort Site (Wahkpa Chu'gn Buffalo Jump & Archaeological Site) |OP|

Jefferson County
W. C. Child Ranch (Kleffner Ranch): County Route 518, near East Helena |NO|

Fraternity Hall: Main Street, Elkhorn |AR|

Jefferson County Courthouse: 200 Centennial, Boulder |OP|

Montana Deaf & Dumb Asylum (Old Administration Building): Boulder River School & Hospital, Boulder |AR|

Boulder Hot Springs: 3 miles southeast of Boulder on Montana Highway 281 |AC|

Lake County
Kootenai Lodge Historic District: 500 Sunburst Drive near Bigfork |AR|

Fort Connah Site: U.S. Highway 93 near Ronan |AR|

Frank Bird Linderman House: Near Lakeside |NO|

St. Ignatius Mission: 1/8 mile southeast of Montana Highway 93, St. Ignatius |OP|

Polson Feed Mill: 501 Main, Polson |AC|

Swan Lake Rock House Historic District: Three Rock Point, Swan Lake |NO|

Lewis & Clark County
Appleton House #13: 2200 Cannon, Helena |NO|

Cathedral of Saint Helena: N. Warren at Lawrence, Helena |OP|

Christmas Gift Evans House: 404 N. Benton, Helena |NO|

Original Governor's Mansion (William Chessman Mansion): Ewing at 6th, Helena |OP|

John T. Murphy House: 418 N. Benton, Helena |NO|

Wassweiler Hotel & Bath Houses: 4528 Highway 12 W., Helena |NO|

Young Women's Christian Association: 501 N. Park, Helena |AR|

Kluge House: 540 W. Main, Helena |AC|

T. H. Kleinschmidt House: 1823 Highland, Helena |NO|

Morris Silverman House: 412 N. Rodney, Helena |NO|

Samuel T. Hauser Mansion: 720 Madison Ave., Helena |NO|

Montana State Capitol Building: Capitol Complex, Helena |OP|

Western Clay Manufacturing Company (Kessler Brickworks, Archie Bray Foundation): 2915 Country Club Rd., Helena |AR|

Helena Historic District Commercial Area: Roughly bounded by Howie, Lawrence, Ewing, & the southern end of Last Chance Gulch |AC, AR|
Westside Residential Area: Roughly bounded by Monroe, Stuart, Dearborn, & the alley between Power & Holter |NO|

Gilman State Bank: Main Street, near Augusta, Gilman |AR|

Methodist-Episcopal Church of Marysville: 3rd Street, Marysville |NO|

Silver Creek School (Little Red School House): East of I-15 on Sierra Road near Helena |OP|

Lincoln County
Eureka Community Hall: Cliff Street, Eureka |AR|

Madison County
Beaverhead Rock State Monument: 14 miles northeast of Dillon |AR|

Madison County Fairgrounds: Twin Bridges |OP|

Robbers' Roost: Montana Highway 287A, 5 miles north of Alder |AC|

Virginia City Historic District: National Historic Landmark, encompasses approximately 20,000 acres, including the hills that rise above the city & a portion of Alder Gulch |AC|

St. Mary of the Assumption: Off Montana Road 287, Laurin |AR|

McCone County
Gladstone Hotel: 101 Main, Circle |AC|

Meagher County
Byron R. Sherman House (The Castle): 310 2nd Ave. N.E., White Sulphur Springs |OP|

Fort Logan & Fort Logan Blockhouse (Camp Baker): 17 miles northwest of White Sulphur Springs on County Road 360 |AR|

Mineral County
Deborgia Schoolhouse: Thompson Falls-Deborgia Road, Deborgia |OP|

Missoula County
Carnegie Public Library (Missoula Museum of the Arts): 335 N. Pattee, Missoula |OP|

Belmont Hotel: 430 N. Higgins Ave., Missoula |AC|

Federal Building, U.S. Post Office, & Courthouse: 200 E. Broadway, Missoula |OP|

Forkenbrock Funeral Home: 234 E. Pine, Missoula |AC|

John R. Toole House (Kappa Kappa Gamma Sorority House): 1005 Gerald Ave., Missoula |NO|

Fred T. Sterling House: 1310 Gerald Ave., Missoula |NO|

Grand Pacific Hotel (Park Hotel, Park Plaza Apartments): 118 W. Alder, Missoula |AC|

John M. Keith House (Sigma Chi Fraternity House): 1110 Gerald Ave., Missoula |NO|

John S. Johnston House: 412 W. Alder, Missoula |NO|

A. J. Gibson House: 402 S. 2nd, Missoula |NO|

Higgins Block: 202 N. Higgins, Missoula |AC|

Milwaukee Depot: 250 Station Drive, Missoula |AC|

Missoula County Courthouse: 220 W. Broadway, Missoula |OP|

Palace Hotel: 147 W. Broadway, Missoula |AC|

St. Francis Xavier Church: 420 W. Pine, Missoula |OP|

Wilma Theatre: 104 S. Higgins, Missoula |AC|

Northern Pacific Railroad Depot: Railroad & Higgins, Missoula |AR|

University Apartments: 400-422 Roosevelt, Missoula |NO|

J. M. Herzog House: 1210 Toole Ave., Missoula |NO|

Clarence R. Prescott House: University of Montana, Missoula |NO|

Flynn Farm: Mullan Road West, near Missoula |NO|

Fort Fizzle Site: Lolo National Forest 5 miles west of Lolo on U.S. 12 |AR|

Lolo Trail: National Historic Landmark, Lolo & Clearwater National Forests, about 150 miles southwest of Lolo to the Weippe Prairie in Idaho |AR|

U.S. Forest Service Remount Depot (Ninemile Ranger Station): Lolo National Forest, 2.4 miles southwest of Huson on I-90, 1.6 miles west on Highway 10, 2.8 miles north on Remount Road |AR|

Travelers' Rest: National Historic Landmark, Near Lolo |AR|

Park County
Sixty-Three Ranch: 8 miles southeast of Livingston on Swingley Road |AC|

Livingston Westside Residential Historic District: 13 blocks centered on 5th & E. Lewis, roughly bounded by the alley between 6th & 7th, the alley between Park & Callender, the alley between Yellowstone & 3rd, & Geyser |NO|

Livingston Commercial Historic District: About 13 blocks & railroad lands, centered on Park & Main, roughly bounded by 3rd, the Burlington Northern Railroad right-of-way, C Street, & Lewis |AC|

Livingston B Street Historic District: 307-317 S. B Street |NO|

Livingston Eastside Residential Historic District: About 6 blocks centered on G & Callender, roughly bounded by the alley between E & F, the alley between Park & Callender, the alley betweeen H & I, & the properties facing the south side of Lewis |NO|

Urback Cabin: 9th Street Island, Livingston |NO|

Krohne Spring House: 329 S. H Street, Livingston |NO|

Trowbridge Dairy: 207 S. M Street, Livingston |NO|

Krohne Island House: Krohne Island, 1500 E. Callender, Livingston |NO|

Detention Hospital: 325 E. Gallatin, Livingston |NO|

Northside School: 118 W. Chinook, Livingston |AR|

KPRK Radio: U.S. 89 east of Livingston |AC|

Rolfson House: Bozeman Road west of Livingston |NO|

Ebert Ranch: Shields Route |NO|

Harvat Ranch: Southeast of Livingston off U.S. 89 |NO|

Phillips County
Phillips County Carnegie Library: S. 1st Street W., Malta |AR|

Pondera County
Conrad City Hall: 154th Ave. S.W., Conrad |OP|

Valier Public School: 820 3rd Street, Valier |NO|

Two Medicine Fight Site: 25 miles east southeast of Browning |AR|

Powell County
N. J. Bielenberg Home: 801 Milwaukee Ave., Deer Lodge |NO|

William E. Coleman House: 500 Missouri Ave., Deer Lodge |NO|

Montana Territorial & State Prison: 925 Main Street, Deer Lodge |OP|

William K. Kohrs Free Memorial Library: Missouri Ave. at 5th, Deer Lodge |OP|

Trask Hall: 703 5th Ave., Deer Lodge |AR|

Deer Lodge American Women's League Chapter House: 802 Missouri Ave., Deer Lodge |AR|

Grant-Kohrs Ranch National Historic Site: North of Deer Lodge on the north end of Main |OP|

Site of the Completion of the Northern Pacific Railroad, 1883: Near Gold Creek |AR|

Fitzpatrick Ranch Station Historic District: Adjacent to Nevada Creek Reservoir near Helmville |AR|

Prairie County
Grandey Elementary School: Park Street, Terry |OP|

Ravalli County
Alta Ranger Station: 27.7 miles south of Conner, .2 miles east on Forest Road 310 |AR|

Dudley C. Bass Mansion: 216 N. College, Stevensville |NO|

George May Residence: 100 Park Ave., Stevensville |NO|

St. Mary's Mission Church & Pharmacy: North Ave., Stevensville |OP|

Fort Owen State Monument: .5 miles northwest of Stevensville |OP|

Big Creek Lake Site |AR|

Marcus Daly Memorial Hospital: 211 S. 4th, Hamilton |AR|

Ravalli County Courthouse: 225 Bedford, Hamilton |OP|

Hamilton City Hall: 175 S. 3rd, Hamilton |OP|

Canyon Creek Laboratory of the U.S. Public Health Service (Ricketts Memorial Museum): About 1 mile west of Hamilton |AR|

Brooks Hotel: County Road 373 near Corvallis |NO|

Richland County
People's Congregational Church (J. K. Ralston Historical Museum): 203 2nd Ave. S.W., Sidney |OP|

Roosevelt County
Fort Peck Agency: U.S. Highway 2 near Poplar |AR|

Fort Union Trading Post National Historic Site: Buford Route near Williston, North Dakota |OP|

Rosebud County
Rosebud County Deaconess Hospital: N. 17th Ave., Forsyth |AC|

Sheridan County
Tipi Hills: Medicine Lake National Wildlife Refuge near Medicine Lake |AR|

Silver Bow County
Butte Historic District: National Historic Landmark, Butte (north of Front Street) & Walkerville |AC, AR|

Burton K. Wheeler House: National Historic Landmark, 1232 E. 2nd, Butte |NO|

Charles W. Clark Mansion: 331 W. Broadway & 108 N. Washington, Butte |OP|

William A. Clark Mansion: 219 W. Granite, Butte |OP|

Silver Bow County Poor Farm Hospital (National Center for Appropriate Technology): 3040 Continental Drive, Butte |AC|

U.S. Post Office: 400 N. Main, Butte |OP|

Silver Bow Brewery Malt House: Nissler Junction, 1 mile east of Silver Bow |NO|

Big Hole Pumpstation: Old Highway 43 near Divide |AR|

Stillwater County
W. H. Norton House: 3rd Ave., Columbus |NO|

Oliver H. Hovda House: N. Woodward, Absarokee |NO|

Sweetgrass County
Yellowstone Crossing, Bozeman Trail: Near Springdale |AR|

Grand Hotel: 139 McLeod, Big Timber |AC|

Toole County
Kevin Depot: Kevin |AR|

Valley County
Charles C. Sargent House: 615 Front, Nashua |NO|

Fort Peck Theatre: Missouri Ave., Fort Peck |OP|

Wheatland County
Graves Hotel: 106 S. Central Ave., Harlowton |AC|

Wibaux County
Pierre Wibaux House: Orgain Ave., Wibaux |NO|

Yellowstone County
Billings Townsite Historic District: 2200, 2300, 2400, & 2500 blocks of Montana Ave. & the south side of the same blocks on 1st Ave., including the Northern Pacific Depot |AC|

Billings Chamber of Commerce Building: 303 N. 27th, Billings |AC|

I. D. O'Donnell House: 105 Clark Ave., Billings |NO|

Austin North House: 622 N. 29th, Billings |AC|

Fire House #2: 201 S. 30th, Billings |OP|

Prescott Commons: Rocky Mountain College Campus, Billings |OP|

Parmly Billings Memorial Library: 2822 Montana Ave., Billings |OP|

Preston B. Moss Residence: 914 Division, Billings |NO|

Christian Yegen House: 208 S. 35th, Billings |NO|

Peter Yegen House: 209 S. 35th, Billings |NO|

Hoskins Basin Archaeological District |AR|

Boothill Cemetery: Swords Park, near Billings |OP|

Pompeys Pillar: National Historic Landmark, 2 miles east of Nibbe |OP|

Pictograph Cave State Monument: National Historic Landmark, 6 miles southeast of Billings |OP|

Antelope Stage Station: Near Broadview |NO|

Select Bibliography

Chapter 1: Lower Yellowstone Country
Beckes, M. R. and J. D. Keyser. *The Prehistory of the Custer National Forest: An Overview*. Billings: Custer National Forest, 1983.

Dusenberry, Verne. *The Northern Cheyenne*. Helena: Montana Historical Society, 1955.

Evans, William B. and Robert L. Peterson. "Decision at Colstrip: The Northern Pacific Railway's Open-Pit Mining Operation." *Pacific Northwest Quarterly* 61 (July 1970): 129-136.

Maximilian, Alexander Philip von. *Travels in the Interior of North America*. New York: Dutton, 1976.

Mulloy, William. *The Hagen Site: A Prehistoric Village on the Lower Yellowstone*. Missoula: University of Montana, 1942.

Oglesby, Richard. *Manuel Lisa and the Opening of the Missouri Fur Trade*. Norman: University of Oklahoma Press, 1963.

Powell, Peter J. *People of the Sacred Mountain*. New York: Harper & Row, 1981.

Renz, Louis T. *The History of the Northern Pacific Railroad*. Fairfield, Washington: Ye Galleon Press, 1980.

Wishart, David J. *The Fur Trade of the American West, 1807-1840: A Geographical Synthesis*. Lincoln: University of Nebraska Press, 1979.

Chapter 2: The Hi-Line Country
Bradley, James H. "Characteristics, Habits and Customs of the Blackfeet Indians." *Contributions to the Historical Society of Montana*. Vol. 9. Helena: Montana Historical Society, 1923, pp. 255-287.

Dusenberry, Verne. "Montana's Displaced Persons: The Rocky Boy Indians." *Montana the Magazine of Western History* 4 (Winter 1954): 1-15.

Ewers, John C. *The Blackfeet: Raiders on the Northwestern Plains*. Norman: University of Oklahoma Press, 1958.

Grinnell, George B. *Blackfoot Lodge Tales: The Story of a Prairie People*. Lincoln: Bison Books, University of Nebraska Press, 1962.

Hardeman, Nicholas P. "Brick Stronghold of the Border: Fort Assinniboine, 1879-1911." *Montana the Magazine of Western History* 29 (Spring 1979): 54-67.

Lowie, Robert H. *The Assiniboine*. New York: American Museum of Natural History, 1909.

Malone, Michael P. and Richard B. Roeder, eds., *The Montana Past: An Anthology*. Missoula: University of Montana, 1969.

Roll, Tom E. et al. *The Bootlegger Trail Site: A Late Prehistoric Spring Bison Kill*. Washington, D.C.: Heritage Conservation & Recreation Service, 1980.

Sharp, Paul F. *Whoop-Up Country: The Canadian-American West, 1865-1885*. Norman: University of Oklahoma Press, 1973.

Stegner, Wallace. *The Big Rock Candy Mountain.* Lincoln: Bison Books, University of Nebraska Press, 1983 |1943|.

_____. *Wolf Willow: A History, a Story, and a Memory of the Last Plains Frontier.* Lincoln: Bison Books, University of Nebraska Press, 1980 |1962|.

Stilgoe, John R. *Metropolitan Corridor: Railroads and the American Scene.* New Haven: Yale University Press, 1983.

Welch, James. *Winter in the Blood.* New York: Harper & Row, 1974.

Chapter 3: The Judith Basin Country

Blouet, Brian W. and F. C. Luebke, eds. *The Great Plains: Environment and Culture.* Lincoln: University of Nebraska Press, 1979.

Derleth, August. *The Milwaukee Road.* New York: Creative Age Press, 1948.

Doig, Ivan. *This House of Sky: Landscapes of a Western Mind.* New York: Harcourt Brace Jovanovich, 1978.

_____. *English Creek.* New York: Atheneum, 1984.

Fletcher, Robert H. *Free Grass to Fences: The Montana Cattle Range Story.* New York: New York University for the Historical Society of Montana, 1960.

Schwieder, Dorothy Hubbard. "Frontier Brethren: The Hutterite Experience in the American West." *Montana the Magazine of Western History* 28 (Winter 1978): 2-15.

Stuart, Granville. *Pioneering in Montana: The Making of a State, 1864-1887.* Lincoln: Bison Books, University of Nebraska Press, 1977 |1925|.

Zellick, Anna. "The Men from Bribir: The Croatian Stonemasons of Lewistown, Montana." *Montana the Magazine of Western History* 28 (Winter 1978): 44-55.

Chapter 4: The Upper Yellowstone Country

Brown, Mark H. *The Plainsmen of the Yellowstone: A History of the Yellowstone Basin.* Lincoln: Bison Books, University of Nebraska Press, 1969 |1961|.

Ewers, John C., ed. *Adventures of Zenas Leonard, Fur Trader.* Norman: University of Oklahoma Press, 1959.

Frison, George C. *Prehistoric Hunters of the High Plains.* New York: Academic Press, 1978.

Lowie, Robert H. *The Crow Indians.* New York: Farrar & Rinehart, 1935.

Nabokov, Peter, ed. *Two Leggings: The Making of a Crow Warrior.* Lincoln: Bison Books, University of Nebraska Press, 1982 |1967|.

Plummer, Norman B. *The Crow Tribe of Indians.* New York: Garland, 1974.

Chapter 5: The Western Valleys

Bakeless, John. *Lewis and Clark: Partners in Discovery.* New York: William Morrow, 1947.

Davis, Leslie B., ed. *Lifeways of Intermontane and Plains Montana Indians.* Bozeman: Montana State University, 1979.

Dunbar, Seymour. *The Journals and Letters of Major John Owen, Pioneer of the North-west*, 1850-1871. Helena: Montana Historical Society, 1927.

Ewers, John C. "Iroquois Indians in the Far West." *Montana the Magazine of Western History* 13 (Spring 1963): 2-10.

Flathead Culture Committee, comp. A *Brief History of the Flathead Tribes*. St. Ignatius: Confederated Salish and Kootenai Tribes, 1978.

Henry, Alexander and David Thompson. *New Light on the Early History of the Greater Northwest*, ed. Elliot Coues. 3 vols. New York: Francis P. Harper, 1897.

Horr, David A., ed. *Interior Salish and Eastern Washington Indians*. Vol. 2. New York: Garland, 1974.

Isch, Flora Mae B. "The Importance of Railroads in the Development of Northwestern Montana." *Pacific Northwest Quarterly* 41 (January 1950): 19-29.

White, M. Catherine, ed. *David Thompson's Journals Relating to Montana and Adjacent Regions, 1808-1812*. Missoula: Montana State University, 1950.

Chapter 6: The Continental Divide Country

"Charles M. Russell—A Special Issue." *Montana the Magazine of Western History* 34 (Summer 1984).

Coues, Elliott, ed. *History of the Expedition Under the Command of Lewis and Clark*. 4 vols. New York: Francis P. Harper, 1893.

Davis, Leslie B. et al. *Stone Circles in the Montana Rockies*. Bozeman: Montana State University, 1982.

Malone, Michael P. *The Battle for Butte: Mining and Politics on the Northern Frontier, 1864-1906*. Seattle: University of Washington Press, 1981.

Miller, Don C. *Ghost Towns of Montana*. Boulder, Colorado: Pruett, 1974.

Toole, K. Ross. "When Big Money Came to Butte: The Migration of Eastern Capital to Montana." *Pacific Northwest Quarterly* 44 (January 1953): 23-29.

Renner, Frederic G. *Charles M. Russell*. New York: Abrams, 1974.

Wolle, Muriel. *Montana Paydirt: A Guide to the Mining Camps of the Treasure State*. Denver: Sage, 1963.

Young, Otis E., Jr. *Western Mining*. Norman: University of Oklahoma Press, 1970.

Chapter 7: The Upper Missouri Country

Barsness, Larry. *Gold Camp: Alder Gulch and Virginia City, Montana*. New York: Hastings House, 1962.

Berthold, Mary Paddock. *Big Hole Journal*. Detroit: Harlo, 1973.

Davison, Stanley R. and Rex C. Myers. "Terminus Town: The Founding of Dillon, 1880." *Montana the Magazine of Western History* 30 (Autumn 1980): 16-29.

Denig, Edwin T. *Five Indian Tribes of the Upper Missouri*, ed. John C. Ewers. Norman: University of Oklahoma Press, 1961.

Dunbar, Robert G. "The Economic Development of the Gallatin Valley." *Pacific Northwest Quarterly* 47 (October 1956): 117-123.

Ewers, John C. *Indian Life on the Upper Missouri*. Norman: University of Oklahoma Press, 1968.

Harris, Burton. *John Colter: His Years in the Rockies*. New York: Scribner's, 1952.

Mentzer, Raymond A., Jr. "Camp Baker/Fort Logan: Microcosm of the Frontier Military Experience." *Montana the Magazine of Western History* 27 (Spring 1977): 34-43.

Merriam, H. G., ed. *Frontier Woman: The Story of Mary Ronan*. Missoula: University of Montana, 1973.

General Reference

Blumenson, John. *Identifying American Architecture: A Pictorial Guide to Styles and Terms, 1600-1945*. Nashville: American Association of State and Local History, 1977.

Burlingame, Merrill. *The Montana Frontier*. Helena: State Publishing, 1942.

Christopherson, Edmund. *Montana's Historic Markers*. Missoula: Earthquake Press, 1970.

Clearman, Mary. *Lambing Out and Other Stories*. Columbia: University of Missouri, 1977.

DeVoto, Bernard, ed. *The Journals of Lewis and Clark*. Boston: Houghton Mifflin, 1953.

Federal Writers' Project. *Montana: A State Guide Book*. New York: Viking, 1939.

Guthrie, A. B., Jr. *The Big Sky*. New York: Sloane, 1947.

_____. *Arfive*. Boston: Houghton Mifflin, 1970.

Harrison, Julia D. *Metis: People Between Two Worlds*. Vancouver and Toronto: Glenbow-Alberta Institute and Douglas and McIntyre, 1985.

"Historical Landscapes and the Western Identity." *Montana the Magazine of Western History* 35 (Spring 1985): 66-68.

Holder, Preston. *The Hoe and the Horse on the Plains: A Study of Cultural Development Among North American Indians*. Lincoln: Bison Books, University of Nebraska Press, 1970.

Howard, Joseph Kinsey. *Montana: High, Wide, and Handsome*. New Haven: Yale University Press, 1943.

Hugo, Richard F. *The Lady in Kicking Horse Reservoir*. New York: Norton, 1973.

Hyde, George E. *Indians of the High Plains: From the Prehistoric Period to the Coming of Europeans*. Norman: University of Oklahoma Press, 1959.

Jackson, W. Turrentine. *Wells Fargo Stagecoaching in Montana Territory*. Helena: Montana Historical Society, 1979.

Lang, William L. and Rex C. Myers. *Montana: Our Land and People*. Boulder, Colorado: Pruett, 1979.

Lowie, Robert H. *Indians of the Plains*. New York: McGraw-Hill, 1954.

Maclean, Norman. *A River Runs Through It and Other Stories*. Chicago: University of Chicago Press, 1976.

Malone, Michael P. and Richard B. Roeder. *Montana: A History of Two Centuries*. Seattle: University of Washington Press, 1976.

Malouf, Carling. "Montana's Aboriginal Inhabitants—The Indians." In *A History of Montana*, ed. Merrill G. Burlingame and K. Ross Toole. Vol. I. New York: Lewis Historical Publishing, 1957, pp. 31-53.

Meinig, D. W., ed. *The Interpretation of Ordinary Landscapes*. New York: Oxford University Press, 1979.

Montana Historical Society. *Not in Precious Metals Alone*. Helena: Montana Historical Society, 1976.

Toole, K. Ross. *Twentieth-Century Montana: A State of Extremes*. Norman: University of Oklahoma Press, 1972.

_____. *Montana: An Uncommon Land*. Norman: University of Oklahoma Press, 1959.

Utley, Robert. *The Indian Frontier of the American West, 1846-1890*. Albuquerque: University of New Mexico Press, 1984.

Vaughan, Thomas, ed. *Space, Style, and Structure: Building in Northwest America*. Portland: Oregon Historical Society, 1974.

Index

CARROLL VAN WEST is Projects Coordinator at the Center for Historic Preservation at Middle Tennessee State University in Murfreesboro. West lived in Helena, Montana, from 1981 to 1985, where he was historical consultant to the State Historic Preservation Office and to several historical societies and museums, including the Western Heritage Center in Billings.

West received his Ph.D. in history from the College of William and Mary in 1982. He has published several book reviews and is the author of a number of scholarly articles, including "Coulson and the Clark's Fork Bottom: The Economic Structure of a Pre-Railroad Community" in *Montana the Magazine of Western History* and "Slumbering on Its Old Foundations: Interpretation at Colonial Williamsburg" in *South Atlantic Quarterly*. In 1983, He received an American Association of State and Local History/National Endowment for the Humanities grant to do demographic research on western Custer County, Montana Territory, from 1876 to 1882.

West is the Historical Landscapes Consultant to *Montana the Magazine of Western History* and is currently preparing a paper on religious missions and reservation "towns" in Montana for the Great Plains Studies Symposium to be held in Lincoln, Nebraska.